Published by J. D. Hamon

Manufactured in the United States of America

SPIKE-35

GENERAL INFORMATION

Why This Is One Of The Safest Of Trading Methods.

This does not try to pick tops or bottoms. It merely gets a slice out of the middle. Very sensitive entry-exit methods are used to get one out quick should the market turn. Unlike most systems, money can be made on slow moving or choppy markets. This helps, because markets that jump around a lot are the ones that are more apt to catch a trader off guard. This method does better if the market is swinging, but traders with very small accounts can trade the slower corn or hogs until they can build up their account.

This Plan Is Mechanical.

There is no question as to where to enter or exit. Trade signals are seen clearly and easily and there are no judgement factors to weigh before a trade is made. Everything is clear-cut to enable a trader to easily see what to do and when to do it.

This makes this safe from emotions that usually ruin plans requiring judgemental decisions. There is no guarantee that this will make money for everyone, because it is possible that the markets may not continue as they have in the past, and markets can change, but things would have to become very different for this not to work.

Why This Works So Wonderfully.

This method is a combination of several old trading techniques that have been used for many years. Those of you who know market history will recognize the use of: 1) Dow Theory, 2) Weekly Rule, 3) Price Patterns, 4) Elliott's work, and 5) Gann's work. To my knowledge they have never before been used in this fashion, however. It is a new and different approach but does use old techniques that have long been proven. These methods worked for years and years individually, and they should continue to work for a long time using my way of combining them.

Furthermore, this system has been tested in a complete and thorough manner. The name SPIKE-35 means that this is the 35th time I have revised the system for testing. This was not simply optimizing, like so many other people have done with their systems (those others work great on past data, but please don't try to use them yourselves). No, what I did was add new theories and ideas, and made sure the system could be totally mechanical.

There can be thirty-five different varieties of this method, but I have picked the one that is most apt to work in all kinds of markets and least apt to lose you money. True, it is possible for a larger amount of money to be made by optimizing and diversifying so that the entries and exits will be better for faster trending markets, but I'm giving you the safest and most realistic way to trade. You never know when a market will go into congestion. It would be better to diversify, although this has not proven necessary as this version always made money in its testing of all markets. I'll talk about this more in my description of money management. Good rules of common sense must be used, however. Real thin markets are more dangerous and should not be traded by the small trader. Stop loss orders should be used, too. I would have had a much better record to show people, had I used a $500.00 stop loss to exit in case of diversity. Since simulated trades must try hard to be like the real market, I felt this might raise questions, so I did not use them. But $500.00 stops should be used by those actually trading so there will be an extra safety precaution. Ordinarily, you will be out long before $500.00 is reached. In fact, there will be many times when you will exit at the same price of entry and only have commission costs. But this $500.00 stop will help keep you out of some of those crazily swinging market periods.

It Tested Out So Good I Could Hardly Believe It.

You'll see all the details later in the manual. I tested the system on 12 commodities over a three year period, from 1980 through the end of 1982. It worked 52% of the time. But more important, gains were 3½ times the size of losses. That's where the money is really made. Some commodities, with higher volatility, did much better. My personal favorites (T-Bills, Swiss Franc, Gold, and Silver) outdid the average performance by an astonishing amount. Like I said before, you'll get all the details. I've provided a profit summary table. There's also trade-by-trade information for the entire three years for each commodity. So there's absolutely nothing hidden. It's all there for you to see for yourself.

This Is A Busy Trader's Dream Come True.

It is a mechanical plan requiring very little time to operate. Everyone should have the same answers. It is easy to do with no fancy equations, no fancy lines to draw, and no computers to run or update.

Since this is designed for the little trader who may have only $5,000.00 to start, we suggest you trade only five commodities. Pick those that move, but do not swing erratically. Get out or do not trade any erratic market. It makes money in wild swinging markets but the small trader may experience larger losses per trade if starting with these kind of markets. Follow the rules and do not let anyone scare you. If you try to pick and choose which trades to take, you may very well come up with the wrong ones and experience a poor average that should not have happened with consistent trading. The main thing about trading is consistency. You must do the same thing on all trades. Those who are not consistent in their trading rules and procedure will eventually lose.

The largest drawdown was only about $9,000.00 and it would not have been nearly this much had stops been put in for getting out at $500.00. Also, diversifying would have shrunk this drawdown to almost nothing. You would have had profits in some commodities to make up for any losses. If one wants to do more work, he can probably make more money. This system is easy to optimize. It can be done very quickly and in less than one hour of time. It is just a matter of changing the entry-exit rules somewhat. The basic theory and operation does not change. I've used the most sensitive possible entry-exit rules to make this more safe for the small trader. Larger traders do not have this concern, but I suggest that they trade more than one contract if they wish more profits; at least in the beginning until they get the feel of how this works and see how it is to adjust the entry-exit rules for different kinds of markets.

So, assuming you keep everything the way I have it, you should not have to spend more than 15 minutes each evening doing the homework needed to do the trading. I have done the hard work for you by spending long hours, months, and years testing, checking, changing and retesting until I found a real winner. This should be the easiest money you ever made trading the market.

Why This Is For Sale.

I am in bad health and have been advised several times not to trade the market myself; I have no other way of making money in commodities because of this.

Managing other people's money would be just as difficult as trading myself. As much as I'd love to trade this system, my life is more important to me than commodity profits. I do trade some but with my temperament (that I cannot do anything about), it always makes me sick even though I am making big money in the market and I always have to quit after a short time. I envy those with stoic natures who are good traders, but I just was not made that way. On the other hand, they are not the creative, sensitive type who can come up with good trading plans like this, either; a person can't be everything. Take the trading method to trade and I'll stick to my creative work.

IN SUMMARY

This is the safest yet most flexible trading system ever designed. It usually only keeps one in the market about four days per trade and may get you out the day after entry. It's not a day trading plan, but could be used to day trade on five minute charts. The rules for using daily price data will work just as well on intraday data.

I have thought long and hard about selling this, especially since the only way to prove to you how good it is, is to use simulated trades. Still, simulated trades can be just as good as regular trades. Everyone knows the uncertainty of the market and nothing can be for sure. There can be just as many losses on something tested by actual trading as one tested by simulated trading. For one thing, an actual trading test will not go back as far as these have (so there won't be as many different market situations tested). Also, in actual trades you do not know how much the ability and skill of the trader may count. Those good trading records never are the same when trying to duplicate them; but simulated trades must take the bad as well as the good. They have to take all trades even though the tester would probably not have traded that way if he had done his regular analysis. This is not some simple moving average or congestion breakout method that you see so often. I feel that it is the best, most fair and trustworthy system anyone can possibly obtain at any price.

Once you use it, I'm sure you'll agree with me.

PUBLISHER'S NOTE

This is the second edition of the Spike 35 Trader's Manual. The following information was supplied by Mr. Hamon since the publication of the first edition:

1. Variance amounts for the Stock Index's are:
   a. S&P 500 40 pts.
   b. NYSE Composite 40 pts.
   c. Value Line 60 pts.

2. On re-entries you must use a "stop order," not an "MIT order." Many brokers will consider an interday MIT order the same as a market order. So a "stop order" must be specified.

3. The following suggestions, especially for users having smaller trading accounts should be helpful.
   a. Have a dollar amount stop according to your account size. I suggest $500.00 for the less volatile and less expensive commodities, and $1000.00 for the more volatile and high-priced commodities like New York Silver. (This is in addition to the regular stop.)
   b. Use limit orders on volatile commodities, or those in a tight congestion. Make the market give you your price so it will not open up away from where you should enter, then come down to stop you out. A tight congestion is defined in the text. The re-entry rule helps here, but similar problems exist with two or three closes within the variance amount. Here is where you need to use limit orders. Also, if a commodity starts jumping around with a lot more volatility than usual, you should use limit orders. These are judgmental factors. But you may want to consider them to further improve your trading.

THE SPIKE-35 SYSTEM

I THE FOUNDATION OF A SUCCESSFUL SYSTEM

The logic of any system is naturally to make a profit. What I've found to be most successful is to trade with the major trend. The Spike System employs two major change of trend rules for defining this. The idea is not to try to call exact tops and bottoms, but rather to get the safest slice—out of the middle. The entry and exit techniques are very sensitive, for two reasons. First, you'll be out with a profit should the major trend turn against you. Second, you'll trade much safer in the choppy, slow-moving markets. By being cautious on both entry and exit, and by trading only in the direction of the major trend, your profits are almost assured.

You may want to just combine your present system with some of the rules presented here. This can also be quite successful. Please remember to paper trade this first. There can be times that combining systems actually makes them worse. So, by all means, go careful—especially at the start. Even if you're going to follow the exact rules of the Spike-35 System, please paper-trade it first. It will take a little time before you develop a daily trading routine...and build a little confidence that you can indeed trade the system yourself.

I'm now going to teach you the rules of Spike. They are all pretty straightforward, and completely automatic. So don't worry if you don't follow them immediately. You'll have plenty of examples to study. Once you get the hang of it, you'll be amazed how easy it is to trade.

In the first section of the rules, I define for you the market High-points and Low-points. This is entirely different from other people's definitions, so don't skip past it. It's important!

In the second section, you'll learn the two Rules for defining a change in trend. This is followed by a section that will teach you *exactly* where to enter and exit each trade.

I'll also show you a few variations of the System for those of you who want something a little different.

Now...On To The System Rules!

Table I
COMMODITY VOLATILITY CHART

Commodity	Point Value	Variance Amount
GNMA	1 pt. = 1/32%	8 pts.
T-Bonds	1 pt. = 1/32%	8 pts.
T-Bills	1 pt. = .01%	10 pts.
Corn	1 pt. = 1/8¢	8 pts.
Oats	1 pt. = 1/8¢	16 pts.
Soybeans	1 pt. = 1/8¢	16 pts.
Wheat	1 pt. = 1/8¢	16 pts.
Cocoa	1 pt. = $1.00	10 pts.
Soybean Meal	1 pt. = $.01	100 pts.
Soybean Oil	1 pt. = $.01	10 pts.
Platinum	1 pt. = $.01	40 pts.
Plywood	1 pt. = $.01	100 pts.
Silver (Chi)	1 pt. = $.01	10 pts.
Silver (NY)	1 pt. = $.01	10 pts.
Gold	1 pt. = $.01	200 pts.
Lumber	1 pt. = $.01	100 pts.
Deutschemark	1 pt. = $.01	10 pts.
Swiss Franc	1 pt. = $.01	10 pts.
British Pound	1 pt. = $.01	10 pts.
Canadian Dollar	1 pt. = $.01	10 pts.
Japanese Yen	1 pt. = $.01	10 pts.
Live Cattle	1 pt. = .01¢	20 pts.
Feeder Cattle	1 pt. = .01¢	20 pts.
Live Hogs	1 pt. = .01¢	20 pts.
Pork Bellies	1 pt. = .01¢	20 pts.
Copper	1 pt. = .01¢	20 pts.
Cotton	1 pt. = .01¢	20 pts.
Coffee	1 pt. = .01¢	40 pts.
Orange Juice	1 pt. = .01¢	40 pts.
Sugar	1 pt. = .01¢	10 pts.
Heating Oil	1 pt. = .01¢	10 pts.

Note: Except in extreme markets, these variance amounts will represent 1-2 grids on the Commodity Perspective charts.

II DEFINING HI-POINTS (HIP'S) AND LOW-POINTS (LOP'S).

Several writers use these terms to identify temporary changes of the market price action. There have been various ways of defining these small turning points, or pauses of the market.

I've developed a definition which works better than most. My definition incorporates a volatility measure in the pattern. So what may be a highpoint on one chart may not be on another chart of a different commodity.

1. The Real Basics

In Figure 1, you see a simple bar chart. The high, low and close are clearly marked. We will be using daily bar charts. Some systems will use weekly bar charts, or 5 minute bar charts. Daily bar charts are the most common, most readily available and easiest to work with. However, the Spike-35 techniques can be used profitably on any other charts you may want to work with.

2. Hi-Point (HIP) Definition

Figure 2 shows a basic version of a high day (not necessarily a HIP). This is defined as: A day with a lower high the day before it and the day after it. In Figure 3, points B, D, and F are all high days. Notice we are dealing with highs, not lows or closes. There are other very important qualifications for determining if a high day is also a high-*point*.

I mentioned earlier that volatility was very important, and included in the system. It's probably the most important step in distinguishing a high day from a HIP. Table 1 lists the volatility measurements for each commodity. This amount is very important! The high of the high day must be at least this amount above the highs on each side of it (see Figure 4). For instance, the variance for Treasury Bills is 10 Ticks, or 10 points. So the high day must reach a price at least 10 points ($250) higher than the highs on each side of it for it to be a high point. The simple version of this occurs in 3 days, as shown in Figure 4.

FIGURE 1

FIGURE 2

High Day

FIGURE 3

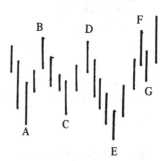

FIGURE 4
T-Bills, Variance is 10 Points

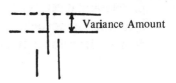

Variance Amount

However, the pattern need not occur in 3 days. As long as the variance amounts, front and back, are met before a new high occurs, the pattern is complete (see Figure 5). Just because a higher high occurs, it doesn't mean there will not be a HIP. The HIP can still form around this higher high...as long as the variance amounts are met before and after the highest high. Also, since there is no requirement that the pattern occur in only 3 days, equal high prices will not cause any problems.

FIGURE 5

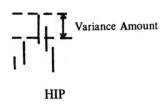

HIP

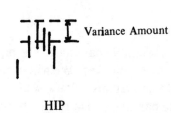

HIP

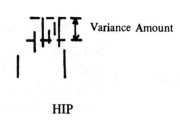

HIP

NOT A HIP - The variance amount was met at the front; but the back variance was not met before the new high.

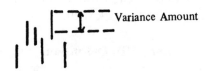

HIP - The next day was much lower, the variance is now met, and a HIP is formed.

If the high is *exactly* the variance amount above the highs on each side of it, this is a valid HIP (see Figure 6).

This should give you a pretty clear explanation of how a HIP is defined. You'll see plenty of examples later on actual charts. If you don't understand it yet, try reading over this section again. It's important that you understand how to find a HIP before you proceed with the Spike-35 System!

FIGURE 6

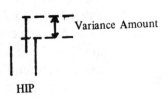

HIP

3. Low-Point (LOP) Definition

This is really identical to the HIP definition, except lows are used instead of highs. Figure 7 shows a basic version of a low day (not necessarily a LOP). This is defined as: a day with a higher low the day before it and the day after it. In Figure 3, Points A, C, E, and G are all low days. Notice we are dealing with lows, not highs or closes.

There are other, very important qualifications for determining if a Low-day is also a Low-*point* (LOP). Volatility applies to LOP's as well as to HIP's. The same variance amounts are used for both high points and low points (see Table I). The low of the low day must be at least this variance amount below the lows on each side of it (see Figure 8). The 10-point Treasury Bill variance (for HIP's) also applies for LOP's. So the low day must be at least 10 points lower than the lows on each side of it. The simple version of this occurs in 3 days, as shown in Figure 8.

FIGURE 7

Low Day

FIGURE 8

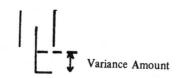

Variance Amount

However, the pattern need not occur in 3 days. As long as the variance amounts, front and back, are met before a new low occurs, the pattern is complete (see Figure 9). Notice that there can be more than one day of lower lows in the LOP formation...as long as the variance amounts are met before and after the lowest low. Also, since there is no requirement that the pattern be complete in 3 days, equal low prices will not cause any problems.

FIGURE 9

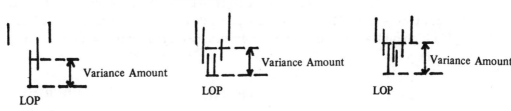

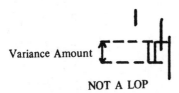

NOT A LOP

The variance amount was met at the front; But the back variance was not met before the new low.

LOP

Assuming the next day was much higher, the variance amount is now met, and a LOP is formed.

If the low is *exactly* the variance amount below the lows on each side of it, this is a valid LOP (see Figure 10).

It should be obvious that HIP's and LOP's are formed identically. The only difference is LOP's are at lows, while HIP's are at highs. Make sure you understand the definitions of High-points (HIP's) and Low-points (LOP's) before you proceed with the Spike-35 System!

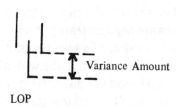

FIGURE 10

LOP

Variance Amount

III CHANGE OF TREND RULES

The Spike System signals a change of trend based on two different rules. The first of these will employ HIP's and LOP's, while the second is a variation of the weekly rule.

The HIP/LOP rule will catch most trend changes. The second rule will serve as a backup. This backup rule is very important, since market action doesn't follow a set pattern 100% of the time. You'll find that in many cases, both rules will signal a change-of-trend on the same day, or within a day of each other. I feel this just further confirms the validity of these rules.

    A. Change of Trend Rule 1 - Market Action Passing Two HIP's or Two LOP's.

If the market reverses and passes the two previous HIP's or LOP's (on the *close*), this is a change of trend.

There is one important qualifier in the definitions of HIP's and LOP's. There must be more than one day between two HIP's (or two LOP's). This is shown in Figures 11 to 13. Notice that the 3 day pattern required to create a HIP cannot overlap and be applied to creation of a second HIP. This is also true for LOP's. Also note in Figure 13 that Day B is the HIP, not Day A. Although you would have originally thought Day A was a HIP, it was later disqualified by the formation of a HIP with a higher high on Day B. (This was only disqualified because of the 1 day between Day A and Day B).

FIGURE 11

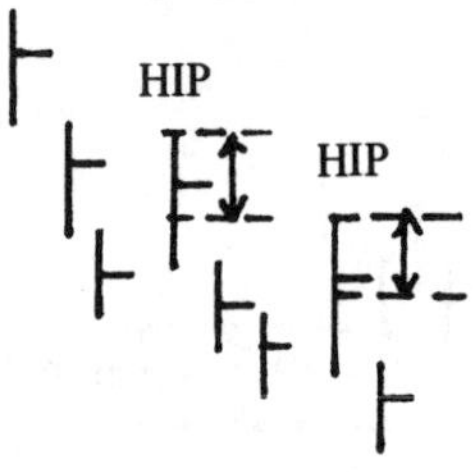

HIP

HIP

FIGURE 12

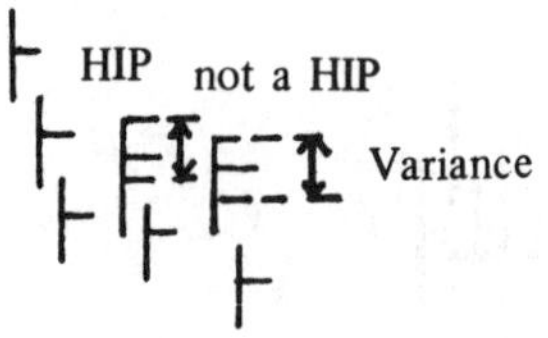

HIP not a HIP

Variance

FIGURE 13

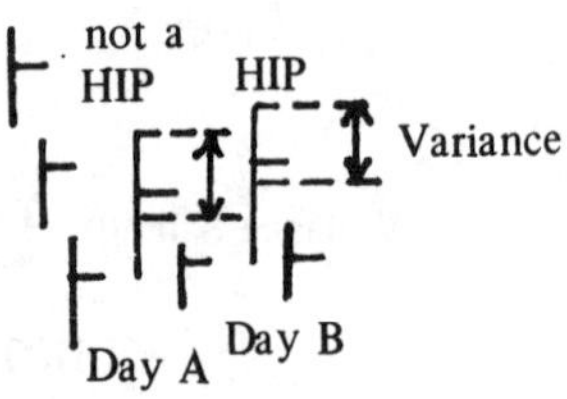

not a HIP HIP

Variance

Day A Day B

This pattern will not occur very often but it is important to watch for it. The logic here is that there haven't been two significant highs. Instead there was just one abnormally low day in between. You should not legitimately anticipate a major change of trend based only on this one pattern. Therefore, a second HIP (or second LOP) must be found before a change of trend can occur.

Reversal of Trend From Down to Up

In a down market, when there is a reversal and the market then closes *above* the two previous HIP's, this is a change of trend (see Figure 14). If the close is at exactly the same price as the higher of the two previous HIP's, this is *not* a change of trend (see Figure 15).

Also, it doesn't matter which of the two previous HIP's is higher (see Figures 14 and 16). As long as the close is above the two immediately previous HIP's, there is a change of trend from down to up.

FIGURE 14   Change of Trend Down to Up

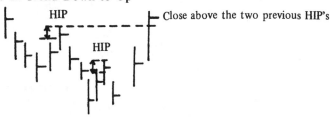

FIGURE 15   NOT a Change of Trend

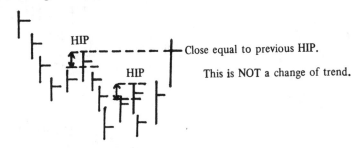

FIGURE 16   Change of Trend Down to Up

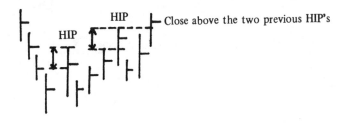

Reversal of Trend From Up to Down

In an up market, when there is a reversal and the market closes *below* the two previous LOP's, this is a change of trend (see Figure 17). If the close is at exactly the same price as the lower of the two previous LOP's, this is *not* a change of trend (see Figure 18).

Also, it doesn't matter which of the two previous LOP's is lower (see Figure 17 and 19). As long as the close is below the two immediately previous LOP's, there is a change of trend from up to down.

FIGURE 17   Change of Trend from Up to Down

Variance Amount

LOP

LOP

close below the two previous LOP's

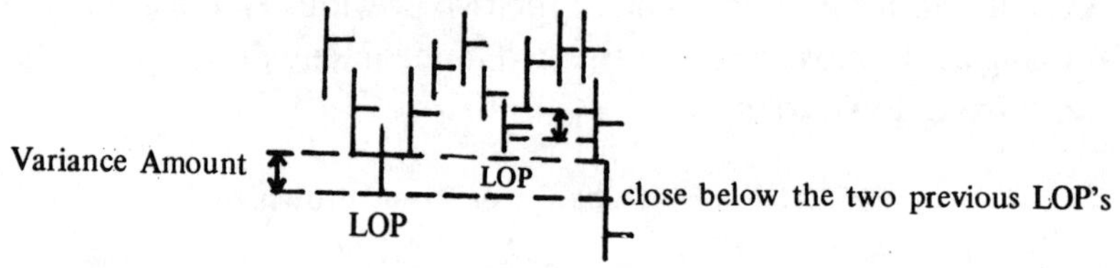

FIGURE 18   NOT a Change of Trend

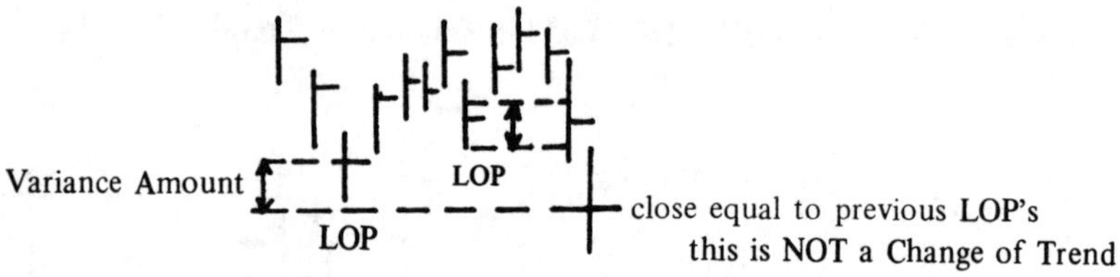

Variance Amount

LOP

LOP

close equal to previous LOP's
this is NOT a Change of Trend

FIGURE 19   Change of Trend from Up to Down

Variance Amount

LOP

LOP

close below the two previous LOP's

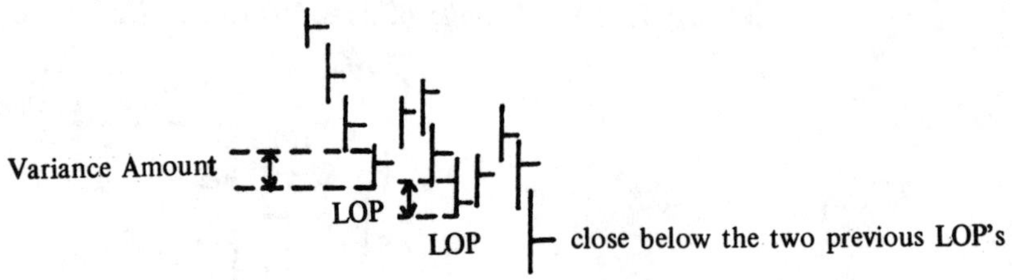

B. Change of Trend Rule 2 - The Thirteen Day Rule (TDR)

This rule is quite simple to follow. Its real strength lies in the fact that *no* price pattern is required. Only price *levels* are used, so if the HIP/LOP Rule does not come into play, the Thirteen Day Rule will still keep you on the right side of the market.

If the market reverses and closes beyond the previous thirteen closes (on the close), this is a change of trend.

Reversal of Trend From Down to Up

In a down market, when there is a reversal and the market then closes *above* the previous thirteen closes, this is a change of trend (see Figure 20). If the close is at exactly the same price as the highest of the previous 13 closes, this is *not* a change of trend (see Figure 21).

FIGURE 20   TDR Change of Trend

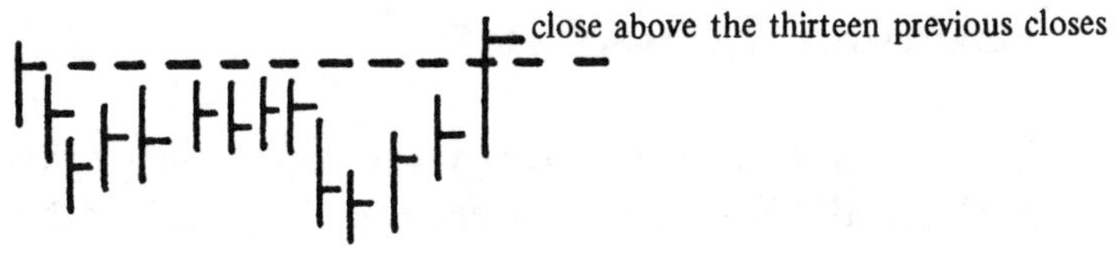

close above the thirteen previous closes

FIGURE 21   NOT a Change of Trend

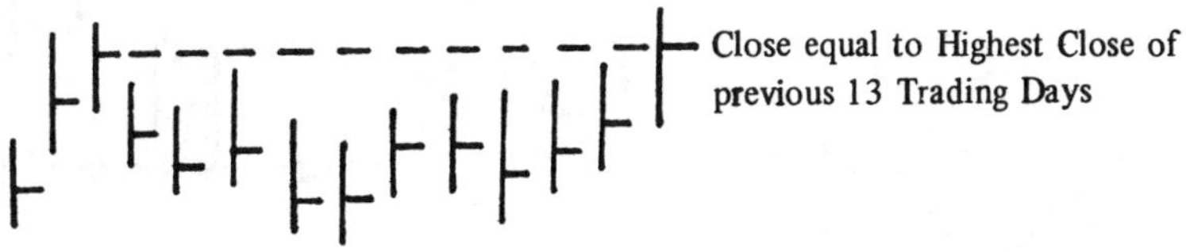

Close equal to Highest Close of previous 13 Trading Days

Remember, we are looking only at closes for this rule. In Figure 22, potential signal A is *not* a change of trend. Although there is a higher high (then the previous 13 days) there is *not* a higher close. For this rule, we don't care about the highs. It's the closes that matter.

Also, we are looking at 13 *previous* days, so today is Day 0, not Day 1. In Figure 22, potential signal B is *not* a change of trend. The day 13 days back has a higher close. However, potential Signal C—on the very next day—is a change of trend. Its close is higher than the previous 13 days. The higher close day is now *14* days back, and no longer is considered for this rule.

FIGURE 22

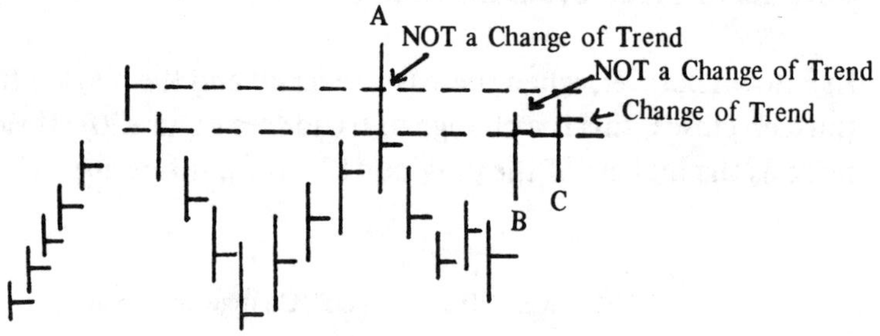

A — NOT a Change of Trend

NOT a Change of Trend

Change of Trend

B C

Reversal of Trend From Up to Down

In an up market, when there is a reversal and the market then closes *below* the previous 13 closes, this is a change of trend (see Figure 23). If the close is at exactly the same price as the lowest of the previous 13 closes, this is *not* a change of trend (see Figure 24).

FIGURE 23

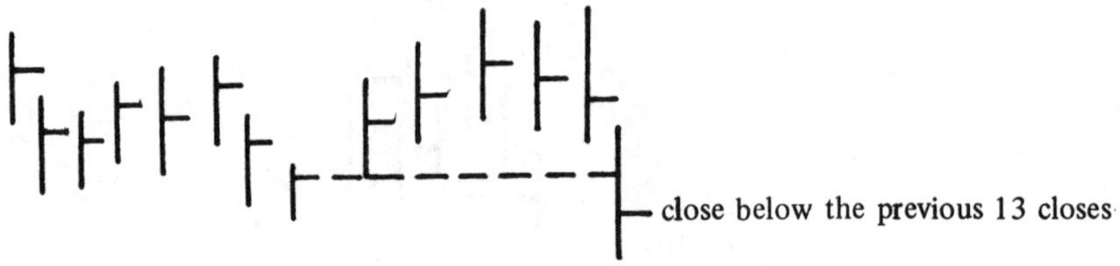

close below the previous 13 closes

FIGURE 24   NOT a Change of Trend

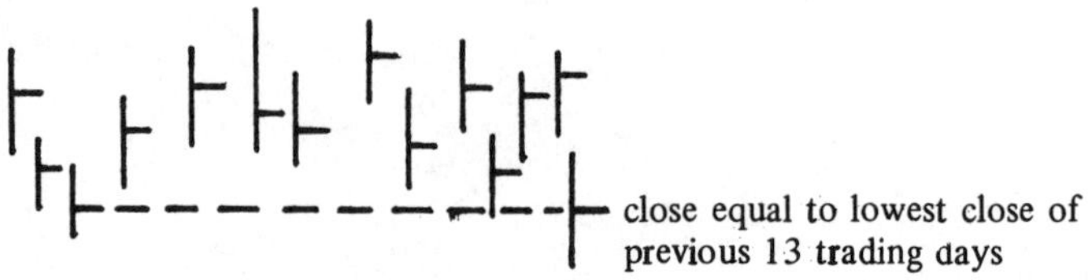

close equal to lowest close of previous 13 trading days

Remember, we are looking only at closes for this rule. In Figure 25, potential signal A is *not* a change of trend. Although there is a lower low (than the previous 13 days) there is *not* a lower close. For the thirteen day rule, we don't care about the lows. It's the closes that matter.

Also, we are looking at 13 *previous* days, so today is Day 0, not Day 1. In Figure 25 potential signal B is *not* a change in trend. The day 13 days back has a lower close. However, potential signal C—on the very next day—is a change of trend. Its close is lower than the previous 13 days. The lower close day is now *14* days back, and no longer is considered for this rule.

FIGURE 25

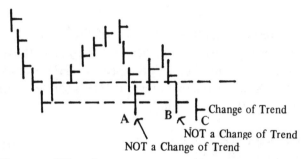

C. Congestions at a Change of Trend

A congestion is a period of a few days, or even weeks, where price stays in a tight trading range. Figure 26 shows an example of a congestion.

FIGURE 26

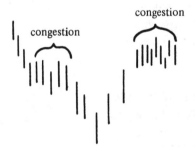

Most trend-following systems get severely whipsawed when there is a congestion period, especially when it occurs at a change of trend. If we were just using the HIP/LOP rule, this may have caused us some problems. This is because the congestions usually prevent a HIP or LOP from forming.

This is nothing to be concerned about. The Thirteen Day Rule is included specifically for these situations. If there is a reversal...and congestions prevent HIP or LOP formation ...the Thirteen Day Rule will still keep you on the right side of the trend.

IV   RULES FOR ENTERING THE MARKET

There will be three different signals that can lead to market entry. The first is based on the Change of Trend Rule 1 - Market Action Passing Two HIP's or Two LOP's. The second is based on the Change of Trend Rule 2 - The Thirteen Day Rule. The third is a re-entry to the market, after exiting from an earlier trade. Reentry will only occur in the market direction that a prior trade was made (based on Rule 1 or 2). This will be very clear once you read through the examples later in the manual.

A. Entry Signal 1

If there is a change of trend, as defined by Change of Trend Rule 1, you will enter the market at the close on the day the trend changes. Look again at the instructions for defining a Change of Trend when market action passes two HIP's or two LOP's. You see that the market must close above the two previous HIP's (or below the two previous LOP's if looking to go short) to get a signal.

Your entry point is at that close. This is shown in Figure 27. You can do this by taking a quick look at your price charts each morning (or previous evening). Then draw a HIP line from the highest high of the two previous HIP's (see Figure 28). Place an order to buy, market-on-close, above this price level. If price is trading below this level at the close, your broker should not place the order. It is imperative that you work well with your broker to trade this way.

FIGURE 27

Entry on Close Above 2 HIP's (CA2H)

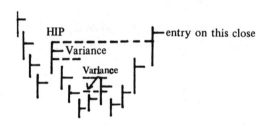

If you prefer, you can also wait until the next day, and get in at the open. This will give you different results, but on balance should be about the same. I prefer to get in right away at the close and my profit results are based on this. The only reason to place the orders at the next day's open is just to simplify the order itself. But once you've cleared up the market-on-close order with your broker, it should be just as easy to handle. And you won't have to worry about any big gaps at the open that may cut into your profits.

FIGURE 28

The Real-Time Analysis

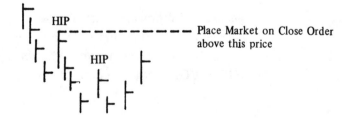

B. Entry Signal 2

If there is a change of trend, as defined by Change of Trend Rule 2, you will enter the market at the close on the day the trend changes. Look again at the instructions for defining a Change of Trend according to the Thirteen Day Rule. You see that the market must close above the highest close for the previous 13 days (or below the lowest close for the previous 13 days if short) to get a signal.

FIGURE 29

. Entry on Close Above Previous 13 Closes (TDR)

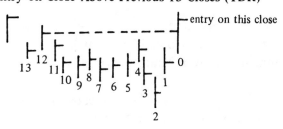

Your entry point is at that close. This is shown in Figure 29. You can do this by taking a quick look at your price charts each morning (or previous evening). Then draw a Thirteen Day Highest Close line from the highest close of the past 13 days (see Figure 30). Place an order to buy, market on close, above this price level.

FIGURE 30

The Real Time Analysis

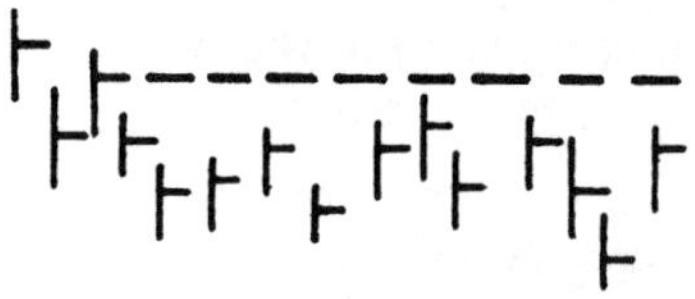

Remember that for Entry Signal 1 and Entry Signal 2, you must be looking at both long and short entries. This will be most important in congestion areas, where you will be close to a potential signal either long or short on the same day (see Figure 31). Of course, this won't occur very often. And as the day's trading begins, it will become obvious that you won't get a close in one of the directions.

FIGURE 31

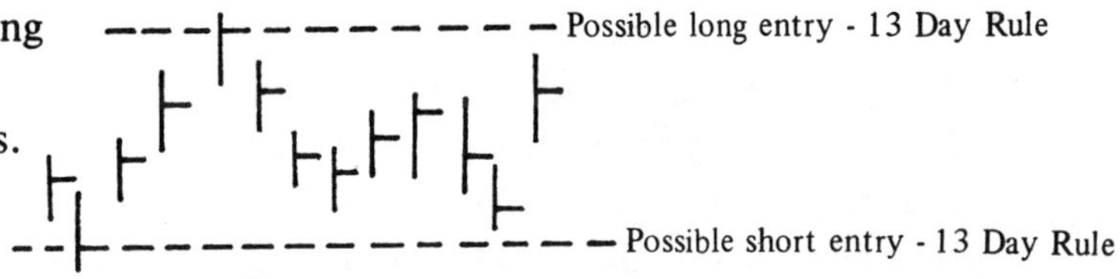

Possible long entry - 13 Day Rule

Possible short entry - 13 Day Rule

C. Multiple Entry Points

You will have a long and short entry point from each of the 2 Change of Trend Rules above. However, you will only use the closer of the entry points in each direction. This is illustrated in Figure 32.

FIGURE 32

Only one long entry point and one short entry point

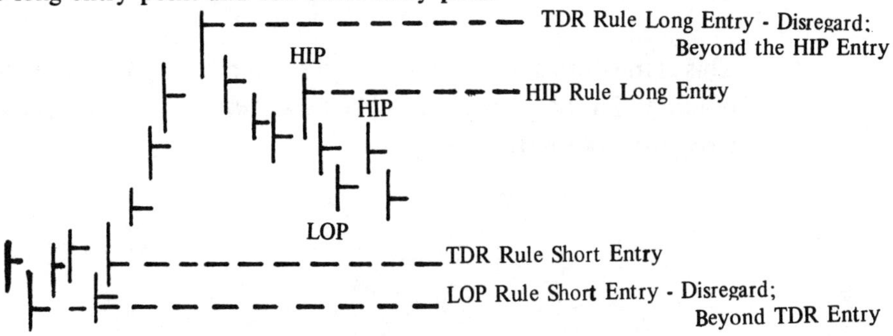

TDR Rule Long Entry - Disregard; Beyond the HIP Entry

HIP

HIP

HIP Rule Long Entry

LOP

TDR Rule Short Entry

LOP Rule Short Entry - Disregard; Beyond TDR Entry

Notice that in order to enter long on the Thirteen Day Rule, you would have already gotten a signal from the HIP Rule. And in order to enter short on the LOP Rule, you would have already gotten a signal from the Thirteen Day Rule.

So you need only watch one long entry and one short entry, *not* all four. And in most cases, either the long or short entry level will be so far away you won't have to worry about it.

V.   RULES FOR EXITING THE MARKET

There is only one exit rule. This rule will get you out whenever there is a potential reversal. If you would like to stay in each trade a little longer, you can alter this rule to match your own trading philosophy.

But I feel its best as will be presented here. It works as an excellent trading stop. It protects your profits, and other than an occasional crazy market, greatly minimizes your losses.

The exit rule is quite simple. Set your stop at the lower (higher if short) of the two previous closes (see Figures 33 and 34). If this level is penetrated, close out your position. Use a market-if-touched (MIT) order. So even if price goes exactly to that point but not further, you should still close your position.

FIGURE 33
Exit From Long Position

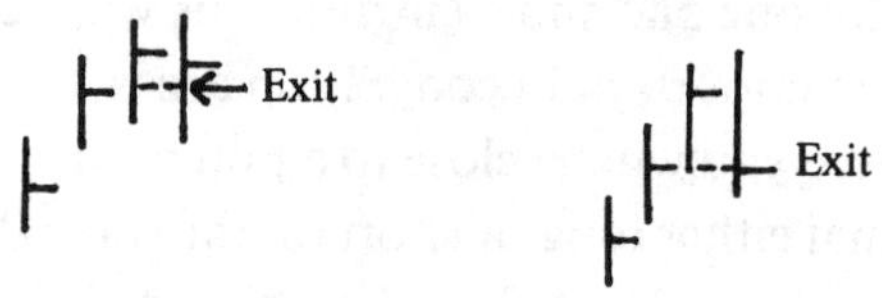

This will get you out before any major losses. It also will get you out prematurely when there is a long trending market. That is where the Re-Entry rules—which I'm about to teach you—come into play with the most success. You'll never miss riding most of the big move.

FIGURE 34
Exit From Short Position

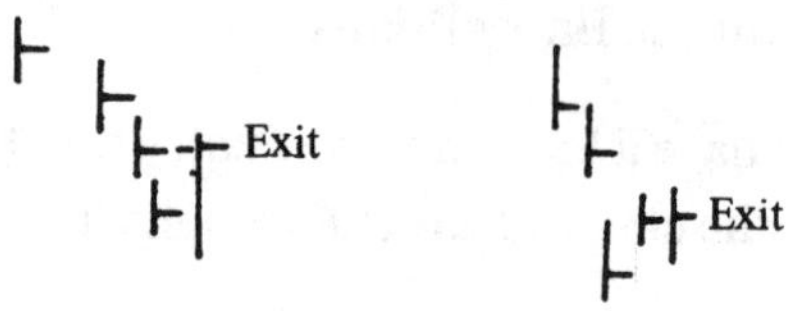

VI   RE-ENTRY RULES

This is the third signal that can lead to market entry. There are two different forms of re-entry. The basic version will be used 99% of the time. Once in a while, the Congestion Re-Entry will be used.

You'll find that most of your trades will be on re-entry. This is due to the very "quick-on-the-trigger" exit rule used to limit losses. It's the exit rule that makes the re-entry rule so important.

A. The Basic Re-Entry Rule

Before any re-entry can occur, there must first, by definition, be an entry. This would have to be based on either the HIP/LOP Rule or the Thirteen Day Rule. This trade would then have to have been exited. If the correct pattern occurs, you would then re-enter the market—**but only in the direction** (Long or Short) of the previous trade (see Figure 35).

FIGURE 35

The Basic Re-Entry Rule

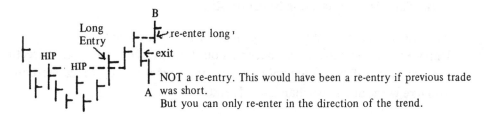

So, for example, let's say you went long T-Bills at 92.50, with a $1250 profit. You are now permitted to apply the re-entry rule. But only for a long trade. Remember you only want to trade in the direction of the major trend, as indicated by the most recent indication of the two Change-of-Trend Rules.

If you're confused, don't worry. This is really quite simple once you see it used. After reading this complete section, look at some of the actual examples. It should then be quite clear how to use the re-entry rule.

Now for the re-entry rule itself. If the market penetrates the four previous closes, without a change of trend, you re-enter the market in the direction of the trend. Figure 35 illustrates this point. Note that Day A penetrated the closes of the four previous days. No re-entry occurred because the major trend was up. Only a long re-entry could occur in an up-market. This then occurred on Day B. Note that re-entry occurs at the price level of the highest of the four previous closes. You don't have to wait for a close above that level. You would use a market-if-touched (MIT) order.

If price goes exactly to that level and then retreats, you would still enter the trade. As long as the price level is met, an entry signal is given.

On the short side, naturally, you would be looking for a penetration below the lowest of the four previous closes.

One more very important point. You can re-enter many times within a major trend. Once your first re-entry is exited, you can look for another re-entry in that direction. This will continue until there is a valid Change-of-Trend (HIP/LOP Rule or Thirteen Day Rule) to the other direction. After that trade is exited, you will look for re-entry only in that direction of the market. This is also simple to understand once you see it applied on some real examples.

B. The Tight Congestion Re-Entry Rule

The only difference between the Basic Re-Entry Rule and the Tight Congestion Re-Entry Rule is the pattern that occurs. You still will trade only in the direction of the major trend, still will trade only after exiting a prior trade; still can re-enter as often as you like without a new Change-of-Trend.

The difference is that you are no longer looking for penetration of the four previous closes. The new pattern is as follows:

A tight congestion is defined as four consecutive closes all within the variance amount of each other (see Figure 36). Variance amounts are shown in Table 1 for each commodity. If there is a tight congestion, you would then re-enter long only on penetration of the highest *high* of the previous 4 days. Likewise, you would re-enter short only on penetration of the lowest low of the previous 4 days (see Figure 37).

This rule will very rarely be used, but will save you from whipsaws when it does come into play. As you can see, this makes it tougher to re-enter the market in a very tight congestion.

FIGURE 36
Tight Congestion

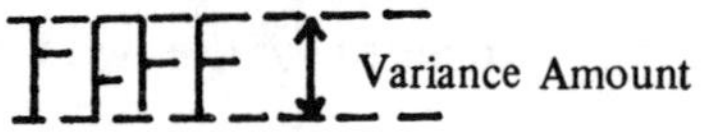

FIGURE 37
The Tight Congestion Re-Entry Rule

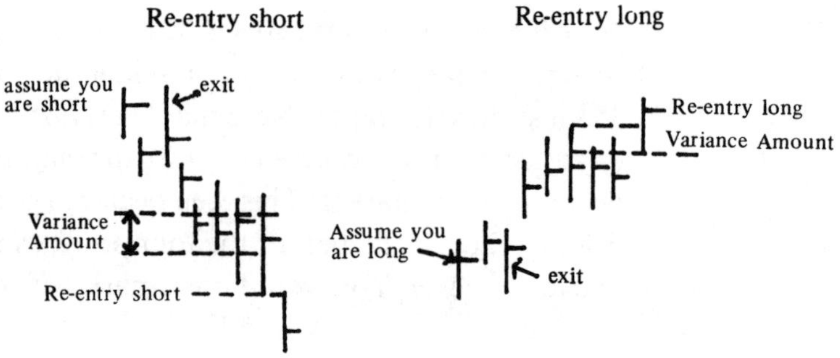

The Spike System can take profits in a choppy market. But when the prices get so tight, the best strategy is to stand aside and wait for prices to start moving again. By waiting to penetrate the highs or lows instead of the closes, this rule can save you quite a bit of unnecessary grief—and a few dollars.

VII   A NOTE ABOUT CONGESTION TRADING

For a long time I thought it would be impossible to make money trading congestions or labored moves—unless a special plan was developed that was different from the rest of the trading system.

With Spike-35, we trade these congestions. Not the very tight one-day swings. But the loose congestions or labored moves of more than one or two day swings. Although you won't make as much money on these choppy markets, there is still a slight profit, enough to warrant not changing any of our methods.

You never know when the swing is going to be the break from the congestion or labored move. If you didn't trade these price patterns, you may miss an excellent trade, or at best, get in late. The Spike-35 method conquers this problem better than any method I've seen in action.

VIII   SUMMARY OF TRADING REQUIREMENTS

1. There must be a Change of Trend, as defined by one of the two following rules.

    A. A close above the highest point of the two previous HIP's, or below the lowest point of the two previous LOP's.

    B. A close above the last thirteen closes, or (to go short) a close below the last thirteen closes.

2.   **Exit** when price penetrates the last two closes (MIT).

3.   **Re-Entry Rule:** If there has been no alteration in the change of trend, when four closes are passed (in the same direction as the previous trade), re-enter (MIT).

In tight congestion, re-enter when four highs, or lows when short, are passed in the trend direction (MIT). You never trade against the trend as defined by the rules above.

IX   HOW TO TRADE SPIKE-35

You must keep charts on the commodities you deem best for your trading. Use those with large open interest and volume, so you'll get better fills on your orders. Try to trade markets that are moving, either up or down. Sometimes a market will be flat or choppy all year. You should not lose much if anything in these markets, but you can utilize your money better elsewhere.

When you have picked the commodities you wish to trade, wait for the entry rules to be validated. You always enter on a Change of Trend at the close only. Put in your order, then when you get your fill back from your broker, put in your order for exit according to the exit rules, which are Market-if-Touched.

If you exit before a Change of Trend, you may re-enter when four closes are passed trading in the same direction (never against the trend) according to the rules. Re-entries are MIT.

X TREATMENT OF LIMIT DAYS

If there is a limit day, you can't reasonably assume that you could have gotten an entry on that day. If the signal is still valid the next day, you will take the trade at that time. However, keep an eye out for a change in the signal. If it's been cancelled (by an exit or whatever) don't take the trade. However, any Change-of-Trend trade can be assumed to have been taken, for purposes of Re-entry trades and determining the direction of the major trend.

FIGURE 38
Limit Day–Delayed Entry

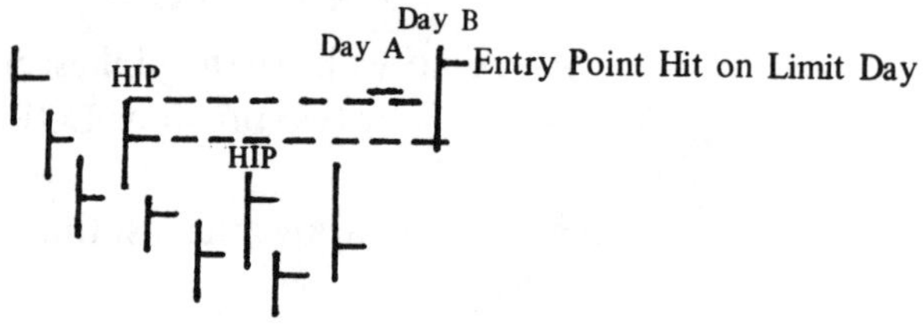

Figure 38 illustrates this. Although the HIP/ LOP Rule signalled an entry on Day A, it was impossible to enter on that day. In Figure 38, you would have entered at the open on Day B. The signal was still valid. In Figure 39, you would not have entered. The open was below the two previous closes, so the trade would have already been exited. Even though the trade was not taken, the major trend is now *long!* A re-entry could now be taken only in the long direction!

FIGURE 39
Limit Day–No Entry

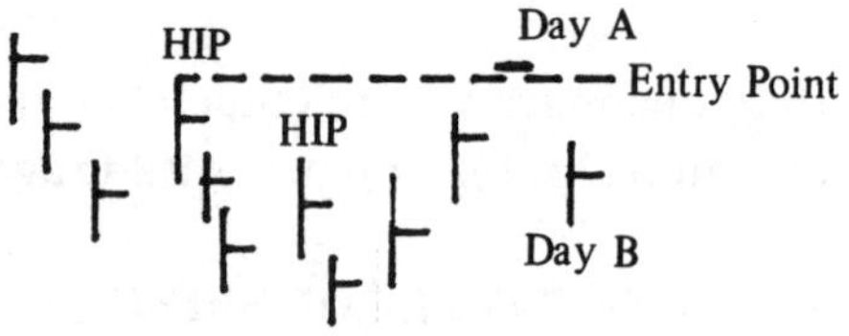

In most instances, the trade will still be okay to enter, as illustrated in Figure 38. The case in Figure 39 will occur very rarely, but please be aware of it after a limit day.

XI   AN OPTIONAL EXIT RULE

Some traders would prefer to ride the trend a little longer, and not exit quite so fast. There are a number of alternative exit methods, which I'm sure you have seen before. When adopting any of these, please be careful! The size of your losses may grow quite large with the wrong exit rule.

One option I can suggest to you that works quite well is something I call a trendline exit. This is illustrated in Figure 40. Note that the trendlines connect the last two HIP's or LOP's, or HIP to LOP if pointed in the direction of the trend. The trend line must be pointed down if you are short, and up if you are long. You would exit when the trend line is passed. If two LOP's, two HIP's or LOP to HIP doesn't make the line intersect with price, use the best of the last several HIP's or LOP's with which to draw a trend line that does intercept price.

As you can see, this rule is a bit subjective. And I didn't analyze it over the long term. But it did look promising, so I'm showing it to you in case you want to pursue it further.

Again, use your own judgement in deciding what to trade. The Spike-35 system works well. But you may find some improvements that make it even better.

XII   AN OPTIONAL RE-ENTRY RULE

If you exit before a change of trend, you may re-enter when four closes are passed trading in the same direction (never against the trend) according to the standard rules I've presented.

An option that you may want to try is a tolerance level for these Market-if-Touched (MIT) orders. This will help prevent those occasional one-day whipsaws. (Of course it will get you into the trend a little later also). An example of this tolerance would be fifteen points for trading Live Hogs. So price must be at least 15 points higher than the highest of the 4 previous closes before you would enter the trade. Pork Bellies is much more volatile so a tolerance of 30 points would be used.

I didn't use this in my system, because I didn't feel it was necessary. It's up to you whether you want to use this rule.

FIGURE 40

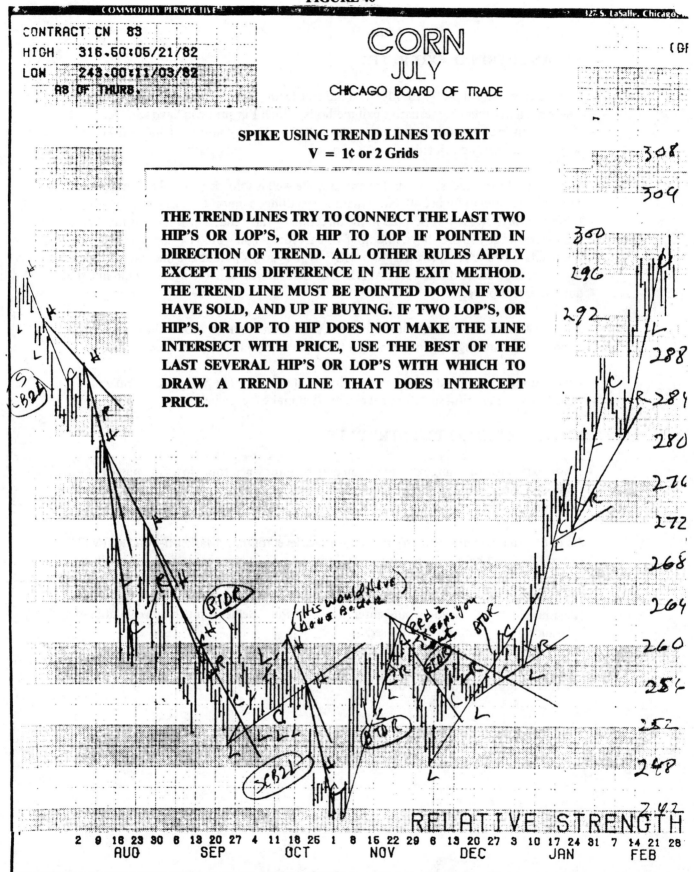

THE TREND LINES TRY TO CONNECT THE LAST TWO HIP'S OR LOP'S, OR HIP TO LOP IF POINTED IN DIRECTION OF TREND. ALL OTHER RULES APPLY EXCEPT THIS DIFFERENCE IN THE EXIT METHOD. THE TREND LINE MUST BE POINTED DOWN IF YOU HAVE SOLD, AND UP IF BUYING. IF TWO LOP'S, OR HIP'S, OR LOP TO HIP DOES NOT MAKE THE LINE INTERSECT WITH PRICE, USE THE BEST OF THE LAST SEVERAL HIP'S OR LOP'S WITH WHICH TO DRAW A TREND LINE THAT DOES INTERCEPT PRICE.

XIII   TRADE *YOUR* SYSTEM

The previous two sections were presented to make a point. Even though this system is totally automatic, each of you has his or her own psychological makeup.

This system will work for you if you trade it correctly. But some traders just can't stick to the exact rules because they just don't trust them enough. They feel they know more about the market than the system does.

Maybe they do. The rules given here are not "cast-in-stone." No one knows what will happen in the future. You may have a little change you'd like to add to the system. Go ahead—if it will make you more willing to stick with it. Just make sure that you first test any changes, to see if they work well with the rest of the system. And once you've got a system, make sure you stick to the rules you use.

EXPLANATION OF TRADE-BY-TRADE RESULTS

In this section I'm going to give you trade-by-trade results on a few actual contracts. The examples you'll see should help clear up any questions you may have on the rules. I've tried to pick contracts that best illustrated the many variations of the rules.

The start of the contract may seem quite arbitrary, but in reality it is based on my analysis methods. I rolled over from one contract to the next based on the charts I had available. You should roll over before the contract expiration month is entered. Try to stay in contracts with a high open interest. But don't roll over too often, as there is some work that must be done to bring each new contract up-to-date. You would have to check for HIP's, LOP's and the Thirteen Day Rule before you could start trading a new contract.

So while the results you see presented here sometimes rolled over at strange times, I would expect you to roll over in a set pattern (e.g. July Bellies, trade until June 15). This shouldn't affect your trading results. But it will help minimize the work you have to do updating contracts.

Each contract in this section will have three areas of analysis. First, you will see a chart, with each trade clearly marked on it. Second, you will have a table summarizing these trades, and the profit or loss on each. Third, will be an explanation of how the trading went. While I will point out many of the HIP's and LOP's, I will not be describing all of them. This would get very time-consuming and, frankly, quite boring and cumbersome. I've tried to point out the important patterns, which result in trades. I've also tried to point out some particular HIP's and LOP's which are good examples of some of the rules and definitions you've learned.

This section should clear up any questions you may have. Study it carefully before proceeding to the Chart-Trading Workshop. And refer back to it once in a while for a refresher. It will help you keep all the rules clear in your mind, and keep you trading the system correctly.

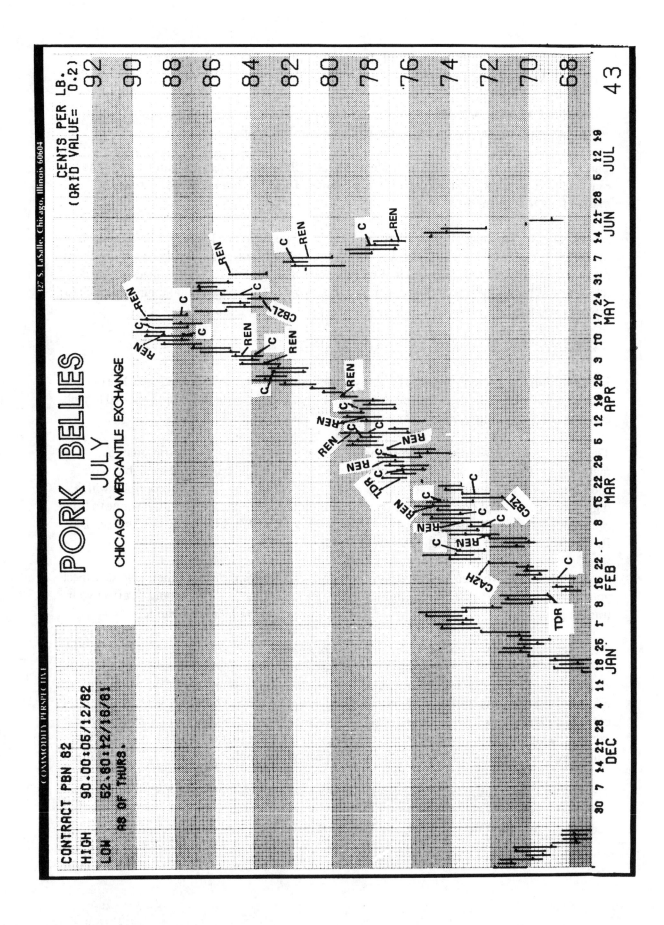

SPIKE-35 TRADING RESULTS
82 July Pork Bellies

Order	Entry and Exit Dates	Entry Rule	Entry and Exit Prices	Gain	Loss
Sell	2-10-82 2-16-82	TDR	69.10 68.75	$ 131.25	
Buy	2-22-82 2-25-82	CA2H	72.05 73.70	618.75	
Buy	3- 3-82 3- 5-82	REN	72.30 72.60	112.50	
Buy	3- 8-82 3-10-82	REN	73.40 73.40	0	0
Buy	3-12-82 3-15-82	REN	75.00 74.60		$ 150.00
Sell	3-16-82 3-17-82	CB2L	71.40 72.80		532.00
Buy	3-21-82 3-25-82	TDR	76.40 76.40	0	0
Buy	3-29-82 3-30-82	REN	77.40 76.80		225.00
Buy	4- 1-82 4- 6-82	REN	77.15 78.50	506.25	
Buy	4- 7-82 4- 7-82	REN	78.90 78.00		337.50
Buy	4-13-82 4-15-82	REN	78.25 78.40	56.25	
Buy	4-20-82 4-28-82	REN	79.10 82.90	1422.00	
Buy	4-30-82 5- 4-82	REN	83.40 83.95	206.25	
Buy	5- 4-82 5-11-82	REN	84.60 87.50	1087.50	

SPIKE-35 TRADING RESULTS
82 July Pork Bellies (Cont'd)

Order	Entry and Exit Dates	Entry Rule	Entry and Exit Prices	Gain	Loss
Buy	5-11-82 5-13-82	REN	88.50 88.80	$ 112.50	
Buy	5-17-82 5-18-82	REN	89.40 87.60		$ 675.00
Sell	5-24-82 5-25-82	CB2L	83.60 84.60		375.00
Sell	6- 1-82 6- 4-82	REN	85.10 81.90	1200.00	
Sell	6- 5-82 6-10-82	REN	81.20 78.00	1200.00	
Sell	6-11-82 6-21-82	REN	76.70 70.20	2437.50	

TRADE-BY-TRADE RESULTS
July 82 Pork Bellies

The rollover from the previous contract occurred at the start of February, 1982. The variance value for Pork Bellies is 20 points. On this chart that is represented by one grid (0.2 cents/lb.).

I'll begin the trade-by-trade analysis on January 25, 1982. You see a LOP formed on Jan. 26. The next pattern is a HIP on Feb. 1, followed by another HIP on Feb. 4. Notice that there was no LOP in between the two HIP's. This is not necessary. There were also two days between the two HIP's, so the one day rule does not apply.

On Feb. 10, there is a sell signal given, based on the Thirteen-Day Rule. Notice that price was lower the day before, but the close is what is important. (The sell occurs at 69.10). This trade is exited on 2/16 at 68.75. Price traded above the highest of the two previous closes.

Note that a HIP also formed on 2/10. This was followed by another HIP on 2/17. So on 2/18 our major trend is still down, and we are looking for a close below the four previous closes to go short. We are also aware that we are close to the high of the two previous HIP's, which is at 71.50. Passing of this (on-close) would signal a Change-of-Trend.

On 2/22, the close was at 72.05, well above the high of the 2 previous HIP's. This is a valid buy signal, and results in a Change-of-Trend from short to long. The trade was closed out on 2/25, when price traded below the two previous closes.

Feb. 26 traded well below the four previous closes. However, this was not a re-entry signal. Remember, the major trend is now long so only a long re-entry can be taken.

The first re-entry occurred on 3/3, when price traded above the four previous closes. The re-entry was MIT at 72.30, the price where the highest of the four previous closes was passed. (Re-entry is MIT, and **not** on-close-only).

A second re-entry occurred on 3/8. Note that this is a second consecutive re-entry in the direction of the major trend. This trade is exited on 3/10 at the same price, as price came back below the two previous closes.

A third re-entry occurred on 3/12. This was 3 trades after only one Change-of-

Trend trade. You would continue to re-enter in the long direction until a new Change-of-Trend signal occurred. Then you would look to re-enter short.

While these re-entries were going on, you should still have been looking for HIP's and LOP's. There is a very obvious LOP on 3/1. A second LOP occurred on 3/5. Notice that this low was two full grids lower than on the preceding and following days. Only one grid is needed on this chart, so this is unquestionably a LOP. A third LOP, which was tough to spot, occurred on 3/11. Notice that the low is more than the variance amount below the lows on either side of it. This one LOP resulted in the trade on 3/16. This price swing now passed two LOP's, reversing our position and giving us a loss instead of a nice gain. You have to learn not to worry about these losses. There will be plenty of profits on other trades.

Getting back to the chart, you should have also been looking for HIP's during this time. On 3/12, a very interesting HIP occurred. This illustrates our 1-Day rule, which states that there must be more than one day between two HIP's or two LOP's. You see that as of 3/11, it appeared that a HIP had formed on 3/10. But on 3/12, price formed a new higher HIP with only 1 day in between. So 3/10 was no longer a HIP. (By the way, before 3/12 the immediately previous HIP had occurred on 3/4).

Now back to where we were—3/17. We were stopped out of our short position when price went above the two previous closes. We are now looking to either reverse by closing above two HIP's or 13 closes, or to re-enter by passing below 4 previous closes.

On 3/22, a very interesting situation occurred. Price traded limit up. This was not yet higher than the highest high of the two previous HIP's. However, it did result in a close above the previous 13 closes. So a buy signal was generated based on the Thirteen-Day Rule. However, because of the limit day, the trade was not entered until 3/23, at the open. On 3/25, price declined. When it passed below the two previous closes, the trade was exited.

You may also notice the LOP on 3/26. This is a good illustration of the LOP definition. The previous day's low was not the full variance amount above the low of 3/26. However, the day before that (3/24) had a much higher low. This is a valid LOP.

On 3/29, we are in a major trend facing up. So re-entry can only occur long. You see that price just reached the highest close of the previous four closes, at 77.40. Since the trades are MIT, we went long at or near this point. The stop is set at the lowest of the two previous closes, or 75.40. At the start of trading on 3/30, we must move our stop to 76.80 based on the two previous closes. As you can see, price then came down and hit the stop, giving us a loss on the trade.

Another re-entry occurs on 4/1, as price went past 77.00, the highest of the four previous closes. On 4/2, price went up, but on 4/5 and 4/6, it stayed in about the same price range. This price action hit our exit on 4/6.

Trading on 4/7 illustrates the one problem with the tight re-entry and exit rules. Trading went above the four previous closes, and we re-entered at about 78.90. At the time we entered the trade, we placed an exit (stop-loss) at the lowest of the two previous closes, or 78.00. After our entry, trading took a nosedive, and eventually reached 78.00, giving us a loss on the trade. This type of trading action gives most technical trading systems a great deal of trouble. We took our loss, but kept it pretty small. And we know that patience will give us a chance for some nice profits.

We re-enter again on 4/13 at 78.20. Price went up a little, but the trade was stopped out with a small profit two days later. Actually, we were lucky to get out with a profit, as price went a bit lower over the next couple of days.

Another re-entry came on 4/20, as price went above the previous 4 closes. This move lasts for quite a substantial gain, getting out on 4/28 with a nice $1422 profit.

There are a couple more straightforward re-entries, taking safe and steady profits out of the up-move. One interesting analysis you may question occurred on 5/11. It is impossible to tell from the chart whether a valid LOP was formed. In a case like this you may have to refer to actual price data, to determine if the minimum variance is met. According to the price data, we seemed to be a couple of ticks short of a LOP. As it turned out, this wouldn't have affected your profits much. There was a legitimate LOP on 5/14, so you would have gone short on the close of 5/19. You would have been stopped out at breakeven on 5/21, so this would not have given you any profits, even though you got in a little earlier.

The Thirteen-Day Rule then finally gave a signal to reverse the trend to short on 5/24. While this trade ended up taking a loss because of a slight correction, a glance ahead shows it certainly called the major trend correctly.

Three straightforward re-entries and exits followed, with a combined profit of over $4800. Trading was then switched to a new Pork Bellies futures contract.

Overall, this 5-month time period had 12 winning trades and 6 losing trades, for a total profit of $6797. An overall look at the chart shows that there was a nice trend, which helped produce profits. But, it's also important that the labored move and whipsaw area did not erode our trading capital. We stayed on top of the market...ready to take the major move when it eventually came...and actually made money instead of taking enormous losses (like most trend-following systems do). I'll show you a few other examples, with different types of markets for trading. You'll then see why I'm so confident that this system will work for you.

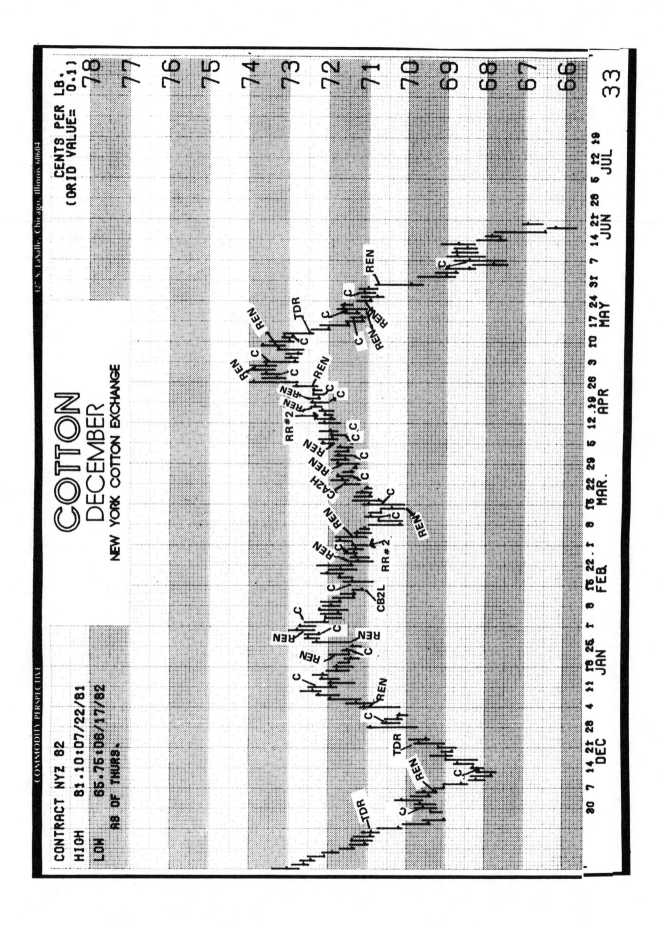

COTTON
DECEMBER
NEW YORK COTTON EXCHANGE

CONTRACT NYZ 82
HIGH 81.10:D7/22/81
LOW   65.75:08/17/82
      AS OF THURS.

CENTS PER LB.
(GRID VALUE= 0.1)

127 S. LaSalle, Chicago, Illinois 60604

78 77 76 75 74 73 72 71 70 69 68 67 66

33

DEC   JAN   FEB   MAR.   APR   MAY   JUN   JUL

SPIKE-35 TRADING RESULTS
82 Dec Cotton

Order	Entry and Exit Dates	Entry Rule	Entry and Exit Prices	Gain	Loss
Sell	11-20-81 11-30-81	TDR	70.90 69.45	$725.00	
Sell	12- 4-81 12-14-81	REN	69.40 68.20	600.00	
Buy	12-22-81 12-30-81	TDR	69.70 70.50	400.00	
Buy	1- 4-82 1-11-82	REN	70.95 72.20	625.00	
Buy	1-21-82 1-22-82	REN	71.80 71.42		$190.00
Buy	1-26-82 1-28-82	REN	71.55 72.25	350.00	
Buy	1-29-82 2- 1-82	REN	72.55 72.50		25.00
Sell	2-12-82 2-16-82	CB2L	71.15 71.40		125.00
Sell	2-23-82 2-24-82	REN	71.40 71.40	0	0

(On Mar lst use reentry Rule #2, and do not enter).

Order	Entry and Exit Dates	Entry Rule	Entry and Exit Prices	Gain	Loss
Sell	3- 3-82 3-10-82	REN	71.25 70.75	250.00	
Sell	3-12-82 3-15-82	REN	70.15 70.70		275.00
Buy	3-22-82 3-24-82	CA2H	71.60 71.50		50.00
Buy	3-30-82 3-31-82	REN	71.85 71.55		200.00
Buy	4- 5-82 4- 7-82	REN	71.90 71.80		50.00
Buy	4- 8-82 4-12-82	REN	72.20 71.85		175.00

(Use reentry Rule #2 until Apr 15).

SPIKE-35 TRADING RESULTS
82 Dec Cotton (Cont'd)

Order	Entry and Exit Dates	Entry Rule	Entry and Exit Prices	Gain	Loss
Buy	4-16-82 4-19-82	REN	72.35 72.15		$100.00
Buy	4-20-82 4-21-82	REN	72.45 72.20		125.00
Buy	4-23-82 4-28-82	REN	72.45 73.25	$400.00	
Buy	4-30-82 5- 3-82	REN	73.95 73.55		200.00
Buy	5- 7-82 5-11-82	REN	73.30 72.95		200.00
Sell	5-12-82 5-19-82	TDR	72.50 71.25	625.00	
Sell	5-21-82 5-21-82	REN	71.15 71.35		100.00
Sell	5-24-82 5-26-82	REN	71.15 71.15	0	0
Sell	5-28-82 6- 7-82	REN	70.75 68.45	1150.00	

TRADE-BY-TRADE RESULTS
Dec 82 Cotton

The rollover from the previous contract occurred in November, 1981. This gave us plenty of time before a new rollover was needed. Volume and open interest are both high on Cotton, and fills shouldn't be a problem. Of course, you could have traded a closer contract if you preferred. Your results would be very similar. The variance amount for Cotton is 20 points, or .2 cents per lb. This is represented by two grids on this particular chart.

On November 20, 1981, price closed below the lowest close of the previous 13 days. This produced a short entry at 70.90, which was closed on 11/30, after producing a nice profit. On 12/4 after a slight up-move, price closed below the four previous closes. We re-entered short at that point, and rode the entire down-move until we were stopped out on 12/14.

The only HIP produced so far was on 12/2, so we could not yet apply Change-of-Trend Rule 1. Another HIP finally formed on 12/18. However, the Thirteen Day Rule (Change-of-Trend Rule 2) gave a buy signal on 12/22. We rode this buy until the first correction 12/30, when we exited at 70.50 with another profit. We re-entered again on 1/4/82 and again rode the move right to the peak.

The preceding trades show the Spike-35 System at its best. Four good winners and no losing trades, in a market that only had a slight trend to it. This system can be tripped up by the occasional wildly swinging day, but will perform very nicely under most circumstances.

The next three re-entries were not unusual. You can follow them from the table without any difficulty. It's important that you remember to keep track of the HIP's and LOP's all the time. Don't get so involved following the re-entries that you accidentally miss a change of trend.

On 1/25, an obvious LOP. On 2/5, the LOP is a little less obvious. You can see that the low of the following day was exactly two grids higher, so the "following-day" requirement was met. The previous day did not meet the two-grid variance amount. Nor did the day preceding that. But 3 days back, on 2/2, the variance amount was met. This is a valid LOP. The variance amount was met without a lower low occurring. Remember, there is no set time limit for meeting the variance amount. It can occur in 1 day...or 2 days...or 3 days...or 10 days...or more. As long as the low of the LOP day is not penetrated.

The two LOP's resulted in a sell signal on 2/12. The close was clearly lower than the low of the two previous LOP's. This position was exited the next trading day with a tiny loss. We re-entered again on 2/23, and were stopped out the very next day with no gain.

This brings us to a very infrequent occurrence. On 2/26, and again on 3/1, we would normally have re-entered the market short. However, this was not a valid re-entry. Re-entry Rule 2, the Tight Congestion Re-entry Rule, kept us out of the market. Look at the closes of the four previous days (2/22 - 2/25). All 4 closes were within the variance amount (2 grids) of each other. We do not re-enter until price moves lower than the lowest *low* (instead of lowest close) of the congestions. We finally do re-enter on 3/3, and ride a small profit until 3/10.

On 3/12, the market goes just below the previous four closes, giving a re-entry. Price then proceeded to move up, catching us with a loss the next trading day. Again notice the HIP's formed on 3/10 and 3/16. Both required extra days to form, but both are indeed valid HIP's.

On 3/22, price closed above those two highs, giving a buy signal. We were closed out of this trade with a small loss. This was followed by three re-entries, as shown on the chart.

On 4/6 a second pattern of four closes within the variance range occurred. On 4/12, we had four closes, all within the two grid variance amount. This is another example of our tight congestion re-entry. This kept us from taking a trade on 4/13, 4/14 and 4/15. (Otherwise, we would have entered on 4/13, been stopped out on 4/14, and re-entered again and been stopped out on 4/15). Our next re-entry occurred on 4/16. This gave us another loss, followed by still another re-entry on 4/20. We finally made a profit with a re-entry on 4/23.

If you glance back at the chart, you see that this type of market would destroy almost any trend-following system. There were a number of little dips in price, and not much of a trend—just enough to keep you re-entering. Still, we only took small losses through this period. We just wait these periods out. We know there will be a large trend coming sooner or later. And that's when we'll make our real profits.

After a couple more re-entries, a sharp drop in price gave us a Change-of-Trend, based on the Thirteen-Day Rule, (5/12). Notice that the day 13 days back (4/23) had a lower low. However, we are only concerned about closes for this rule. Since the close on 5/12 was lower than the previous 13 closes, this was a valid trend reversal. We rode out a nice profit on this trade, which was followed by a couple of small re-entries. Our last trade on this chart was a re-entry, which as you can see, gave us a nice profit.

Trading for the 6½ month period shown here produced 9 winners and 13 losers. However, the profits were much larger than the losses, resulting in a $3310 profit. This is an excellent example of how the Spike-35 System functions in many different types of markets.

The first two months were fantastic. A perfect example of how well the system can perform. There was then a very choppy period. This was followed by a very strong trend, which produced nice profits. So we had examples of two of the best types of market for Spike, and an example of one of the worst types of markets. But the system still did very well.

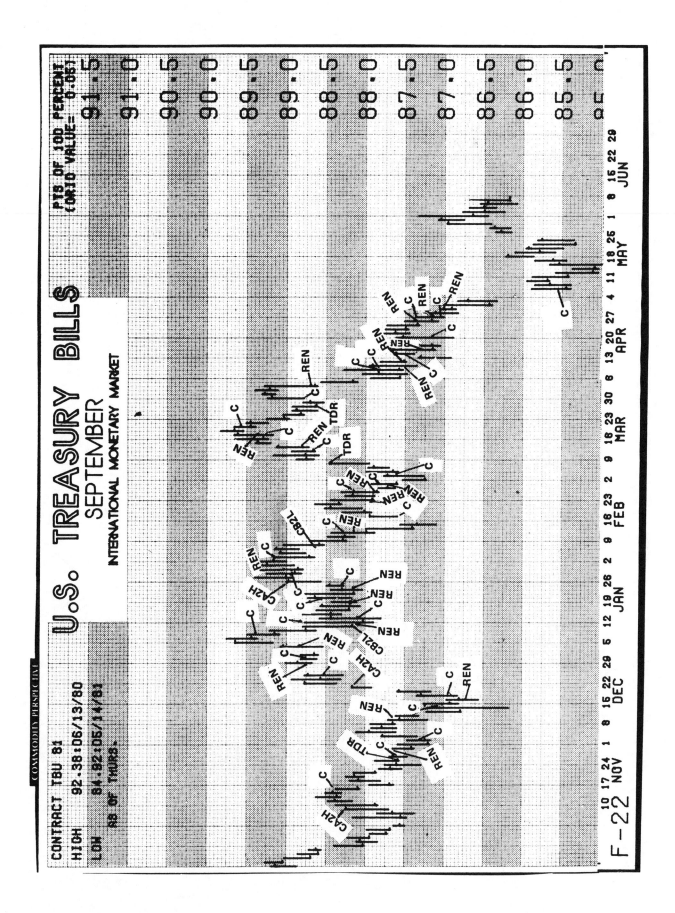

CONTRACT TBU 81
HIGH 92.38:06/13/80
LOW   84.82:06/14/81
AS OF THURS.

PTS OF 100 PERCENT
(ONE VALUE = 0.05)

U.S. TREASURY BILLS
SEPTEMBER
INTERNATIONAL MONETARY MARKET

COMMODITY PERSPECTIVE

F-22

SPIKE-35 TRADING RESULTS
81 Sept T-Bills

Order	Exit and Exit Dates	Entry Rule	Entry and Exit Prices	Gain	Loss
Buy	11- 7-80 11-13-80	CA2H	88.24 88.34	$ 250.00	
Sell	11-25-80 11-26-80	TDR	87.57 87.57	0	0
Sell	11-28-80 12- 2-80	REN	87.57 87.37	500.00	
Sell	12- 9-80 12-15-80	REN	87.64 87.37	1350.00	
Sell	12-16-80 12-18-80	REN	86.77 86.92		$ 375.00
Buy	12-19-80 12-24-80	CA2H	88.16 88.55	975.00	
Buy	12-29-80 12-30-82	REN	88.76 88.76	0	0
Buy	1- 2-81 1- 7-81	REN	88.82 89.43	1525.00	
Sell	1- 9-81 1-12-81	CB2L	88.15 88.75		1500.00
Sell	1-12-81 1-13-81	REN	88.15 88.15	0	0
Sell	1-19-81 1-20-81	REN	88.20 88.55		875.00
Sell	1-22-81 1-23-81	REN	88.15 88.30		375.00
Buy	1-26-81 1-28-81	CA2H	88.97 88.97	0	0
Buy	1-30-81 2- 3-81	REN	89.04 89.15	275.00	
Sell	2- 6-81 2-11-81	CB2L	88.57 88.30	675.00	
Sell	2-11-81 2-17-81	REN	88.25 87.60	1625.00	

SPIKE-35 TRADING RESULTS
81 Sept T-Bills (Cont'd)

Order	Entry and Exit Dates	Entry Rule	Entry and Exit Prices	Gain	Loss
Sell	2-23-81 2-25-81	REN	87.94 88.17		$575.00
Sell	2-25-81 2-27-81	REN	87.90 87.85	125.00	
Sell	2-27-81 3- 3-81	REN	87.70 87.61	225.00	
Buy	3- 6-81 3-11-81	TDR	88.46 88.74	700.00	
Buy	3-12-81 3-17-81	REN	88.77 89.27	1250.00	
Buy	3-17-81 3-19-81	REN	89.37 89.60	575.00	
Sell	3-26-81 3-30-81	TDR	88.62 88.80		550.00
Sell	4- 2-81 4- 8-81	REN	88.69 87.85	2100.00	
Sell	4- 9-81 4- 9-81	REN	87.55 88.90		875.00
Sell	4-10-81 4-14-81	REN	87.55 87.50	125.00	
Sell	4-15-81 4-20-81	REN	87.30 87.17	325.00	
Sell	4-24-81 4-27-81	REN	87.35 87.35	0	0
Sell	4-27-81 4-28-81	REN	87.15 87.15	0	0
Sell	4-29-81 5- 6-81	REN	87.03 85.53	3750.00	

TRADE-BY-TRADE RESULTS
Sept 81 T-Bills

The rollover from the previous contract occurred in November, 1980. You might have traded a different, sooner-to-expire contract. That would be fine, and probably smart. But T-Bills have a high open interest and trading volume, so even the distant contract should give you reasonable fills on your orders. The variance amount for Treasury Bills is 10 points, or $250. This is represented by two grids on this particular chart.

The analysis begins on October 20. We are looking for a Change-of-Trend to start trading. You can see two HIP's, one on 10/29, and the other on 11/5. A Buy signal was given on 11/7, when trading closed at 88.24. You can see that the Thirteen-Day Rule would not have come into play for a few more days, so the HIP/LOP Rule got us in a little quicker. We exited the trade on 11/13, right near the top of the move.

Always remember to keep track of the HIP's and LOP's, so watch for a reversal. LOP's occurred on 11/6 and again on 11/17. As of 11/17, our major trend is still long. So on 11/18, we are looking for either a re-entry long or a Change-of-Trend to short. An informative point can be made on 11/24. Note that the low was lower than either of the two previous LOP's. **This is not a signal.** The **close** must be below the lows of the previous two LOP's. The next day (11/25) the Thirteeen-Day Rule reversed us to short anyway. Note that the close had to be lower than the previous 13 closes (not lows). On 11/24, the close was lower than the previous 12 closes, but the close on 11/5 prevented our reversal. On 11/25, we only looked back to 11/6, and the trade was entered. Our stop was very close, and we exited the trade the next day.

We re-entered again on 11/28, and rode the down move until 12/2. Note the HIP formed on 11/25, and a second one formed on 12/4. These will be important later.

We re-entered again on 12/9 and rode the down move until 12/15. It looked like the trend would continue, so we re-entered again on 12/16. The market then broke upwards, but we got out with a pretty small loss.

Please look back at 12/15. A HIP was **not** formed here. The variance is two grids, and the preceding was only one grid lower.

The big jump in price on 12/19 signalled a Change-of-Trend from short to long. This was a close above the 2 previous HIP's, and also a close above the previous 13 closes. So both Change-of-Trend Rules gave buy signals. We exited the trade on 12/24 with a nice profit.

Our first re-entry (on 12/29) showed no gain. A second re-entry on 1/2/81 caught the tail of the move, and gave us another nice profit.

The low on 12/24 formed a LOP, as did the low on 1/2/81. Although there was not a two grid space from the previous day's low (on either LOP), both gave more than the two grid variance when looking at the low two day's previous. Remember—the variance need not be met in only one day. As long as it is met, a LOP is formed.

The price fallout led to a Change of Trend on 1/9/81. Price closed below the lowest low of the two previous LOP's. We were stopped on 1/12/81 with a loss. You'll notice price went just to our stop (highest of two previous closes) and then went back down. This gave us a loss on our first trade, followed by a re-entry short later in the day (when price traded below the four previous closes). Our tight stop took us out of this trade the very next day with no gain.

A slight congestion occurred over the next week, but price didn't trade below the four previous closes. We were out of the market until 1/19, which gave us a loss. We re-entered short one more time, on 1/22, and took another loss.

Keep track of HIP's and LOP's. You see an obvious HIP on 1/14. Another HIP formed on 1/21. Although the high of 1/20 was only one and lower than the high of 1/21, the high on 1/19 more than met our variance requirement. (This does not have to be met in **one** day. As long as the HIP high is at least the variance amount higher than the preceding and following highs within the pattern). On 1/26, the close was above the two previous HIP's, producing a Change-of-Trend from short to long. After exiting, we re-entered a few days later and took a small profit.

During that time two new LOP's formed, one on 1/29 and the other on 2/3. The close on 2/6 was below both of these LOP's, giving a short signal and change of trend. This gave us a nice profit, as did the following re-entry signal on 2/11. Notice that on 2/11, you exited the first trade because of the close stop, and then re-enter later in the day. We caught almost the entire down-move, despite the early exit on 2/11.

There were three more re-entries before the next Change-of-Trend. They all were quite straightforward. The re-entries were each at the lowest of four previous closes, and the exits at the highest of the two previous closes.

An obvious HIP formed on 2/20. However, 2/25 did **not** qualify as a HIP. The following day met the variance amount, but the previous day did not quite meet that amount. Trading on 2/23 was well above the high of 2/25, so 2/25 **could not qualify** as a HIP. Because there was only one low HIP, the Thirteen-Day Rule was more important. On 3/6, we reversed to long based on the Thirteen-Day Rule. The close here was just one tick higher than on 2/20, but that was enough to give a signal. If the close was at **exactly** the same price, this would not have been a signal.

Price then went up nicely. We were exited at 3/11, but re-entered the next day. This re-entry caught a bit of a profit, as did the next re-entry on 3/17. We exited this trade on 3/19 right near the top.

Surprisingly, no LOP's formed between 3/2 and 3/27. The Thirteeen-Day-Rule gave a short signal on 3/26. This was stopped out on 3/30, but the following re-entry on 4/2 gave a profit of over $2000!

The re-entry on 4/9 was stopped out that very same day. It is important to place a stop whenever you enter the market. Do not wait until the next day. In this case we eventually re-entered short the next day. But you never know when a major reversal may occur. That's why we are so quick to exit a market whenever a move shows weakness. We don't want to be in the market in the wrong direction when a strong breakout occurs.

There were a number of re-entries after this, all either breaking even or making money. The last one, on 4/29, made $3750. All these re-entries were straightforward. Details are all in the accompanying trade table.

At this point trading was switched to another T-Bills contract. This switch occurred at this time for the simple reason that that is when my chart expired. You could easily have stayed in this contract up until August.

Trading for the six months shown produced 17 profitable trades and only 7 losers. We made $11,225 total profit for the six months. If you look at the chart, you see a nice trend at the end, which gave us a nice profit. But we also did very well through February and March, where most trend-following systems would have had problems.

By now, you should be getting a good handle on how to use the system. But bear with me, and follow some more trades before trying it yourself. I want to be sure you understand how to trade the system.

You've now seen some real examples of the Spike-35 System in action. I didn't pick the best commodities, nor the worst. I picked three charts that would show you a diverse use of the different Spike-35 Trading Rules. Between this section and the section outlining the rules, you should have no trouble learning how to trade using the Spike-35 System.

As a further tool for you, I've presented the system's performance results with a little twist. Instead of just showing results, I'm giving you a Chart Trading Workshop. You can work the system on as many different charts as you like. Then check your results against mine. After just 1 or 2 charts, I think you'll start to feel quite confident. Confident in both your ability to trade the system and in the system's ability to make you a substantial profit.

CHART TRADING WORKSHOP

I've seen a number of commodity trading systems. Some are quite easy to follow and understand. Most, however, are very poorly presented and leave a great deal of room for misinterpretation.

I hope I've presented the rules clearly and concisely. I've also given some real-life examples for you to study. But this next section should give you an even better understanding of how to use the Spike-35 System.

Instead of simply giving you a listing of results, I've decided to give you an additional learning tool. A price chart is reproduced for each commodity contract I analyzed in my 3 year study. I've purposely avoided marking the trades on these charts. They are there for you to practice using the Spike-35 System. After you try it yourself, you can refer to the table of trades included for each chart.

Only by trading yourself will you develop a feel for the Spike System. Any questions you may have will be answered by the rules and actual examples sections of the manual. Please refer back to them if you get confused on any of the charts.

There is one important point I must make before you proceed with the charts. The start-up and end of trading on each chart may be slightly confusing to you. This was *not* based on any set rule. It simply was based on the particular charts I had available at the time. So don't feel you're missing anything when you see the track record pick up in the middle of the chart, or end well before the charts end. Also, if the trading on any chart starts with a re-entry, it is based on an earlier Change-of-Trend signal. This Change-of-Trend signal does not appear on your chart because it overlapped with an earlier contract for that commodity. I eliminated these overlap trades from my track record because they would have overstated my results.

TRADE RESULTS SUMMARY

The results given in the following table are a summary of the trades taken on 12 different commodities over the years 1980, 1981, and 1982. There may be some slight gaps between the contracts. This is due to the charts I used for analysis.

I think the results speak for themselves. Profits were much larger than losses, and there were many more winners than losers. And the profits were quite substantial. Also, there were no losing commodities. Every commodity was either a big moneymaker or gave consistent, steady profits over the full 3 years.

This 3-year period was not a strong one for trending systems. Most commodity trading systems were quite weak during stretches of this time frame. I did not try to optimize anything, or pick an especially good time-frame.

You cannot assume that results in actual trading will necessarily be the same as results in simulated trading. The markets can change so that this will not perform as well as it has in the past. However, I fully expect it to continue to perform well. I've bent over backwards to give allowances and to try to underestimate the trade. Mistakes in trading can occur, and there may be a few mistakes in the simulated examples. These should not signficantly affect the overall results.

Please don't let the bad performance of other systems scare you off. There is real value in this system. I think once you see the simulated performance and try the system yourself, you'll agree that **this is a system which will earn you substantial commodity profits.**

HAMON SPIKE-35 RESULTS

Commodity	Time Period	Wins	Losses	$ Winners	$ Losers	$ Profit	Longest Loss String	Drawdown
Coffee	12/79 - 7/80	13	12	20,250	8,237	12,013	6	4112
Coffee	7/80 - 2/81	12	13	17,362	7,049	10,313	4	2587
Coffee	2/81 - 5/81	5	8	6,563	2,175	4,388	4	937
Coffee	5/81 - 12/81	14	6	33,037	2,305	30,732	2	750
Coffee	12/81 - 6/82	6	15	8,813	5,139	3,674	6	1781
Coffee	6/82 - 12/82	10	16	11,063	4,087	6,976	8	2137
Coffee	**80 - 82**	**60**	**70**	**97,088**	**28,,992**	**68,096**	**8**	**4112**
Japanese Yen	1/80 - 7/80	12	12	7,725	4,075	3,650	3	1200
Japanese Yen	7/80 - 12/80	9	6	7,275	2,962	4,313	2	1500
Japanese Yen	12/80 - 5/81	13	5	6,924	1,537	5,387	2	675
Japanese Yen	5/81 - 11/81	10	14	7,612	3,900	3,712	3	1225
Japanese Yen	12/81 - 2/82	5	3	4,313	725	3,588	2	675
Japanese Yen	2/82 - 7/82	11	9	5,225	2,360	2,865	4	937
Japanese Yen	8/82 - 12/82	10	9	6,275	1,587	4,688	5	825
Japanese Yen	**80 - 82**	**70**	**58**	**45,349**	**17,146**	**28,203**	**5**	**1500**
Chicago Silver	12/79 - 5/80	9	2	197,000	4,000	193,000	2	4000
Chicago Silver	5/80 - 12/80	12	8	68,300	14,900	53,400	3	6500
Chicago Silver	12/80 - 5/81	8	10	32,300	9,750	22,550	3	4400
Chicago Silver	5/81 - 11/81	12	8	32,000	4,100	27,900	4	2000
Chicago Silver	12/81 - 6/82	9	10	17,650	4,600	13,050	5	2750
Chicago Silver	6/82 - 12/82	11	10	22,800	9,450	13,350	2	1750
Chicago Silver	**80 - 82**	**61**	**48**	**370,250**	**47,000**	**323,250**	**5**	**6500**
Cotton	12/79 - 4/80	8	7	3,050	2,125	925	3	1325
Cotton	5/80 - 11/80	12	13	12,550	3,750	8,800	6	1700
Cotton	11/80 - 5/81	10	12	5,750	4,335	1,415	5	2210
Cotton	5/81 - 11/81	19	8	6,820	2,350	4,470	2	1025
Cotton	11/81 - 6/82	9	13	5,125	1,815	3,310	7	925
Cotton	6/82 - 12/82	10	14	5,800	3,625	2,175	6	1175
Cotton	**80 - 82**	**68**	**67**	**39,095**	**18,000**	**21,095**	**7**	**2210**
T-Bills	12/79 - 5/80	12	9	16,525	4,075	12,450	5	2025
T-Bills	5/80 - 11/80	17	6	14,425	2,075	12,350	3	1275
T-Bills	11/81 - 5/81	17	7	16,350	5,125	11,225	3	2750
T-Bills	5/81 - 11/81	12	5	10,000	1,200	8,800	1	375
T-Bills	12/81 - 5/82	12	12	7,950	5,175	2,775	3	1750
T-Bills	6/82 - 12/82	14	16	12,100	4,100	8,000	3	875
T-Bills	**80 - 82**	**84**	**55**	**77,350**	**21,750**	**55,600**	**5**	**2750**

HAMON SPIKE-35 RESULTS

Commodity	Time Period	Wins	Losses	$ Winners	$ Losers	$ Profit	Longest Loss String	Drawdown
Gold	12/79 - 5/80	8	8	22,800	11,850	10,950	6	9300
Gold	5/80 - 11/80	14	12	33,380	9,570	23,810	3	3300
Gold	11/80 - 5/81	9	10	23,750	6,600	17,150	3	2600
Gold	5/81 - 9/81	10	4	12,650	2,000	10,650	1	800
Gold	9/81 - 4/82	12	10	14,700	4,600	10,100	3	1300
Gold	6/82 - 12/82	11	13	20,900	7,650	13,250	6	4200
Gold	**80-82**	**64**	**57**	**128,180**	**42,270**	**85,910**	**6**	**9300**
Pork Bellies	12/79 - 6/80	12	12	6,713	3,488	3,225	4	975
Pork Bellies	6/80 - 12/80	9	12	7,166	5,082	2,084	3	2280
Pork Bellies	12/80 - 6/81	13	7	12,712	2,175	10,537	2	637
Pork Bellies	6/81 - 2/82	17	12	12,404	3,056	9,348	3	1026
Pork Bellies	2/82 - 6/82	12	6	9,092	2,295	6,797	2	1050
Pork Bellies	6/82 - 1/83	12	17	8,360	5,984	2,376	3	1543
Pork Bellies	**80 - 82**	**75**	**66**	**56,447**	**22,080**	**34,367**	**4**	**2280**
Soybeans	1/80 - 6/80	8	12	4,700	3,200	1,500	5	1500
Soybeans	6/80 - 1/81	14	12	18,775	4,250	14,525	5	1325
Soybeans	1/81 - 6/81	9	12	7,350	4,050	3,300	3	1100
Soybeans	6/81 - 1/82	15	14	6,875	2,825	4,050	3	550
Soybeans	1/82 - 6/82	9	13	5,750	2,600	3,150	3	1000
Soybeans	6/82 - 1/83	15	10	6,775	1,650	4,875	5	875
Soybeans	**80 - 82**	**70**	**73**	**50,225**	**18,575**	**31,650**	**5**	**1500**
T-Bonds	12/79 - 6/80	15	7	22,657	3,625	19,032	2	1375
T-Bonds	6/80 - 1/81	16	13	14.210	6,128	8,082	4	1657
T-Bonds	1/81 - 5/81	11	7	11,251	2,219	9,032	2	1000
T-Bonds	6/81 - 1/82	15	16	13,875	8,289	5,586	5	2477
T-Bonds	1/82 - 6/82	10	11	6,750	3,094	3,656	5	1562
T-Bonds	7/82 - 2/83	11	17	16,617	5,407	9,960	6	1687
T-Bonds	**80 - 82**	**78**	**71**	**85,360**	**28,762**	**56,598**	**6**	**2477**
S&P Index	**5/82 - 12/82**	**12**	**21**	**14,500**	**11,525**	**2,975**	**7**	**3500**
Corn	12/79 - 5/80	5	12	1,050	1,050	0	4	325
Corn	5/80 - 11/80	8	19	3,100	1,600	1,500	5	400
Corn	11/80 - 4/81	12	10	3,550	1,350	2,200	2	387
Corn	4/81 - 11/81	15	12	4,900	1,850	3,050	2	350
Corn	11/81 - 6/82	13	12	3,553	877	2,676	4	325
Corn	6/82 - 12/82	14	8	3,174	675	2,499	4	375
Corn	**80 - 82**	**67**	**73**	**19,327**	**7,402**	**11,925**	**5**	**400**

HAMON SPIKE-35 RESULTS

Commodity	Time Period	Wins	Losses	$ Winners	$ Losers	$ Profit	Longest Loss String	Drawdown
Swiss Franc	12/79 - 6/80	12	14	9,512	4,738	4,774	4	1512
Swiss Franc	7/80 - 11/80	9	8	6,587	3,151	3,436	2	1125
Swiss Franc	11/80 - 6/81	15	7	13,000	3,237	9,763	2	2162
Swiss Franc	7/81 - 1/82	11	11	13,824	3,387	10,437	3	1437
Swiss Franc	1/82 - 6/82	9	8	7,738	2,300	5,438	4	1437
Swiss Franc	7/82 - 1/83	14	11	10,825	2,625	8,200	2	987
Swiss Franc	**80 - 82**	**71**	**59**	**61,486**	**19,438**	**42,048**	**4**	**2162**
Feeder Cattle	1/80 - 6/80	11	5	11,450	1,737	9,713	3	1098
Feeder Cattle	6/80 - 11/80	6	12	2,152	2,328	-176	5	977
Feeder Cattle	11/80 - 6/81	13	16	7,678	4,191	3,487	3	1012
Feeder Cattle	6/81 - 2/82	14	9	7,707	1,584	6,123	2	374
Feeder Cattle	2/82 - 6/82	9	4	3,234	396	2,838	2	176
Feeder Cattle	7/82 - 1/83	9	12	4,048	1,848	2,200	3	792
Feeder Cattle	**80 - 82**	**62**	**58**	**36,269**	**11,984**	**24,285**	**5**	**1098**

TOTALS

Commodity	Time Period	Wins	Losses	$ Winners	$ Losers	$ Profit
Coffee	80 - 82	60	70	97,088	28,992	68,096
Japanese Yen	80 - 82	70	58	45,349	17,146	28,203
Chicago Silver	80 - 82	61	48	370,250	47,000	323,250
Cotton	80 - 82	68	67	39,095	18,000	21,095
T-Bills	80 - 82	84	55	77,350	21,750	55,600
Gold	80 - 82	64	57	128,180	42,270	85,910
Pork Bellies	80 - 82	75	66	56,447	22,080	34,367
Soybeans	80 - 82	70	73	50,225	18,575	31,650
T-Bonds	80 - 82	78	71	85,360	28,762	56,598
S&P Index	5/82 - 12/82	12	21	14,500	11,525	3,475
Corn	80 - 82	67	73	19,327	7,402	11,925
Swiss Franc	80 - 82	71	59	61,487	19,439	42,048
Feeder Cattle	80 - 82	62	58	36,269	11,984	24,285
Totals - 3 years 12 commodities (+ S&P)	**80 - 82**	**843**	**776**	**1,080,927**	**294,925**	**786,002**

1619 Total Trades
52.1% Correct   Avg. Profit   1282.24 = 3.37 to 1
(47.9% Wrong)   Avg. Loss   380.06

$$\text{Profit Factor} = \frac{1282.24}{380.06} \times \frac{52.14}{47.86} = 3.67$$

COMMODITY PROFITS MONTH-BY-MONTH

Month	Coffee	Jap. Yen	Chi. Silver	Cotton	T-Bills	Gold	Pork Bellies	Soy Beans	T-Bonds	Corn	Swiss Franc	Feeder Cattle	S&P Index	Total
12/79	975	*	19,000	375	300	1,800	-600	*	188	*	-312	*	*	21,726
1/80	-2,913	-525	67,500	1,250	-425	100	1,125	-1,500	5,031	-325	-88	1,264	*	70,494
2/80	2,625	1,050	0	-1,325	4,175	-5,900	-225	850	5,781	-62	613	1,650	*	9,232
3/80	3,375	-237	0	800	1,425	13,700	993	2,400	-687	513	2,462	3,608	*	28,352
4/80	675	950	105,000	-175	5,400	1,050	1,688	-300	3,218	-325	3,250	1,542	*	121,973
5/80	1,800	2,637	5,400	300	5,150	-1,400	-75	-350	2,250	-125	-1,137	483	*	14,933
6/80	3,975	825	14,000	225	900	7,130	1,628	725	3,250	-200	-13	1,156	*	33,601
7/80	7,575	363	4,800	1,375	-1,275	8,180	1,076	3,425	1,023	1,075	-325	87	*	27,379
8/80	1,312	200	750	4,800	4,650	1,100	1,162	-650	3,969	300	1,762	-757	*	18,598
9/80	-712	1,426	26,200	1,200	2,575	7,300	-1,748	2,975	1,875	225	737	374	*	42,427
10/80	713	1,337	-600	600	1,300	-500	342	775	2,625	475	187	-372	*	6,882
11/80	1,538	-800	4,350	975	875	1,200	152	-300	-1,347	838	1,075	198	*	8,754
12/80	375	1,337	16,850	-1,110	2,450	5,600	2,341	8,350	-563	1,225	2,263	396	*	39,514
1/81	1,013	2,211	3,750	475	-1,225	0	488	1,175	125	-362	1,062	528	*	9,240
2/81	-412	-350	-3,900	525	2,125	6,800	731	-1,000	2,944	-225	5,275	682	*	13,195
3/81	2,137	1,675	2,700	-1,025	2,200	6,350	4,050	1,200	1,562	400	-525	1,915	*	22,639
4/81	-262	749	2,350	975	1,675	-800	600	-200	250	700	1,562	-1,144	*	6,455
5/81	2,925	1,887	2,950	1,170	3,625	400	2,156	600	4,094	500	124	1,738	*	22,169
6/81	7,687	1,038	2,150	350	1,550	1,400	-37	1,150	562	750	*	-220	*	16,380
7/81	10,819	712	6,750	150	1,475	4,850	1,919	300	0	-400	-125	857	*	27,307
8/81	-450	-600	2,900	2,400	1,375	3,300	1,007	1,775	2,469	875	125	0	*	15,176
9/81	7,538	-450	12,850	775	650	850	399	-200	-468	700	4,362	616	*	27,622
10/81	2,663	-162	-1,050	225	175	1,750	-836	50	-250	-150	2,712	-111	*	5,016
11/81	1,424	1,787	2,150	1,025	3,700	3,400	2,033	875	3,812	875	2,275	207	*	23,563
12/81	507	0	550	1,000	350	-150	1,539	75	938	688	313	2,156	*	7,966
1/82	-19	1,925	850	785	-75	1,450	1,786	1,175	-915	125	725	1,122	*	8,934
2/82	-1,219	975	1,650	-150	-1,200	1,400	2,251	1,350	1,593	512	500	1,738	*	9,400
3/82	2,400	812	2,400	-275	1,425	2,300	-795	500	1,562	225	1,600	88	*	12,242
4/82	2,362	-112	-1,000	-50	175	*	1,647	0	-625	50	362	880	*	3,689
5/82	-375	-150	1,600	125	2,100	*	356	-100	-1,000	450	238	198	*	3,442
6/82	1,069	2,786	7,000	1,900	-300	300	4,534	1,400	2,125	250	2,787	1,210	400	25,461
7/82	2,250	213	1,500	1,450	1,400	2,350	19	1,025	-531	1,124	188	484	-1,325	10,147
8/82	1,125	-237	1,300	725	1,950	5,500	317	2,250	3,656	925	912	462	2,350	21,235
9/82	3,411	313	4,500	-775	1,375	5,750	1,148	1,475	1,710	425	1,125	462	-1,750	19,169
10/82	-1,350	-675	800	650	1,700	-1,000	1,843	100	2,281	-225	-388	440	1,250	5,425
11/82	225	3,224	1,100	50	1,100	50	246	-275	3,313	-100	-187	-418	3,400	11,723
12/82	1,313	2,062	4,150	-675	775	300	-342	-175	-531	200	4,625	154	-1,350	10,506
1/83	*	*	*	*	*	*	-551	725	1,313	*	1,925	616	*	4,028
	68,095	28,200	323,250	21,095	55,600	85,910	34,367	31,650	56,598	11,926	42,048	24,289	2,975	786,002

MONEY MANAGEMENT

There have been a number of books and publications discussing money management for commodities. These have run from very complex, sophisticated risk distribution and portfolio balancing criteria to simple obvious statements like "buy only commodities that will go up."

I'm not going to give you any exact rules to follow. But this is not to downplay the value of money management. It may be more important than the system you use. One excellent discussion of money management is in *Winning in the Commodities Market* by George Angell. Also, money management is discussed in my two books, *Advanced Commodity Trading Techniques* and *Eight New Commodity Technical Trading Methods.*

Money management rules, even more than trading systems, are subject to your own personal feelings, whims, and emotions. So be sure you work with rules you can stick with. If you break your rules, you'll suffer the consequences eventually. One important component of any money management "battle plan" is diversification. I would highly recommend this to anyone trading any commodity system. While some commodities interact with each other, there is quite a difference between the moves of different commodities. Pork Bellies and S&P 500 may be experiencing the same general market condition, but will have different fundamentals. By diversifying, you will lessen your risk and potential drawdown (drawdown is the largest loss you suffer at any one time). Trade 5 very different commodities, instead of 5 contracts of your favorite commodity. If you lose a bit of money in one commodity, you've got four others backing you up.

There is one other money management rule I'd like you to follow. Don't trade beyond your means. Every system will have a losing period. Make sure you have enough money in your commodity account to ride out these weak periods. Don't overcommit yourself at any one time—and don't trade commodities with money you need. Use only your speculative funds. I'll end this discussion with what is probably the most important money management rule of all: Use common sense and don't let your emotions control your trading.

A PERSONAL NOTE

What you've learned here should make you a successful commodity trader. You can trade the Spike-35 System exactly as its presented, or make modifications where you see fit.

The most important thing I can tell you is to trade intelligently. Anyone can just place an order. But, if you're using your brain, you'll be more confident in your trading. Think while you use the system. Maybe you'll find something that works even better.

The Spike-35 System is not the ultimate answer. There are always new ideas or improvements. I'm sure you'll make money trading the Spike-35 as is. But real winners are not sheep, blindly following rules. Question what I've taught you. You may find something better—and you may not. But the important thing is to think. It will give you confidence. And you'd be amazed at how much better a system works when you trade it with confidence.

Whether you trade Spike-35 or your own Spike-36, Spike-37, or Spike-100, you are now better prepared for commodities trading than almost every other trader in the market.

Good luck and happy trading!

COMMODITY PERSPECTIVE/CHICAGO, ILLINOIS 60604

Coffee, Sugar and Cocoa Exchange, Inc., N.Y.

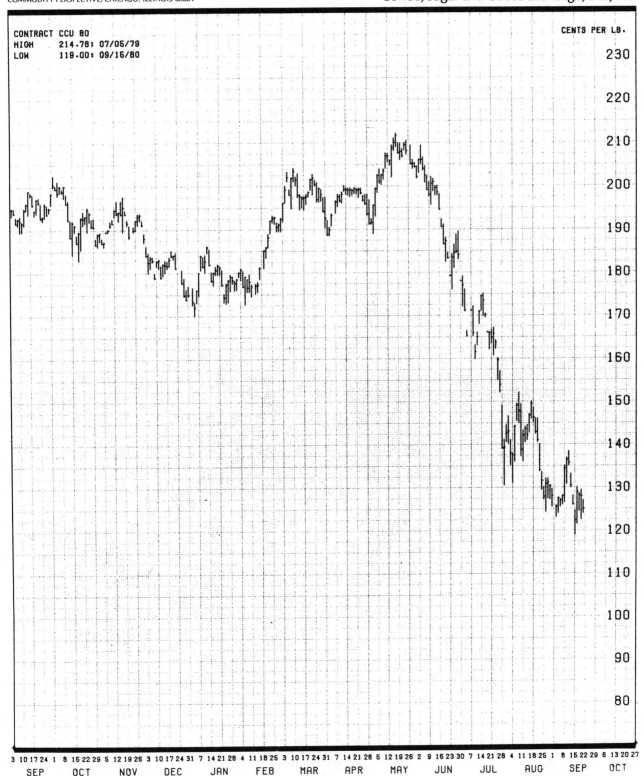

CONTRACT CCU 80
HIGH   214.78: 07/06/79
LOW   119.00: 09/16/80

CENTS PER LB.

SPIKE-35 TRADING RESULTS
80 Sept Coffee

Order	Entry and Exit Dates	Entry Rule	Entry and Exit Prices	Gain	Loss
Sell	12-26-79 12-31-79	CB2L	177.60 175.00	$ 975.00	
Sell	1- 3-80 1- 5-80	REN	173.60 173.40	75.00	
Buy	1-11-80 1-12-80	CA2H	186.00 182.50		$ 962.50
Sell	1-23-80 1-24-80	CB2L	174.30 177.00		1012.50
Sell	1-25-80 1-25-80	REN	174.30 177.00		1012.50
Sell	1-30-80 2- 1-80	REN	177.00 178.00		375.00
Sell	2- 5-80 2- 8-80	REN	177.50 179.00		562.50
Sell	2-11-80 2-14-80	REN	176.50 177.00		187.50
Buy	2-15-80 2-26-80	CA2H	181.00 192.00	3750.00	
Buy	3- 3-80 3- 6-80	REN	193.00 199.00	2250.00	
Buy	3-10-80 3-11-80	REN	202.00 201.50		187.50
Buy	3-19-80 3-24-80	RR#2	198.00 201.50	1312.50	
Sell	3-28-80 4- 3-80	CB2L	194.00 191.00	1125.00	
Sell	4-22-80 4-23-80	RR#2	197.40 199.40		750.00
Sell	4-24-80 4-28-80	REN	197.50 196.70	300.00	
Sell	4-28-80 4-29-80	REN	195.70 195.70	0	0

SPIKE-35 TRADING RESULTS
80 Sept Coffee (Cont'd)

Order	Entry and Exit Dates	Entry Rule	Entry and Exit Prices	Gain	Loss
Sell	4-29-80 5- 1-80	REN	193.40 191.40	$ 750.00	
Buy	5- 6-80 5- 7-80	TDR	202.40 201.00		$ 525.00
Buy	5- 8-80 5-13-80	REN	202.50 206.00	$1312.50	
Buy	5-14-80 5-19-80	REN	207.30 209.70	900.00	
Buy	5-23-80 5-27-80	REN	209.70 208.00		637.50
Sell	5-30-80 6- 2-80	CB2L	202.00 204.40		900.00
Sell	6- 5-80 6-10-80	REN	202.00 199.50	1125.00	
Sell	6-16-80 6-24-80	REN	198.00 188.00	3750.00	
Sell	7- 1-80 7- 8-80	REN	178.00 171.00	2625.00	
Sell	7- 9-80 7-10-80	REN	163.00 166.00		1125.00

COFFEE

MAY 1981

COMMODITY PERSPECTIVE/CHICAGO, ILLINOIS 60604

Coffee, Sugar and Cocoa Exchange, Inc., N.Y.

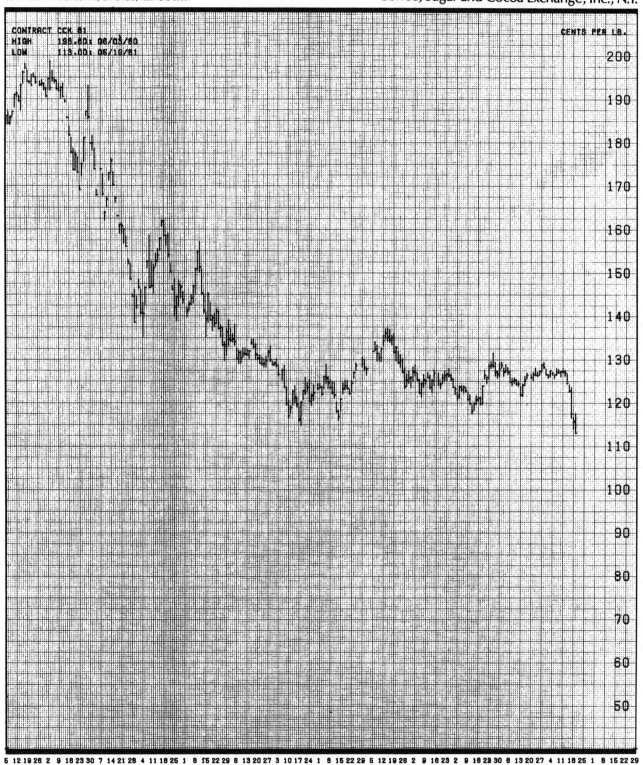

CONTRACT CCK 81
HIGH   198.60: 06/05/80
LOW   113.00: 06/18/81

CENTS PER LB.

SPIKE-35 TRADING RESULTS
81 May Coffee

Order	Entry and Exit Dates	Entry Rule	Entry and Exit Prices	Gain	Loss
Sell	7-18-80 7-30-80	CB2L	160.70 144.50	$6075.00	
Sell	8- 4-80 8- 5-80	REN	138.50 142.50		$1500.00
Buy	8-12-80 8-19-80	TDR	152.50 158.50	2250.00	
Sell	8-22-80 8-26-80	TDR	146.00 144.50	562.50	
Sell	9- 2-80 9- 4-80	REN	142.00 142.60		225.00
Buy	9- 9-80 9-10-80	TDR	154.50 150.70		1425.00
Sell	9-15-80 9-16-80	CB2L	139.20 141.20		750.00
Sell	9-18-80 9-19-80	REN	139.00 139.50		187.50
Sell	9-23-80 9-29-80	REN	138.00 133.00	1875.00	
Sell	10- 3-80 10- 8-80	REN	134.00 131.50	937.50	
Sell	10-14-80 10-15-80	REN	130.00 131.10		412.50
Sell	10-20-80 10-23-80	REN	130.00 129.00	375.00	
Sell	10-23-80 10-24-80	REN	128.50 129.00		187.50
Sell	10-29-80 10-31-80	REN	129.00 129.00	0	0
Sell	11- 3-80 11- 6-80	REN	128.50 127.50	375.00	
Sell	11- 6-80 11-12-80	REN	126.50 119.40	2662.50	

SPIKE-35 TRADING RESULTS
81 May Coffee (Cont'd)

Order	Entry and Exit Dates	Entry Rule	Entry and Exit Prices	Gain	Loss
Sell	11-17-80 11-18-80	REN	117.00 119.50		$937.50
Sell	11-25-80 11-26-80	REN	120.00 121.50		562.50
Buy	12- 3-80 12- 5-80	CA2H	126.00 125.00		187.50
Sell	12-11-80 12-15-80	CA2L	118.00 118.00	0	0
Buy	12-23-80 12-30-80	TDR	127.00 128.50	$562.50	
Buy	1- 6-81 1- 7-81	REN	132.00 131.50		187.50
Buy	1-12-81 1-15-81	REN	133.00 135.00	750.00	
Sell	1-21-81 1-23-81	TDR	129.20 130.00		300.00
Sell	1-23-81 1-28-81	TDR	127.00 125.00	750.00	
Sell	2- 3-81 2- 5-81	REN	125.00 124.50	187.50	
Sell	2-11-81 2-13-81	REN	124.50 125.00		187.50

COFFEE

SEPTEMBER 1981

Coffee, Sugar and Cocoa Exchange, Inc., N.Y.

COMMODITY PERSPECTIVE/CHICAGO, ILLINOIS 60604

CONTRACT CCU 81
HIGH   198.05, 06/05/80
LOW   88.75, 06/26/81

CENTS PER LB.

SEP OCT NOV DEC JAN FEB MAR APR MAY JUN JUL AUG SEP OCT

SPIKE-35 TRADING RESULTS
81 Sept Coffee

Order	Entry and Exit Dates	Entry Rule	Entry and Exit Prices	Gain	Loss
Sell	2-18-81 2-19-81	REN	129.80 130.10		$412.50
Sell	2-25-81 3- 4-81	REN	131.10 125.60	$2062.50	
Sell	3- 9-81 3-13-81	REN	125.10 123.50	600.00	
Buy	3-19-81 3-25-81	TDR	128.00 127.60		150.00
Buy	3-30-81 3-31-81	REN	127.60 126.60		375.00
Buy	4- 2-81 4- 4-81	REN	127.40 126.40		375.00
Sell	4- 6-81 4- 8-81	CB2L	125.10 125.20		37.50
Sell	4-10-81 4-15-81	REN	124.90 124.10	300.00	
Sell	4-23-81 4-24-81	REN	124.60 125.60		375.00
Buy	4-24-81 4-29-81	TDR	126.20 126.80	225.00	
Buy	5- 7-81 5- 9-81	REN	127.40 126.60		337.50
Buy	5-11-81 5-12-81	REN	127.30 127.00		112.50
Sell	5-13-81 5-21-81	TDR	124.60 115.60	3375.00	

COFFEE

MARCH 1982

Coffee, Sugar and Cocoa Exchange, Inc., N.Y.

COMMODITY PERSPECTIVE/CHICAGO, ILLINOIS 60604

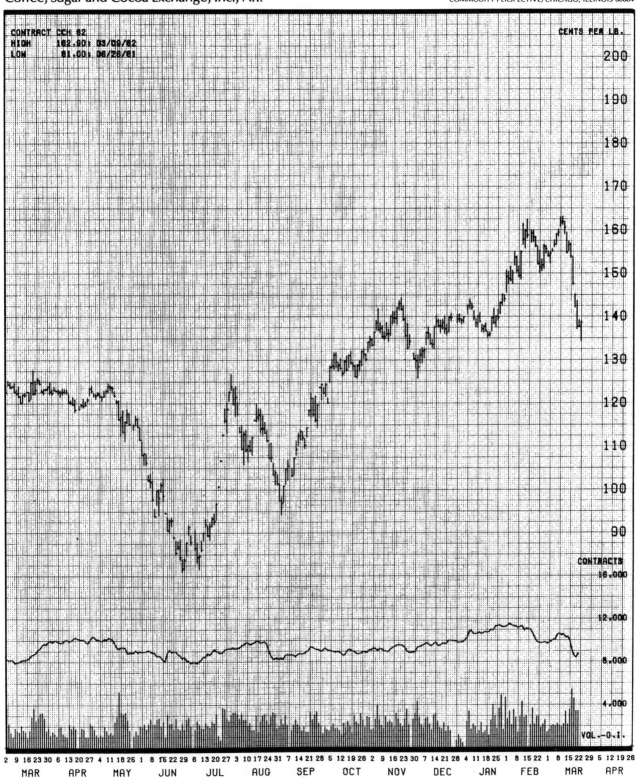

CONTRACT CCH 82
HIGH   162.30: 03/09/82
LOW   81.00: 06/26/81

CENTS PER LB.

SPIKE-35 TRADING RESULTS
82 Mar Coffee

Order	Entry and Exit Dates	Entry Rule	Entry and Exit Prices	Gain	Loss
Sell	5-28-81	REN	114.50		
	6-10-81		97.50	6,375.00	
Sell	6-17-81	REN	93.50		
	6-19-81		92.50	375.00	
Sell	6-22-81	REN	88.50		
	6-25-81		86.50	750.00	
Sell	6-25-81	REN	85.00		
	6-30-81		84.50	187.50	
Sell	7- 7-81	REN	85.60		
	7- 9-81		85.60	0	0
Buy	7-13-81	CA2H	91.60		
	7-14-81		89.95		$618.75
Buy	7-16-81	REN	92.00		
	7-30-81		122.50	11,437.50	
Sell	8-11-81	TDR	108.80		
	8-12-81		110.00		450.00
Sell	8-19-81	REN	114.00		
	8-20-81		114.00	0	0
Sell	8-20-81	REN	113.00		
	9- 2-81		97.40	5,850.00	
Buy	9-11-81	TDR	112.50		
	9-15-81		112.50	0	0
Buy	9-17-81	REN	113.00		
	9-22-81		118.00	1,875.00	
Buy	9-28-81	REN	123.50		
	9-29-81		123.00		187.50

SPIKE-35 TRADING RESULTS
82 Mar Coffee (Cont'd)

Order	Entry and Exit Dates	Entry Rule	Entry and Exit Prices	Gain	Loss
Buy	10- 2-81	REN	124.60		
	10- 6-81		128.60	$1,500.00	
Buy	10- 6-81	REN	129.50		
	10- 8-81		129.00		$187.50
Buy	10-13-81	REN	129.50		
	10-19-81		129.20		112.50
Buy	10-22-81	REN	129.60		
	10-27-81		131.10	562.50	
Buy	10-28-81	REN	131.60		
	10-30-81		134.00	900.00	
Buy	11- 2-81	REN	135.00		
	11- 5-81		136.70	637.50	
Buy	11-10-81	REN	137.10		
	11-11-81		135.10		750.00
Buy	11-12-81	REN	137.10		
	11-16-81		139.40	862.50	
Buy	11-17-81	REN	140.00		
	11-19-81		141.80	675.00	
Sell	11-24-81	CB2L	132.40		
	12- 1-81		129.60	1,050.00	

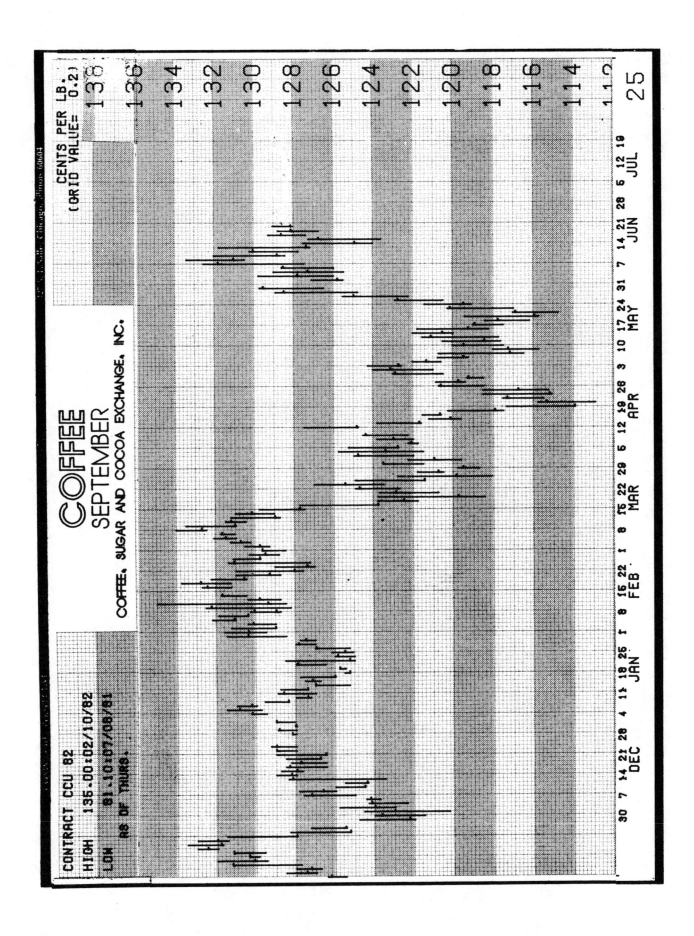

SPIKE-35 TRADING RESULTS
82 Sept. Coffee

Order	Exit and Exit Dates	Entry Rule	Entry and Exit Prices	Gain	Loss
Sell	12-11-81	REN	124.30		
	12-11-81		124.45		$ 56.25
Buy	12-11-81	CA2H	128.20		
	12-13-81		128.00		75.00
Buy	12-16-81	REN	128.30		
	12-16-81		128.00		112.50
Buy	12-18-81	REN	128.40		
	12-21-81		127.80		225.00
Buy	12-22-81	REN	128.40		
	12-28-81		128.20		75.00
Buy	12-31-81	REN	129.00		
	1- 6-82		130.00	$ 375.00	
Sell	1-15-82	STDR	126.00		
	1-20-82		126.40		150.00
Sell	1-21-82	REN	125.25		
	1-25-82		125.90		243.75
Buy	1-29-82	CA2H	130.40		
	2- 1-82		130.10		112.50
Buy	2- 4-82	REN	131.05		
	2- 8-82		130.15		337.50
Buy	2- 9-82	REN	131.05		
	2-10-82		129.00		768.75
Buy	2-16-82	REN	132.25		
	2-18-82		132.25	0	0
Sell	2-22-82	CB2L	128.00		
	2-24-82		128.00	0	0
Sell	3- 2-82	REN	129.50		
	3- 2-82		129.50	0	0
Sell	3-10-82	REN	130.75		
	3-11-82		131.20		168.75

SPIKE-35 TRADING RESULTS
82 Sept Coffe (Cont'd)

Order	Entry and Exit Dates	Entry Rule	Entry and Exit Prices	Gain	Loss
Sell	3-12-82	REN	131.00		
	3-19-82		122.45	$3206.25	
Sell	3-25-82	REN	121.40		
	3-26-82		121.40	0	0
Sell	3-29-82	REN	119.80		
	3-30-82		121.50		$637.50
Sell	4-13-82	REN	121.70		
	4-21-82		115.40	2362.50	
Buy	4-29-82	CA2H	122.90		
	5- 3-82		122.90	0	0
Buy	5-11-82	REN	119.45		
	5-12-82		118.45		375.00
Buy	5-12-82	REN	119.45		
	5-14-82		120.45	375.00	
Sell	5-19-82	TDR	116.00		
	5-21-82		117.00		375.00
Buy	5-25-82	CA2H	122.80		
	6- 1-82		127.00	1575.00	
Buy	6- 2-82	REN	129.60		
	6- 3-82		125.80		1425.00
Buy	6- 7-82	REN	128.50		
	6- 9-82		130.95	918.75	

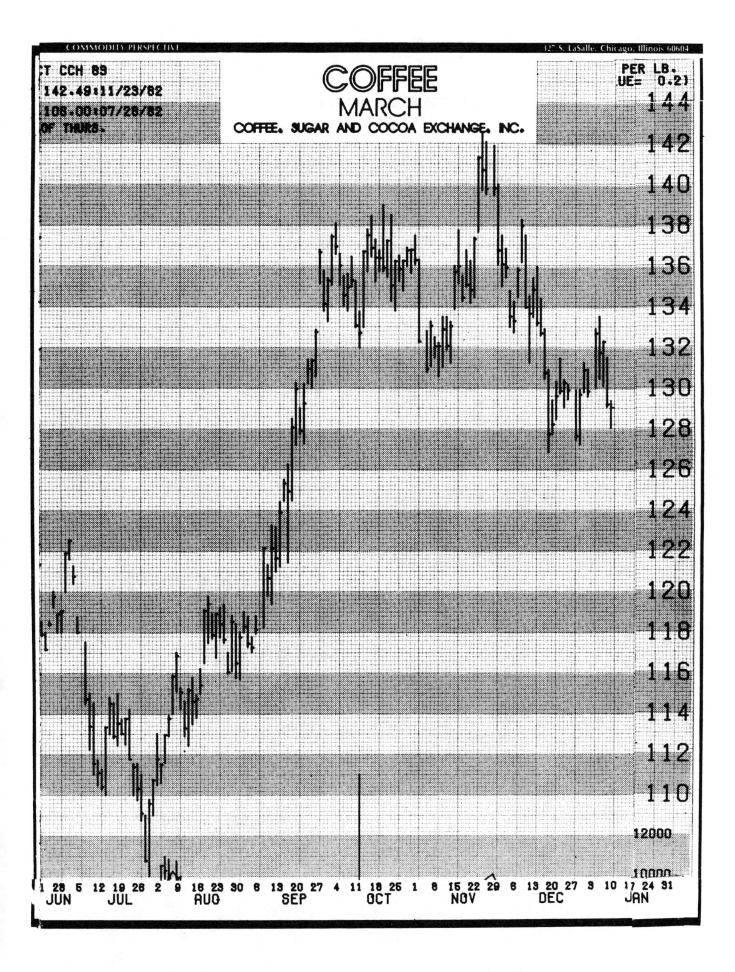

COFFEE
MARCH
COFFEE, SUGAR AND COCOA EXCHANGE, INC.

CT CCH 89
142.49:11/23/82
106.00:07/28/82
OF THURS.

PER LB.
UE= 0.2)

SPIKE-35 TRADING RESULTS
83 Mar Coffee

Order	Entry and Exit Dates	Entry Rule	Entry and Exit Prices	Gain	Loss
Buy	6-29-82	CA2H	121.80		
	7- 1-82		121.30		$187.50
Sell	7- 6-82	CB2L	114.80		
	7-13-82		111.10	$1387.50	
Sell	7-20-82	REN	112.80		
	7-20-82		113.60		300.00
Sell	7-21-82	REN	112.80		
	7-28-82		109.20	1350.00	
Buy	8- 5-82	CA2H	115.80		
	8- 9-82		115.30		187.50
Buy	8-16-82	REN	115.40		
	8-19-82		118.90	1312.50	
Buy	8-31-82	REN	118.60		
	9- 1-82		117.80		300.00
Buy	9- 3-82	REN	118.40		
	9- 9-82		120.70	862.50	
Buy	9- 9-82	REN	122.20		
	9-13-82		121.70		187.50
Buy	9-13-82	REN	122.20		
	9-15-82		124.00	675.00	
Buy	9-16-82	REN	125.40		
	9-20-82		128.10	1012.50	
Buy	9-21-82	REN	130.00		
	9-24-82		130.90	337.50	
Buy	9-24-82	REN	131.50		
	9-29-82		134.20	1012.50	
Buy	9-30-82	REN	136.80		
	10- 4-82		136.60		$ 75.00
Sell	10- 8-82	CB2L	133.20		
	10-12-82		133.20	0	0

SPIKE-35 TRADING RESULTS
83 Mar Coffee (Cont'd)

Order	Entry and Exit Dates	Entry Rule	Entry and Exit Prices	Gain	Loss
Buy	10-13-82	TDR	137.60		
	10-14-82		136.60		$375.00
Buy	10-19-82	REN	137.60		
	10-19-82		136.40		450.00
Buy	10-20-82	REN	136.90		
	10-21-82		135.90		375.00
Buy	10-27-82	REN	136.40		
	10-28-82		136.30		37.50
Buy	10-29-82	REN	136.90		
	10-30-82		136.80		37.50
Sell	11- 1-82	CB2L	132.30		
	11- 3-82		132.30	0	0
Sell	11- 8-82	REN	131.00		
	11- 9-82		132.10		412.50
Sell	11-11-82	REN	131.90		
	11-11-82		132.90		375.00
Buy	11-19-82	TDR	137.40		
	11-24-82		140.70	$1237.50	
Buy	11-26-82	REN	141.40		
	11-26-82		140.80		225.00
Sell	12- 2-82	CB2L	133.60		
	12- 6-82		134.50		337.50
Sell	12- 9-82	REN	133.50		
	12-10-82		134.10		225.00
Sell	12-13-82	REN	133.50		
	12-20-82		128.50	1875.00	
Sell	12-27-82	REN	129.80		
	12-28-82		129.80	0	0

JAPANESE YEN

SEPTEMBER 1980

International Monetary Market

COMMODITY PERSPECTIVE/CHICAGO, ILLINOIS 60604

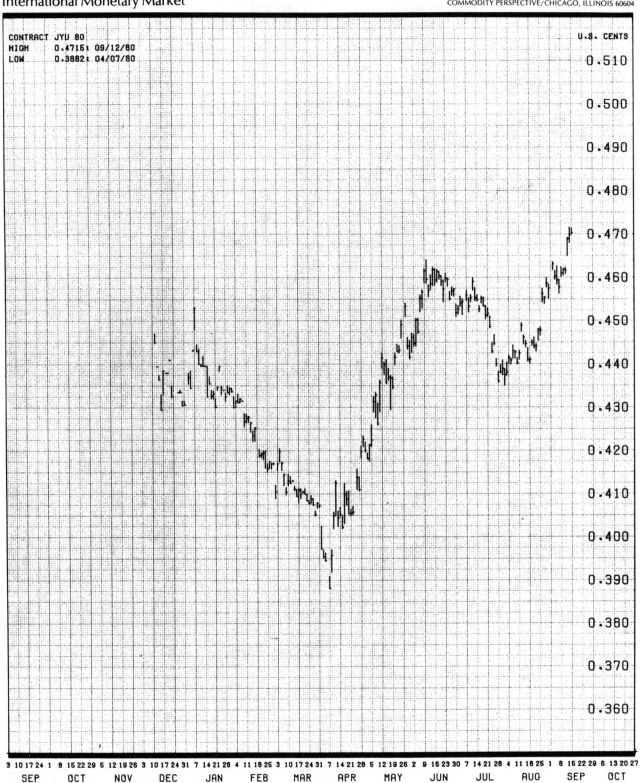

```
CONTRACT  JYU 80                                    U.S. CENTS
HIGH      0.4715: 09/12/80
LOW       0.3882: 04/07/80
```

0.510

0.500

0.490

0.480

0.470

0.460

0.450

0.440

0.430

0.420

0.410

0.400

0.390

0.380

0.370

0.360

3 10 17 24 1 8 15 22 29 5 12 19 26 3 10 17 24 31 7 14 21 28 4 11 18 25 3 10 17 24 31 7 14 21 28 5 12 19 26 2 9 16 23 30 7 14 21 28 4 11 18 25 1 8 15 22 29 6 13 20 27

SEP   OCT   NOV   DEC   JAN   FEB   MAR   APR   MAY   JUN   JUL   AUG   SEP   OCT

SPIKE-35 TRADING RESULTS
80 Sept Yen

Order	Entry and Exit Dates	Entry Rule	Entry and Exit Prices	Gain	Loss
Sell	1-21-80 1-22-80	CB2H	43.03 43.40		$462.50
Sell	1-28-80 1-29-80	REN	43.35 43.40		62.50
Sell	2- 1-80 2- 5-80	REN	43.25 43.16	$ 112.50	
Sell	2- 8-80 2-12-80	REN	42.80 42.75	62.50	
Sell	2-13-80 2-21-80	REN	42.65 41.95	875.00	
Sell	2-22-80 3- 3-80	REN	41.90 41.70	250.00	
Sell	3- 7-80 3-10-80	REN	41.15 41.45		375.00
Sell	3-14-80 3-17-80	REN	41.05 41.12		87.50
Sell	3-18-80 3-20-80	REN	40.95 41.05		125.00
Sell	3-21-80 3-22-80	REN	40.95 40.87	100.00	
Sell	3-26-80 3-28-80	REN	40.75 40.75	0	0
Sell	4- 1-80 4- 8-80	REN	40.25 39.50	937.50	
Buy	4-10-80 4-11-80	CA2H	41.25 40.50		937.50
Buy	4-17-80 4-19-80	REN	41.02 40.88		175.00
Buy	4-24-80 4-30-80	REN	41.10 42.00	1125.00	

SPIKE-35 TRADING RESULTS
80 Sept Yen (Cont'd)

Order	Entry and Exit Dates	Entry Rule	Entry and Exit Prices	Gain	Loss
Buy	5- 5-80	REN	42.27		
	5- 8-80		43.10	$1037.50	
Buy	5- 9-80	REN	43.30		
	5-14-80		43.98	850.00	
Buy	5-20-80	REN	44.00		
	5-28-80		44.60	750.00	
Buy	6- 3-80	REN	44.63		
	6-11-80		45.81	1475.00	
Buy	6-13-80	REN	46.17		
	6-14-80		45.85		$400.00
Sell	6-25-80	TDR	45.50		
	6-27-80		45.70		250.00
Sell	6-30-80	REN	45.39		
	7- 2-80		45.27	150.00	
Sell	7- 3-80	REN	45.17		
	7- 3-80		45.40		287.50
Sell	7- 8-80	REN	45.25		
	7- 9-80		45.60		437.50
Buy	7-10-80	CA2H	45.92		
	7-11-80		45.54		475.00

JAPANESE YEN

MARCH 1981

International Monetary Market

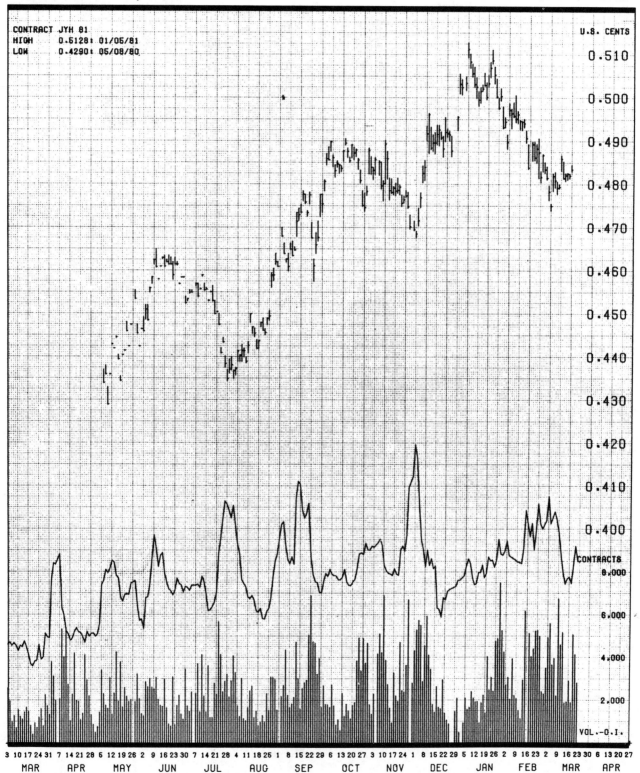COMMODITY PERSPECTIVE/CHICAGO, ILLINOIS 60604

CONTRACT JYH 81
HIGH 0.5128: 01/06/81
LOW 0.4290: 05/08/80

U.S. CENTS

0.510
0.500
0.490
0.480
0.470
0.460
0.450
0.440
0.430
0.420
0.410
0.400

CONTRACTS
8,000
6,000
4,000
2,000

VOL.-O.I.

3 10 17 24 31 7 14 21 28 5 12 19 26 2 9 16 23 30 7 14 21 28 4 11 18 25 1 8 15 22 29 6 13 20 27 3 10 17 24 1 8 15 22 29 5 12 19 26 2 9 16 23 2 9 16 23 30 6 13 20 27

MAR APR MAY JUN JUL AUG SEP OCT NOV DEC JAN FEB MAR APR

SPIKE-35 TRADING RESULTS
81 Mar Yen

Order	Entry and Exit Dates	Entry Rule	Entry and Exit Prices	Gain	Loss
Sell	7-18-80 7-29-80	CB2L	45.00 43.87	$1412.50	
Sell	8- 8-80 8-11-80	REN	44.00 44.15		$187.50
Buy	8-11-80 8-14-80	CA2H	44.28 44.67	487.50	
Buy	8-19-80 8-21-80	REN	44.70 44.62		100.00
Buy	8-22-80 9- 4-80	REN	44.80 46.28	1850.00	
Buy	9- 9-80 9-18-80	REN	46.50 47.36	1075.00	
Buy	9-19-80 9-22-80	REN	47.75 47.12		787.50
Sell	9-23-80 9-25-80	CB2L	46.13 46.70		712.50
Buy	9-30-80 10- 6-80	TDR	48.07 48.57	625.00	
Buy	10-13-80 10-15-80	REN	48.55 48.77	275.00	
Sell	10-23-80 10-28-80	CB2L	48.10 47.75	437.50	
Sell	11- 5-80 11-10-80	REN	48.34 48.04	375.00	
Buy	11-10-80 11-12-80	CA2H	48.95 48.15		1000.00
Sell	11-20-80 11-24-80	CB2L	47.57 47.71		175.00
Sell	11-25-80 12- 2-80	REN	47.56 46.97	737.50	

JAPANESE YEN

JUNE 1981

International Monetary Market

COMMODITY PERSPECTIVE/CHICAGO, ILLINOIS 60604

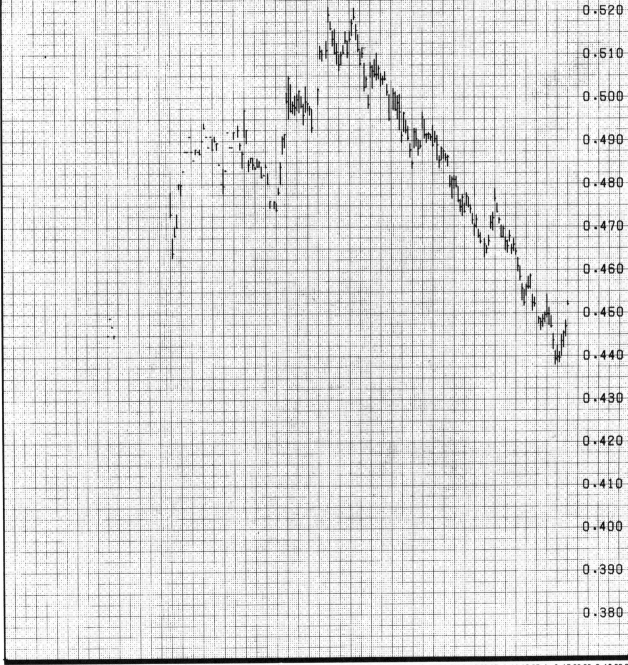

CONTRACT JYM 81
HIGH   0.5208 x 01/06/81
LOW   0.4379 x 06/06/81

U.S. CENTS

0.530
0.520
0.510
0.500
0.490
0.480
0.470
0.460
0.450
0.440
0.430
0.420
0.410
0.400
0.390
0.380

2 9 16 23 30 7 14 21 28 4 11 18 25 1 8 15 22 29 6 13 20 27 3 10 17 24 1 8 15 22 29 5 12 19 26 2 9 16 23 2 9 16 23 30 6 13 20 27 4 11 18 25 1 8 15 22 29 6 13 20 27

JUN   JUL   AUG   SEP   OCT   NOV   DEC   JAN   FEB   MAR   APR   MAY   JUN   JUL

SPIKE-35 TRADING RESULTS
81 June Japanese Yen

Order	Entry and Exit Dates	Entry Rule	Entry and Exit Prices	Gain	Loss
Buy	12- 4-80 12-10-80	CA2H	49.05 49.87	$1025.00	
Buy	12-16-80 12-17-80	REN	49.93 49.93	0	0
Buy	12-19-80 12-23-80	REN	50.14 49.80		425.00
Buy	12-29-80 1- 2-81	REN	49.85 51.00	1437.50	
Buy	1- 2-81 1- 7-81	REN	51.03 51.50	587.50	
Buy	1-14-81 1-16-81	REN	51.01 51.01	0	0
Buy	1-19-81 1-22-81	REN	51.31 51.46	187.50	
Sell	1-28-81 2- 2-81	CB2L	50.22 50.45		600.00
Sell	2- 6-81 2- 6-81	REN	50.49 50.55		75.00
Sell	2- 9-81 2-11-81	REN	50.49 50.43	75.00	
Sell	2-12-81 2-17-81	REN	50.30 50.10	250.00	
Sell	2-20-81 3- 2-81	REN	49.50 48.80	875.00	
Sell	3-13-81 3-16-81	REN	49.05 49.15		125.00
Sell	3-16-81 3-17-81	REN	49.05 49.05	0	0
Sell	3-18-81 3-20-81	REN	48.87 48.55	400.00	

SPIKE-35 TRADING RESULTS
81 June Japanese Yen (Cont'd)

Order	Entry and Exit Dates	Entry Rule	Entry and Exit Prices	Gain	Loss
Sell	3-24-81 3-30-81	REN	48.53 48.11	$ 525.00	
Sell	3-31-81 4- 3-81	REN	47.96 47.61	437.50	
Sell	4- 6-81 4- 7-81	REN	47.45 47.70		$312.50
Sell	4- 9-81 4-14-81	REN	47.33 47.16	212.50	
Sell	4-15-81 4-22-81	REN	46.93 46.60	412.50	
Sell	4-29-81 5- 6-81	REN	47.07 46.67	500.00	

JAPANESE YEN

DECEMBER 1981

International Monetary Market

COMMODITY PERSPECTIVE/CHICAGO, ILLINOIS 60604

CONTRACT JYZ 81
HIGH   0.5320 01/21/81
LOW   0.4232 08/04/81

U.S. CENTS

0.530
0.520
0.510
0.500
0.490
0.480
0.470
0.460
0.450
0.440
0.430
0.420
0.410
0.400
0.390
0.380

1 8 15 22 29   5 12 19 26   2 9 16 23   2 9 16 23 30   6 13 20 27   4 11 18 25   1 8 15 22 29   6 13 20 27   3 10 17 24 31   7 14 21 28   5 12 19 26   2 9 16 23 30   7 14 21 28   4 11 18 25

DEC   JAN   FEB   MAR   APR   MAY   JUN   JUL   AUG   SEP   OCT   NOV   DEC   JAN

SPIKE-35 TRADING RESULTS
81 Dec Japanese Yen

Order	Entry and Exit Dates	Entry Rule	Entry and Exit Prices	Gain	Loss
Sell	5-12-81	TDR	48.30		
	5-19-81		47.74	$ 700.00	
Sell	5-21-81	REN	47.50		
	5-29-81		46.95	687.50	
Sell	6- 2-81	REN	46.85		
	6- 9-81		45.97	1100.00	
Buy	6-15-81	TDR	47.30		
	6-17-81		47.25		$ 62.50
Sell	6-30-81	CB2L	45.72		
	7- 2-81		45.82		125.00
Sell	7- 6-81	REN	45.40		
	7- 8-81		45.56		200.00
Sell	7-14-81	REN	45.27		
	7-23-81		44.52	937.50	
Sell	7-23-81	REN	44.32		
	7-24-81		44.52		250.00
Sell	7-27-81	REN	44.30		
	7-29-81		44.02	350.00	
Sell	7-29-81	REN	43.75		
	8- 5-81		43.35	500.00	
Buy	8-12-81	CA2H	45.07		
	8-14-81		44.72		437.50
Buy	8-17-81	REN	45.07		
	8-19-81		45.17	125.00	
Buy	8-21-81	REN	45.47		
	8-24-81		45.17		375.00
Buy	8-28-81	REN	45.14		
	8-31-81		44.81		412.50

SPIKE-35 TRADING RESULTS
81 Dec Japanese Yen (Cont'd)

Order	Entry and Exit Dates	Entry Rule	Entry and Exit Prices	Gain	Loss
Sell	8-31-81	CB2L	44.40		
	9- 2-81		44.75		$437.50
Sell	9- 8-81	REN	44.55		
	9-10-81		44.20	$ 437.50	
Buy	9-14-81	TDR	45.20		
	9-16-81		45.20	0	0
Buy	9-21-81	REN	45.56		
	9-22-81		45.20		450.00
Sell	9-29-81	CB2L	43.71		
	10- 1-81		43.75		50.00
Buy	10- 9-81	CA2H	44.89		
	10-12-81		44.58		387.50
Sell	10-15-81	CB2L	43.85		
	10-23-81		43.40	562.50	
Sell	10-26-81	REN	42.92		
	10-28-81		43.15		287.50
Buy	11- 3-81	TDR	44.66		
	11- 5-81		44.40		325.00
Buy	11-12-81	REN	44.28		
	11-13-81		44.20		100.00
Buy	11-16-81	REN	44.38		
	11-24-81		46.15	2212.50	

JAPANESE YEN

MARCH 1982

International Monetary Market

COMMODITY PERSPECTIVE/CHICAGO, ILLINOIS 60604

CONTRACT JYH 82
HIGH   0.4820: 06/16/81
LOW   0.4150: 03/12/82

SPIKE-35 TRADING RESULTS
82 Mar Japanese Yen

Order	Entry and Exit Dates	Entry Rule	Entry and Exit Prices	Gain	Loss
Buy	12- 2-81	REN	47.46		
	12- 3-81		47.00		$575.00
Sell	12-11-81	TDR	46.35		
	12-15-81		46.35	0	0
Sell	12-21-81	REN	46.22		
	12-22-81		46.30		100.00
Sell	12-23-81	REN	46.14		
	12-29-81		45.60	$ 675.00	
Sell	1- 6-82	REN	46.20		
	1-15-82		45.12	1350.00	
Sell	1-18-82	REN	45.05		
	1-19-82		45.05	0	0
Sell	1-19-82	REN	44.94		
	1-20-82		44.98		50.00
Sell	1-21-82	REN	44.85		
	1-27-82		44.35	625.00	
Sell	1-27-82	REN	44.14		
	2- 4-82		43.25	1112.50	
Sell	2- 8-82	REN	43.20		
	2-11-82		42.76	550.00	

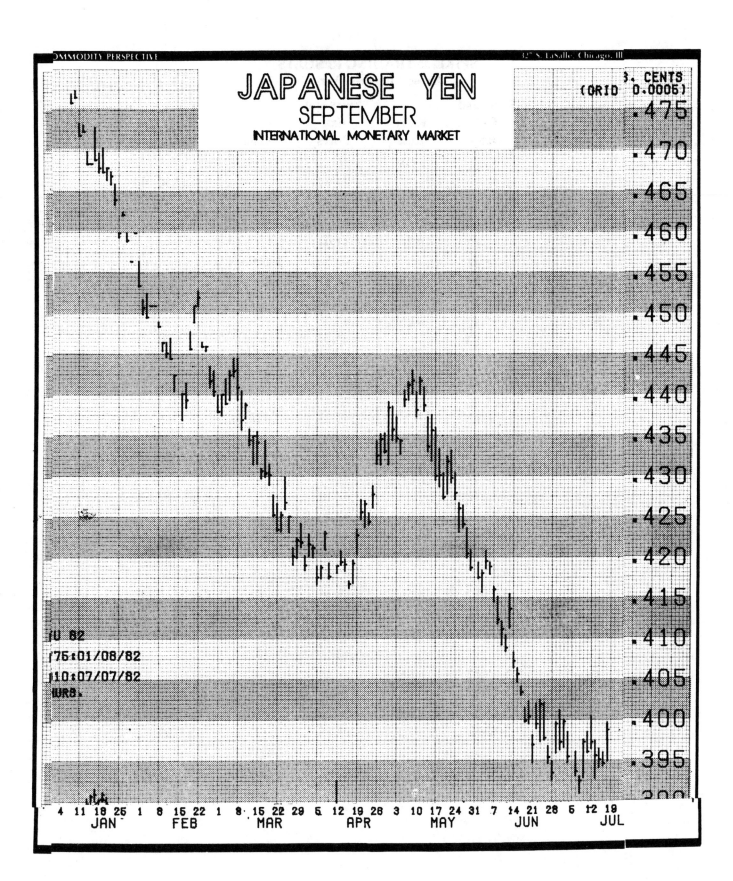

JAPANESE YEN
SEPTEMBER
INTERNATIONAL MONETARY MARKET

3. CENTS
(GRID 0.0005)

.475
.470
.465
.460
.455
.450
.445
.440
.435
.430
.425
.420
.415
.410
.405
.400
.395

U 82
75:01/08/82
10:07/07/82
WR8:

4 11 18 25   1   8 15 22   1   8 15 22 29   5 12 19 26   3 10 17 24 31   7 14 21 28   5 12 19
   JAN   FEB   MAR   APR   MAY   JUN   JUL

SPIKE-35 TRADING RESULTS
82 Sept Japanese Yen

Order	Entry and Exit Dates	Entry Rule	Entry and Exit Prices	Gain	Loss
Buy	2-22-82	TDR	45.20		
	2-23-82		44.65		$687.50
Sell	3- 1-82	TDR	43.80		
	3- 2-82		44.00		250.00
Sell	3- 9-82	REN	43.90		
	3-15-82		43.50	$ 500.00	
Sell	3-15-82	REN	43.35		
	3-17-82		43.42		87.50
Sell	3-17-82	REN	43.04		
	3-18-82		43.06		25.00
Sell	3-18-82	REN	42.97		
	3-23-82		42.52	562.50	
Sell	3-25-82	REN	42.32		
	3-30-82		42.23	112.50	
Sell	3-31-82	REN	42.00		
	4- 1-82		42.19		237.50
Sell	4- 5-82	REN	41.87		
	4- 7-82		42.10		287.50
Sell	4-15-82	REN	41.70		
	4-16-82		41.92		275.00
Buy	4-20-82	CA2H	42.55		
	4-22-82		42.54		12.50
Buy	4-23-82	REN	42.71		
	4-29-82		43.27	700.00	
Buy	4-29-82	REN	43.45		
	5- 3-82		43.55	125.00	
Buy	5- 5-82	REN	43.85		
	5-10-82		44.03	225.00	
Buy	5-11-82	REN	44.20		
	5-12-82		43.80		500.00

SPIKE-35 TRADING RESULTS
82 Sept Japanese Yen (Cont'd)

Order	Entry and Exit Dates	Entry Rule	Entry and Exit Prices	Gain	Loss
Sell	5-17-82 5-19-82	CB2L	43.00 43.00	0	0
Sell	5-24-82 6- 3-82	REN	42.72 41.85	$1087.50	
Sell	6- 7-82 6-11-82	REN	41.64 41.12	650.00	
Sell	6-14-82 6-22-82	REN	40.82 40.05	962.50	
Sell	6-25-82 6-29-82	REN	39.67 39.60	87.50	
Sell	7- 6-82 7- 8-82	REN	39.52 39.35	212.50	
Sell	7-14-82 7-15-82	REN	39.55 39.55	0	0

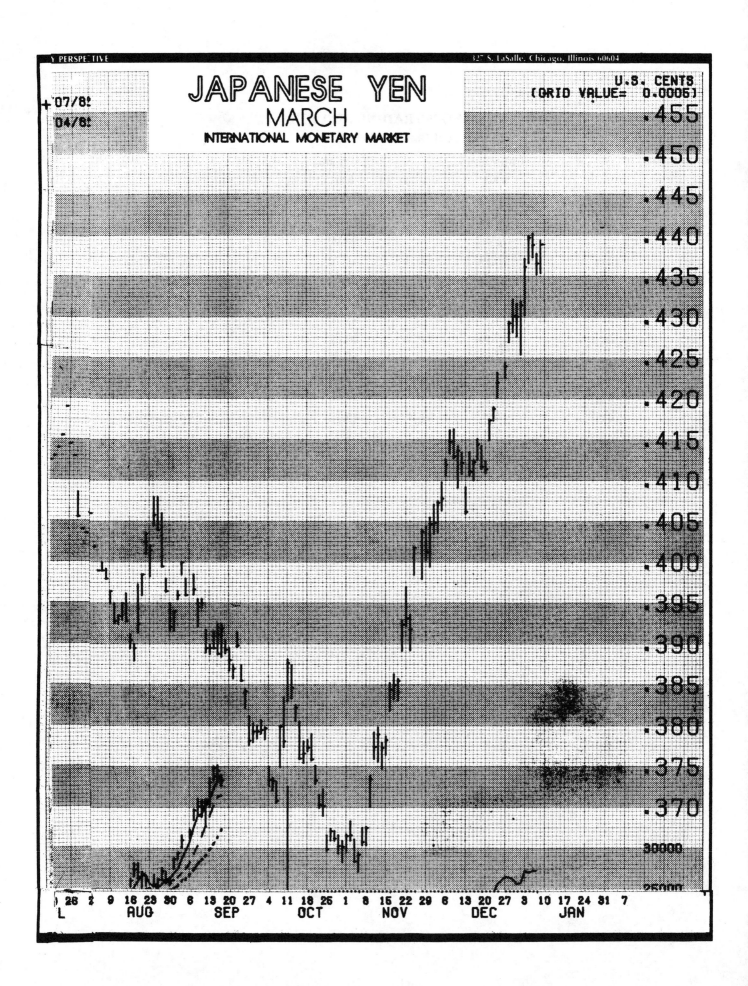

SPIKE-35 TRADING RESULTS
83 Mar Japanese Yen

Order	Entry and Exit Dates	Entry Rule	Entry and Exit Prices	Gain	Loss
Buy	8-24-82	CA2H	40.60		
	8-26-82		40.41		$237.50
Buy	9- 2-82	REN	39.85		
	9- 3-82		39.60		312.50
Sell	9-10-82	CB2L	38.95		
	9-14-82		38.97		50.00
Sell	9-15-82	REN	38.90		
	9-16-82		38.99		62.50
Sell	9-20-82	REN	38.87		
	9-22-82		39.00		162.50
Sell	9-23-82	REN	38.67		
	9-29-82		37.95	$ 900.00	
Sell	10- 4-82	REN	37.51		
	10- 7-81		37.52		12.50
Buy	10-11-82	TDR	38.78		
	10-13-82		38.25		662.50
Sell	10-21-82	CB2L	37.05		
	11- 1-82		36.55	625.00	
Sell	11- 3-82	REN	36.52		
	11- 5-82		36.56		50.00
Buy	11- 9-82	TDR	37.36		
	11-12-82		37.74	475.00	
Buy	11-16-82	REN	38.20		
	11-18-82		38.45	312.50	
Buy	11-18-82	REN	38.53		
	11-23-82		39.24	887.50	
Buy	11-23-82	REN	39.35		
	11-30-82		40.13	975.00	
Buy	11-30-82	REN	40.42		
	12- 1-82		40.46	50.00	
Buy	12- 2-82	REN	40.52		
	12- 9-82		41.30	975.00	

SPIKE-35 TRADING RESULTS
83 Mar Japanese Yen (Cont'd)

Order	Entry and Exit Dates	Entry Rule	Entry and Exit Prices	Gain	Loss
Buy	12-16-82	REN	41.26		
	12-17-82		41.23		37.50
Buy	12-21-82	REN	41.51		
	12-23-82		41.74	287.50	
Buy	12-27-82	REN	42.27		
	12-30-82		42.90	787.50	

COMMODITY PERSPECTIVE/CHICAGO, ILLINOIS 60604

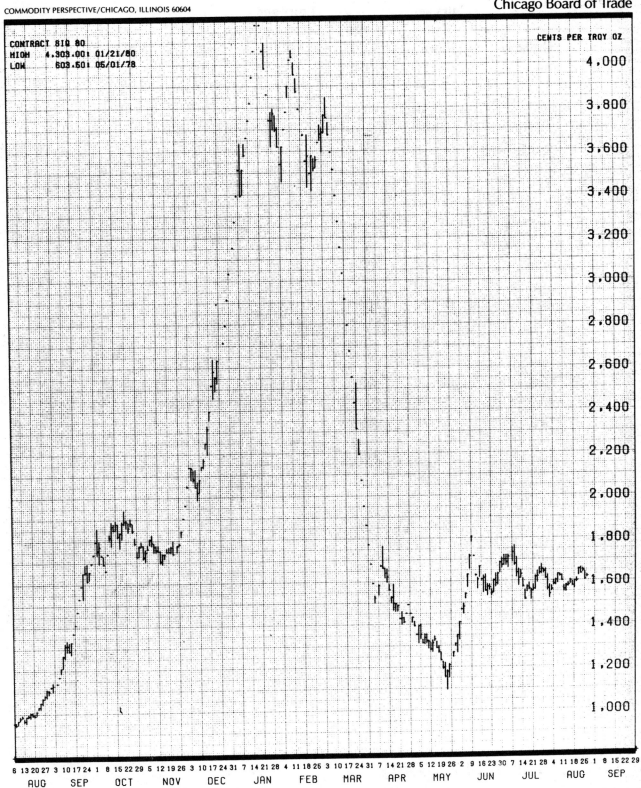

CONTRACT 810 80
HIGH   4,303.00: 01/21/80
LOW   603.50: 05/01/78

CENTS PER TROY OZ.

4,000
3,800
3,600
3,400
3,200
3,000
2,800
2,600
2,400
2,200
2,000
1,800
1,600
1,400
1,200
1,000

6 13 20 27 3 10 17 24 1 8 15 22 29 5 12 19 26 3 10 17 24 31 7 14 21 28 4 11 18 25 3 10 17 24 31 7 14 21 28 5 12 19 26 2 9 16 23 30 7 14 21 28 4 11 18 25 1 8 15 22 29

AUG   SEP   OCT   NOV   DEC   JAN   FEB   MAR   APR   MAY   JUN   JUL   AUG   SEP

SPIKE-35 TRADING RESULTS
80 Aug Chicago Silver

Order	Entry and Exit Dates	Entry Rule	Entry and Exit Prices	Gain	Loss
Buy	12-11-79	TDR	21.40		
	12-20-79		25.20	$ 19,000.00	
Buy	12-21-79	REN	25.90		
	1- 8-80		34.00	40,500.00	
Buy	1- 9-80	REN	35.20		
	1-24-80		40.60	27,000.00	
Sell	1-31-80	TDR	37.00		
	2- 5-80		36.20	4,000.00	
Buy	2-12-80	TDR	40.21		
	2-13-80		40.10		$1,000.00
Sell	2-25-80	TDR	35.20		
	2-27-80		35.80		3,000.00
Sell	3- 6-80	REN	36.80		
	4- 9-80		16.80	100,000.00	
Sell	4-14-80	REN	15.85		
	4-16-80		15.65	1,000.00	
Sell	4-16-80	REN	15.20		
	4-23-80		14.40	4,000.00	
Sell	4-30-80	REN	14.20		
	5- 2-80		14.00	1,000.00	
Sell	5- 5-80	REN	13.60		
	5- 8-80		13.50	500.00	

SILVER

FEBRUARY 1981

Chicago Board of Trade

COMMODITY PERSPECTIVE/CHICAGO, ILLINOIS 60604

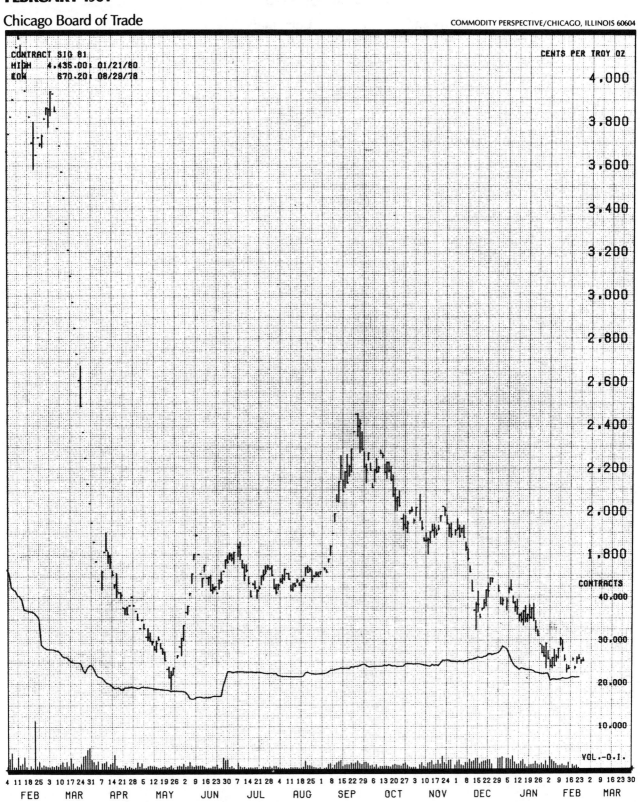

CONTRACT SIG 81
HIGH 4.436.00: 01/21/80
LOW 670.20: 08/29/78

CENTS PER TROY OZ

4.000
3.800
3.600
3.400
3.200
3.000
2.800
2.600
2.400
2.200
2.000
1.800

CONTRACTS
40.000
30.000
20.000
10.000

VOL.-O.I.

4 11 18 25 3 10 17 24 31 7 14 21 28 5 12 19 26 2 9 16 23 30 7 14 21 28 4 11 18 25 1 8 15 22 29 6 13 20 27 3 10 17 24 1 8 15 22 29 5 12 19 26 2 9 16 23 2 9 16 23 30

FEB   MAR   APR   MAY   JUN   JUL   AUG   SEP   OCT   NOV   DEC   JAN   FEB   MAR

SPIKE-35 TRADING RESULTS
81 Feb Chicago Silver

Order	Entry and Exit Dates	Entry Rule	Entry and Exit Prices	Gain	Loss
Sell	5-16-80	CB2L	13.50		
	5-23-80		12.72	$ 3,900.00	
Buy	5-29-80	TDR	14.11		
	6-12-80		16.91	14,000.00	
Buy	6-24-80	REN	16.52		
	7- 3-80		17.80	6,400.00	
Buy	7- 3-80	REN	18.00		
	7- 8-80		18.10	500.00	
Sell	7-14-80	SCB2L	16.68		
	7-16-80		16.62	300.00	
Sell	7-18-80	REN	16.03		
	7-21-80		16.51		$2,400.00
Sell	7-29-80	REN	17.08		
	8- 1-80		16.50	2,900.00	
Sell	8-11-80	REN	16.60		
	8-13-80		16.70		500.00
Sell	8-18-80	REN	16.57		
	8-18-80		16.80		1,150.00
Buy	8-20-80	CA2H	17.40		
	8-25-80		17.30		500.00
Buy	8-29-80	REN	17.10		
	9- 3-80		17.10	0	0
Buy	9- 4-80	REN	17.70		
	9-15-80		21.40	18,500.00	
Buy	9-17-80	REN	22.16		
	9-24-80		23.70	7,700.00	
Sell	10- 3-80	CB2L	21.11		
	10- 6-80		21.91		4,000.00
Sell	10-13-80	REN	21.81		
	10-15-80		22.31		2,500.00

SPIKE-35 TRADING RESULTS
81 Feb Chicago Silver (Cont'd)

Order	Entry and Exit Dates	Entry Rule	Entry and Exit Prices	Gain	Loss
Sell	10-16-80 10-22-80	REN	21.80 20.69	$5,550.00	
Sell	10-22-80 10-27-80	REN	20.47 19.70	3,850.00	
Sell	10-28-80 10-29-80	REN	19.20 19.90		$3,500.00
Sell	11- 6-80 11-11-80	REN	19.57 18.67	4,500.00	
Sell	11-12-80 11-12-80	REN	18.63 18.70		350.00
Sell	11-25-80 11-26-80	REN	19.40 19.40	0	0
Sell	11-26-80 11-29-80	REN	19.19 19.15	200.00	

SILVER

AUGUST 1981

Chicago Board of Trade

COMMODITY PERSPECTIVE/CHICAGO, ILLINOIS 60604

CONTRACT SEQ 81
HIGH   4.570.00% 01/21/80
LOW   737.00% 01/11/79

CENTS PER TROY OZ

3,000
2,800
2,600
2,400
2,200
2,000
1,800
1,600
1,400
1,200
1,000
800
600
400
200
0

4 11 18 25 1 8 15 22 29 6 13 20 27 3 10 17 24 1 8 15 22 29 5 12 19 26 2 9 16 23 2 9 16 23 30 6 13 20 27 4 11 18 25 1 8 15 22 29 6 13 20 27 3 10 17 24 31 7 14 21 28

AUG   SEP   OCT   NOV   DEC   JAN   FEB   MAR   APR   MAY   JUN   JUL   AUG   SEP

SPIKE-35 TRADING RESULTS
81 Aug Chicago Silver

Order	Entry and Exit Dates	Entry Rule	Entry and Exit Prices	Gain	Loss
Sell	12- 4-80 12-15-80	CB2L	20.45 17.01	$17,200.00	
Sell	12-15-80 12-18-80	REN	16.94 17.01		$ 350.00
Sell	12-30-80 1- 1-81	REN	17.10 17.10	0	0
Sell	1- 7-81 1- 9-81	REN	17.05 17.01	200.00	
Sell	1- 9-81 1-14-81	REN	16.80 16.46	1,700.00	
Sell	1-21-81 1-29-81	REN	16.27 14.70	1,850.00	
Sell	1-30-81 2- 4-81	REN	14.32 14.22	500.00	
Sell	2- 4-81 2- 6-81	REN	13.90 14.12		1,100.00
Sell	2-13-81 2-18-81	REN	13.80 14.11		1,550.00
Sell	2-18-81 2-20-81	REN	13.75 14.10		1,750.00
Sell	2-25-81 3- 6-81	REN	13.67 12.50	5,850.00	
Sell	3-11-81 3-13-81	REN	12.30 12.80		2,500.00
Buy	3-18-81 3-24-81	CA2H	13.80 13.67		650.00
Sell	4- 1-81 4- 2-81	TDR	12.60 12.70		500.00
Sell	4- 7-81 4-13-81	REN	12.50 11.80	4,000.00	

SPIKE-35 TRADING RESULTS
81 Aug Chicago Silver (Cont'd)

Order	Entry and Exit Dates	Entry Rule	Entry and Exit Prices	Gain	Loss
Sell	4-15-81	REN	11.67		
	4-16-81		11.85		$900.00
Sell	4-23-81	REN	11.85		
	4-24-81		11.90		250.00
Sell	4-24-81	REN	11.80		
	5- 1-81		11.60	$1,000	
Sell	5- 4-81	REN	11.48		
	5- 7-81		11.52		200.00

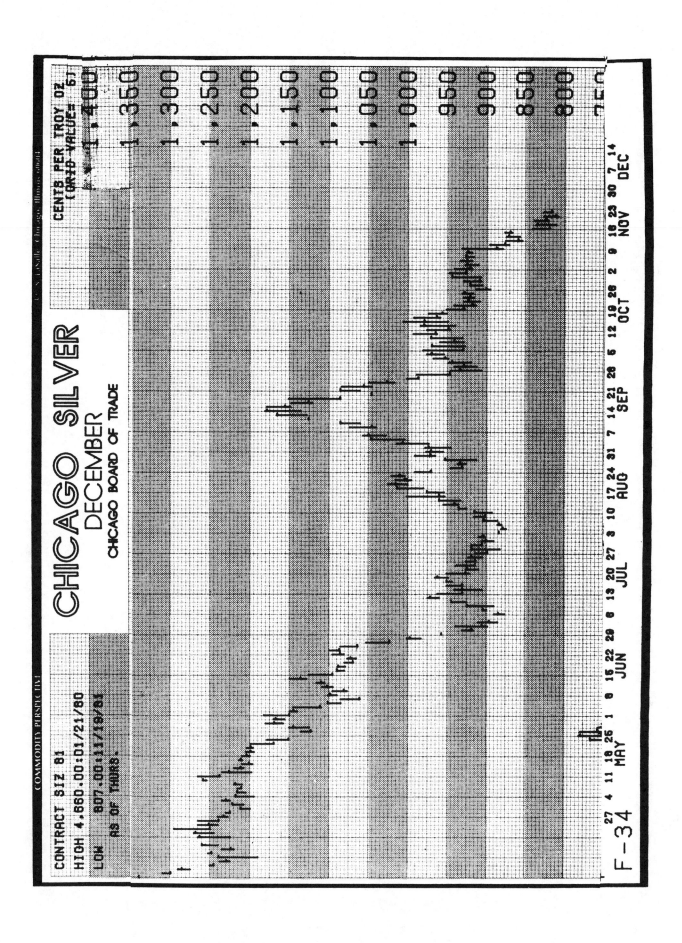

SPIKE-35 TRADING RESULTS
81 Dec Chicago Silver

Order	Entry and Exit Dates	Entry Rule	Entry and Exit Prices	Gain	Loss
Sell	5-13-81	REN	12.11		
	5-15-81		12.11	0	0
Sell	5-19-81	REN	12.00		
	5-28-81		11.57	$2150.00	
Sell	6- 2-81	REN	11.45		
	6- 8-81		11.02	2150.00	
Sell	6-16-81	REN	10.85		
	6-22-81		10.85	0	0
Sell	6-24-81	REN	10.65		
	7- 7-81		9.05	8000.00	
Sell	7-14-81	REN	9.25		
	7-15-81		9.31		$300.00
Sell	7-20-81	REN	9.27		
	7-22-81		9.25	100.00	
Sell	7-24-81	REN	9.10		
	7-24-81		9.15		250.00
Sell	7-27-81	REN	9.10		
	7-28-81		9.20		500.00
Sell	7-30-81	REN	9.00		
	7-31-81		9.06		300.00
Sell	8- 4-81	REN	8.81		
	8- 6-81		8.85		200.00
Buy	8-11-81	TDR	9.35		
	8-13-81		9.35	0	0
Buy	8-13-81	REN	9.45		
	8-17-81		9.60	750.00	

SPIKE-35 TRADING RESULTS
81 Dec Chicago Silver (Cont'd)

Order	Entry and Exit Dates	Entry Rule	Entry and Exit Prices	Gain	Loss
Buy	8-17-81	REN	9.65		
	8-20-81		10.12	$2350.00	
Buy	8-28-81	REN	9.72		
	9- 1-81		9.69		$150.00
Buy	9- 2-81	REN	9.78		
	9- 8-81		10.45	3350.00	
Buy	9- 9-81	REN	10.60		
	9-15-81		11.60	5000.00	
Sell	9-23-81	TDR	10.26		
	9-30-81		9.33	4650.00	
Sell	10- 5-81	REN	9.30		
	10- 6-81		9.70		2000.00
Sell	10-19-81	REN	9.50		
	10-22-81		9.23	1350.00	
Sell	10-26-81	REN	9.14		
	10-28-81		9.22		400.00
Sell	11- 9-81	REN	9.10		
	11-13-81		8.72	1900.00	
Sell	11-16-81	REN	8.40		
	11-18-81		8.35	250.00	

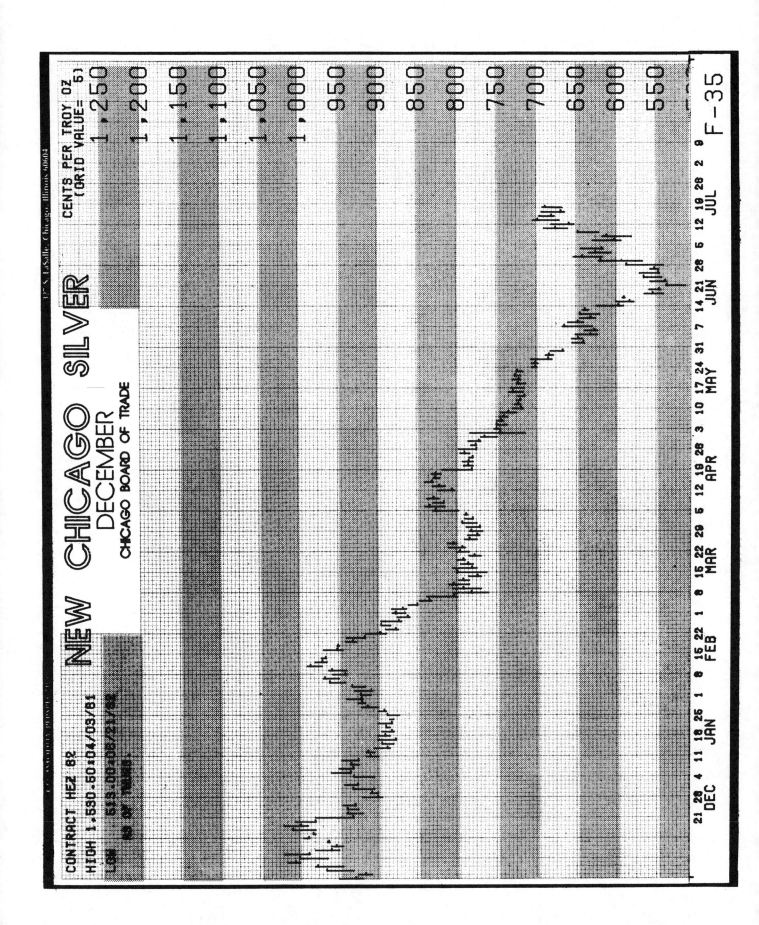

SPIKE-35 TRADING RESULTS
82 Dec Chicago Silver

Order	Entry and Exit Dates	Entry Rule	Entry and Exit Prices	Gain	Loss
Sell	12-21-81 12-23-81	CB2L	9.30 9.40		$500.00
Sell	12-24-81 12-30-81	REN	9.30 9.09	$1050.00	
Sell	1- 8-82 1-15-82	REN	9.27 8.95	1600.00	
Sell	1-15-82 1-16-82	REN	8.85 8.95		500.00
Sell	1-25-82 1-25-82	REN	8.30 8.35		250.00
Buy	1-28-82 2- 1-82	TDR	9.20 9.20	0	0
Buy	2- 3-82 2- 8-82	REN	9.22 9.57	1750.00	
Buy	2-10-82 2-12-82	REN	9.70 9.68		100.00
Sell	2-22-82 3- 1-82	CB2L	9.00 8.75	1250.00	
Sell	3- 3-82 3- 9-82	REN	8.60 8.02	2900.00	
Sell	3-12-82 3-15-82	REN	8.85 8.95		500.00
Sell	3-19-82 3-22-82	REN	8.77 8.95		900.00
Sell	3-25-82 3-30-82	REN	8.76 8.83		350.00
Buy	4- 5-82 4- 7-82	CA2H	8.25 8.25	0	0
Buy	4-14-82 4-16-82	REN	8.30 8.25		250.00

SPIKE-35 TRADING RESULTS
82 Dec Chicago Silver (Cont'd)

Order	Entry and Exit Dates	Entry Rule	Entry and Exit Prices	Gain	Loss
Sell	4-26-82	TDR	7.75		
	4-28-82		7.75	0	0
Sell	4-29-82	REN	7.68		
	4-30-82		7.73		$750.00
Sell	4-30-82	REN	7.62		
	5-12-82		7.20	$2100.00	
Sell	5-13-82	REN	7.20		
	5-13-82		7.20	0	0
Sell	5-18-82	REN	7.15		
	5-20-82		7.25		500.00
Sell	5-24-82	REN	7.07		
	5-26-82		7.07	0	0
Sell	5-26-82	REN	6.98		
	6- 3-82		6.48	2500.00	
Sell	6- 3-82	REN	6.38		
	6- 7-82		6.32	250.00	
Sell	6-10-82	REN	6.30		
	6-22-82		5.45	4250.00	

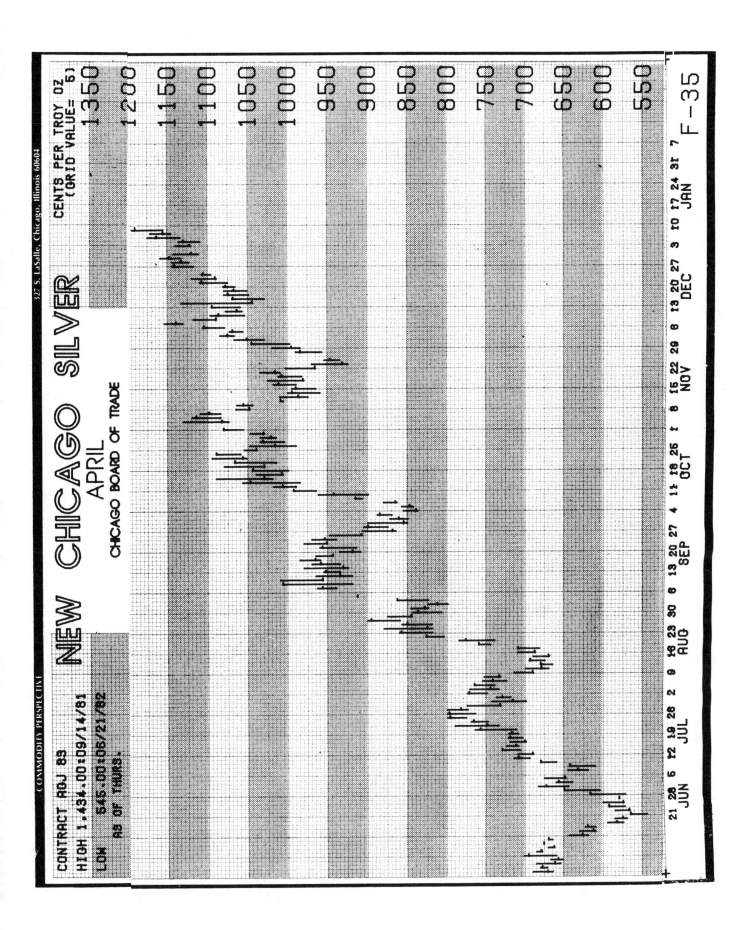

COMMODITY PERSPECTIVE

NEW CHICAGO SILVER

APRIL

CHICAGO BOARD OF TRADE

CONTRACT AOJ 83

HIGH 1.434.00:09/14/81

LOW 545.00:05/21/82

AS OF THURS.

CENTS PER TROY OZ
(GRID VALUE= 5)

327 S. LaSalle, Chicago, Illinois 60604

F-35

SPIKE-35 TRADING RESULTS
83 Apr Chicago Silver

Order	Entry and Exit Dates	Entry Rule	Entry and Exit Prices	Gain	Loss
Buy	6-30-82	TDR	6.74		
	7- 1-82		6.50		$1200.00
Buy	7- 8-82	REN	6.60		
	7-15-82		7.14	$2300.00	
Buy	7-20-82	REN	7.30		
	7-22-82		7.50	1000.00	
Buy	7-23-82	REN	7.77		
	7-26-82		7.65		600.00
Sell	8- 9-82	CB2L	6.90		
	8-12-82		6.82	400.00	
Sell	8-13-82	REN	6.75		
	8-16-82		6.95		1000.00
Buy	8-19-82	TDR	7.77		
	8-24-82		8.25	2400.00	
Buy	8-26-82	REN	8.60		
	8-27-82		8.50		500.00
Buy	9- 2-82	REN	8.50		
	9- 9-82		9.56	5300.00	
Buy	9-15-82	REN	9.60		
	9-17-82		9.60	0	0
Buy	9-22-82	REN	9.68		
	9-23-82		9.52		800.00
Sell	9-24-82	CB2L	9.09		
	10- 1-82		8.70	1950.00	
Sell	10- 4-82	REN	8.55		
	10- 6-82		8.65		500.00
Buy	10-11-82	CA2H	9.94		
	10-13-82		9.94	0	0
Buy	10-13-82	REN	10.08		
	10-15-82		10.30	1100.00	

SPIKE-35 TRADING RESULTS
83 Apr Chicago Silver (Cont'd)

Order	Entry and Exit Dates	Entry Rule	Entry and Exit Prices	Gain	Loss
Buy	10-19-82	REN	10.50		
	10-20-82		10.30		$1000.00
Buy	10-21-82	REN	10.70		
	10-25-82		10.55		750.00
Buy	10-29-82	REN	10.33		
	11- 8-82		10.65	$1600.00	
Sell	11-10-82	TDR	10.10		
	11-13-82		9.97	650.00	
Sell	11-14-82	REN	9.85		
	11-16-82		10.15		1500.00
Sell	11-22-82	REN	9.80		
	11-26-82		9.60	1000.00	
Buy	11-30-82	TDR	10.45		
	12- 8-82		11.05	3000.00	
Buy	12-14-82	REN	10.97		
	12-14-82		10.65		1600.00
Buy	12-20-82	REN	10.80		
	12-30-82		11.35	2750.00	

COTTON

DECEMBER 1980

New York Cotton Exchange

COMMODITY PERSPECTIVE/CHICAGO, ILLINOIS 60604

CONTRACT NYZ 80
HIGH   96.96 : 09/12/80
LOW   65.75 : 06/28/79

CENTS PER LB.

96
94
92
90
88
86
84
82
80
78
76
74
72
70
68
66

3 10 17 24 31 | 7 14 21 28 | 4 11 18 25 | 3 10 17 24 31 | 7 14 21 28 | 5 12 19 26 | 2 9 16 23 30 | 7 14 21 28 | 4 11 18 25 | 1 8 15 22 29 | 6 13 20 27 | 3 10 17 24 1 | 8 15 22 29 | 5 12 19 26

DEC | JAN | FEB | MAR | APR | MAY | JUN | JUL | AUG | SEP | OCT | NOV | DEC | JAN

SPIKE-35 TRADING RESULTS
80 Dec Cotton

Order	Entry and Exit Dates	Entry Rule	Entry and Exit Prices	Gain	Loss
Buy	12-12-79 12-18-79	CA2H	72.40 73.00	$300.00	
Buy	12-21-79 12-28-79	REN	73.10 73.25	75.00	
Buy	12-31-79 1- 4-80	REN	73.70 73.85	75.00	
Sell	1- 7-80 1- 9-80	TDR	72.10 72.30		$100.00
Buy	1-22-80 1-25-80	TDR	74.75 76.00	625.00	
Buy	1-29-80 1-31-80	REN	76.30 77.60	650.00	
Buy	2- 4-80 2- 6-80	REN	77.95 77.65		150.00
Buy	2-11-80 2-12-80	REN	78.70 78.00		350.00
Sell	2-19-80 2-21-80	CB2L	75.15 76.80		825.00
Buy	3- 3-80 3- 5-80	TDR	78.45 78.45	0	0
Sell	3-12-80 3-17-80	CB2L	75.25 73.65	800.00	
Sell	3-25-80 3-26-80	REN	75.75 75.75	0	0
Sell	4- 1-80 4- 3-80	REN	75.00 74.15	425.00	
Sell	4- 8-80 4-10-80	REN	73.60 74.30		350.00

SPIKE-35 TRADING RESULTS
80 Dec Cotton (Cont'd)

Order	Entry and Exit Dates	Entry Rule	Entry and Exit Prices	Gain	Loss
Sell	4-15-80	REN	74.20		
	4-16-80		74.70		$250.00
Sell	4-17-80	REN	74.10		
	4-18-80		74.30		100.00
Sell	4-18-80	REN	73.45		
	4-22-80		73.45	0	0
Sell	4-28-80	REN	73.40		
	4-30-80		73.20	$100.00	

COTTON

MARCH 1981

New York Cotton Exchange

COMMODITY PERSPECTIVE/CHICAGO, ILLINOIS 60604

CONTRACT NYH 81
HIGH   97.00: 09/16/80
LOW   69.00: 09/17/79

CENTS PER LB.

SPIKE-35 TRADING RESULTS
81 Mar Cotton

Order	Entry and Exit Dates	Entry Rule	Entry and Exit Prices	Gain	Loss
Sell	5- 5-80	REN	74.10		
	5- 6-80		74.40		$150.00
Buy	5- 8-80	CA2H	75.90		
	5-13-80		76.80	$450.00	
Sell	5-29-80	TDR	74.20		
	6- 4-80		72.75	725.00	
Sell	6- 5-80	REN	72.30		
	6- 9-80		72.40		50.00
Sell	6-10-80	REN	72.00		
	6-11-80		72.10		50.00
Sell	6-13-80	REN	72.05		
	6-17-80		72.15		50.00
Buy	6-18-80	CA2H	73.20		
	6-20-80		72.70		250.00
Buy	6-25-80	REN	73.20		
	6-26-80		73.00		100.00
Sell	6-26-80	TDR	71.80		
	7- 1-80		74.20		1200.00
Buy	7- 1-80	CA2H	75.00		
	7- 9-80		76.80	900.00	
Buy	7- 9-80	REN	77.70		
	7-10-80		76.80		450.00
Buy	7-11-80	REN	77.70		
	7-18-80		81.95	2125.00	
Buy	7-25-80	REN	79.50		
	8- 1-80		84.70	2600.00	
Buy	8- 1-80	REN	84.80		
	8- 5-80		83.70		550.00

SPIKE-35 TRADING RESULTS
81 Mar Cotton (Cont'd)

Order	Entry and Exit Dates	Entry Rule	Entry and Exit Prices	Gain	Loss
Buy	8-11-80 8-15-80	REN	83.95 86.40	$1225.00	
Buy	8-16-80 8-16-80	REN	87.70 87.00		$ 100.00
Buy	8-18-80 8-18-80	REN	87.30 87.00		150.00
Buy	8-19-80 8-22-80	REN	87.30 88.50	600.00	
Buy	8-22-80 8-28-80	REN	89.35 91.70	1175.00	
Buy	8-29-80 9- 3-80	REN	93.60 93.60	0	0
Buy	9- 8-80 9- 9-80	REN	94.30 93.20		550.00
Buy	9-11-80 9-15-80	REN	93.60 95.00	700.00	
Sell	9-22-80 9-30-80	CB2L	91.20 89.10	1050.00	
Sell	10-10-80 10-15-80	REN	91.30 89.90	700.00	
Buy	10-21-80 10-23-80	CA2H	92.80 92.60		100.00
Sell	11- 3-80 11- 7-80	TDR	89.65 89.05	300.00	

COTTON

JULY 1981

New York Cotton Exchange

COMMODITY PERSPECTIVE/CHICAGO, ILLINOIS 60604

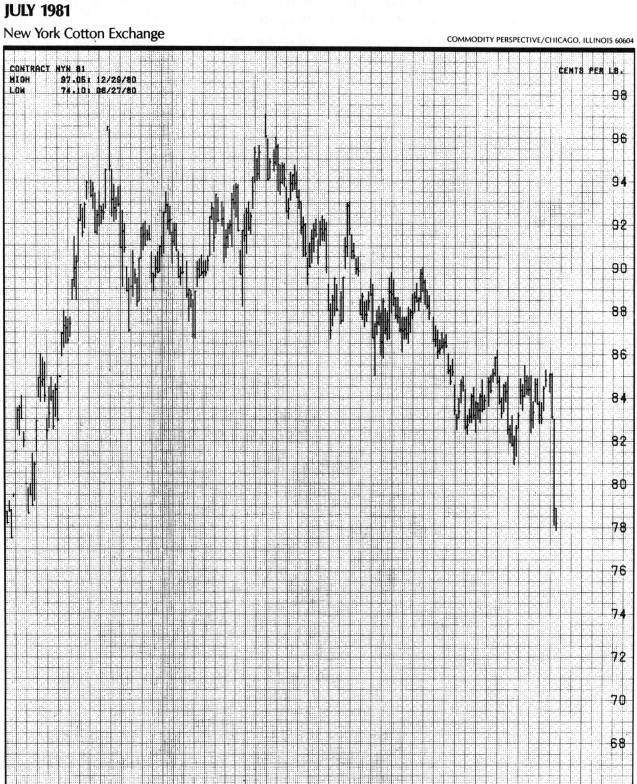

CONTRACT NYN 81
HIGH   97.05: 12/29/80
LOW   74.10: 06/27/80

CENTS PER LB.

JUL AUG SEP OCT NOV DEC JAN FEB MAR APR MAY JUN JUL AUG

SPIKE-35 TRADING RESULTS
81 July Cotton

Order	Entry and Exit Dates	Entry Rule	Entry and Exit Prices	Gain	Loss
Sell	11- 5-80	CB2L	88.70		
	11-11-80		88.70	0	0
Buy	11-19-80	TDR	90.30		
	11-24-80		92.30	$1000.00	
Buy	11-25-80	REN	92.75		
	11-28-80		92.10		$ 325.00
Buy	12- 5-80	REN	92.00		
	12- 9-80		92.90	450.00	
Buy	12- 9-80	REN	93.16		
	12-10-80		93.00		60.00
Sell	12-11-80	CB2L	89.70		
	12-12-80		91.70		1000.00
Buy	12-22-80	CA2H	95.30		
	12-24-80		94.30		500.00
Buy	12-24-80	REN	95.30		
	12-30-80		95.30	0	0
Buy	1- 6-81	REN	95.55		
	1- 6-81		94.80		375.00
Sell	1-12-81	CB2L	92.55		
	1-14-81		93.10		275.00
Sell	1-20-81	REN	93.15		
	1-23-81		92.00	575.00	
Sell	1-23-81	REN	91.75		
	1-27-81		90.65	550.00	
Sell	2- 6-81	REN	90.40		
	2-11-81		88.05	1175.00	
Buy	2-20-81	CA2H	92.80		
	2-22-80		91.50		650.00
Buy	3- 6-81	REN	88.65		
	3-10-81		88.40		125.00
Sell	3-10-81	CB2L	86.70		
	3-12-81		87.30		300.00
Sell	3-16-81	REN	86.70		
	3-17-81		87.70		500.00

SPIKE-35 TRADING RESULTS
81 July Cotton (Cont'd)

Order	Entry and Exit Dates	Entry Rule	Entry and Exit Prices	Gain	Loss
Buy	3-20-81	TDR	88.85		
	3-24-81		88.65		$ 100.00
Buy	4- 2-81	REN	87.20		
	4- 9-81		88.40	$ 600.00	
Buy	4-10-81	REN	88.65		
	4-14-81		89.25	300.00	
Sell	4-20-81	TDR	86.65		
	4-22-81		86.65	0	0
Sell	4-22-81	REN	86.60		
	4-25-81		86.25	200.00	
Sell	4-27-81	REN	86.10		
	4-27-81		86.35		125.00
Sell	4-29-81	REN	86.00		
	5- 1-81		85.25	375.00	
Sell	5- 4-81	REN	84.50		
	5- 6-81		83.45	525.00	

COTTON

MARCH 1982

New York Cotton Exchange

COMMODITY PERSPECTIVE/CHICAGO, ILLINOIS 60604

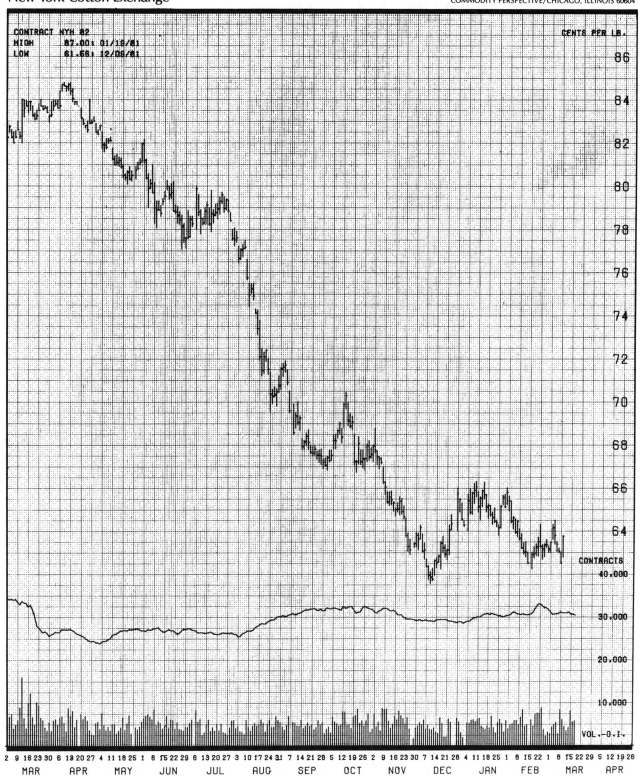

CONTRACT NYH 82
HIGH   87.00: 01/18/81
LOW   61.66: 12/09/81

CENTS PER LB.

SPIKE-35 TRADING RESULTS
82 Mar Cotton

Order	Entry and Exit Dates	Entry Rule	Entry and Exit Prices	Gain	Loss
Sell	5-11-81 5-13-81	REN	81.85 81.20	$ 320.00	
Sell	5-14-81 5-15-81	REN	80.95 81.20		$ 125.00
Sell	5-15-81 5-20-81	REN	80.95 80.50	225.00	
Sell	5-22-81 5-26-81	REN	80.20 80.50		150.00
Buy	5-29-81 6- 2-81	CA2H	81.95 80.20		875.00
Sell	6- 2-81 6- 5-81	TDR	80.25 80.10	75.00	
Sell	6- 5-81 6-10-81	REN	79.60 78.95	325.00	
Sell	6-19-81 6-23-81	REN	79.45 78.80	325.00	
Sell	6-23-81 6-30-81	REN	78.65 77.65	500.00	
Sell	7- 8-81 7- 9-81	REN	78.10 78.40		150.00
Sell	7-15-81 7-16-81	REN	78.10 78.70		300.00
Sell	7-27-81 7-31-81	REN	78.80 77.60	600.00	
Sell	8- 3-81 8- 5-81	REN	77.20 77.10	50.00	
Sell	8- 7-81 8-12-81	REN	76.60 75.20	700.00	

SPIKE-35 TRADING RESULTS
82 Mar Cotton (Cont'd)

Order	Entry and Exit Dates	Entry Rule	Entry and Exit Prices	Gain	Loss
Sell	8-12-81 8-19-81	REN	74.80 72.10	$1350.00	
Sell	8-21-81 8-26-81	REN	71.50 70.40	550.00	
Sell	8-27-81 8-28-81	REN	70.10 70.60		$250.00
Sell	9- 4-81 9-10-81	REN	70.50 69.45	525.00	
Sell	9-14-8. 9-16-81	REN	68.30 68.20	50.00	
Sell	9-18-81 9-22-81	REN	67.90 67.80	50.00	
Sell	9-23-81 9-30-81	REN	67.50 67.20	150.00	
Buy	10- 6-81 10- 9-81	TDR	68.25 68.60	175.00	
Buy	10-12-81 10-14-81	REN	69.10 69.90	400.00	
Buy	10-28-81 10-30-81	REN	68.10 67.40		350.00
Buy	11- 2-81 11- 3-81	REN	68.00 67.40		150.00
Sell	11- 6-81 11-12-81	CB2L	66.30 65.60	350.00	
Sell	11-12-81 11-18-81	REN	65.30 65.10	100.00	

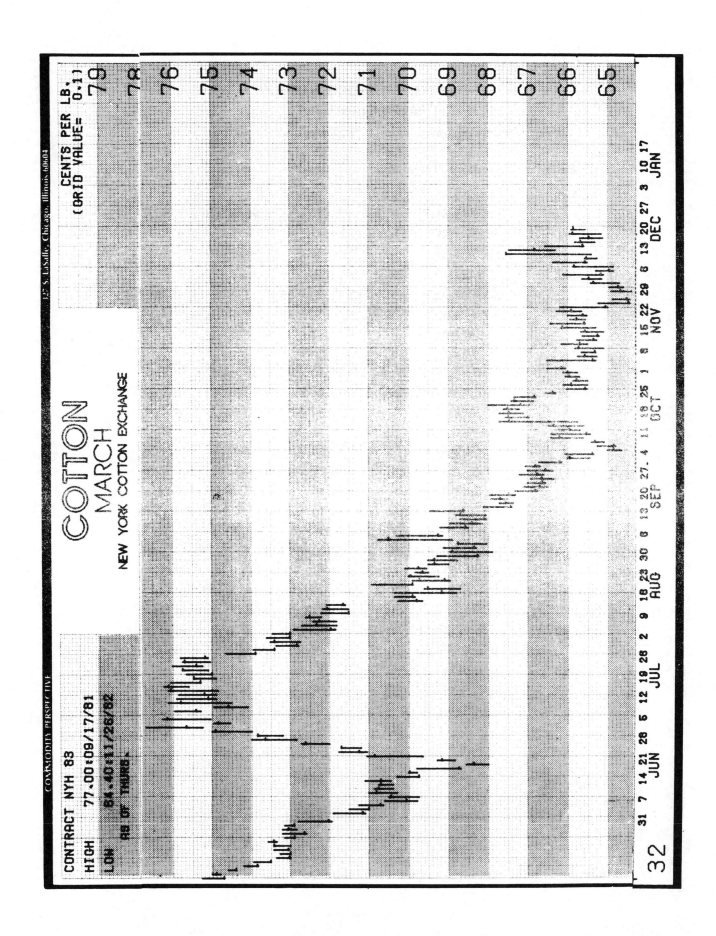

COTTON
MARCH
NEW YORK COTTON EXCHANGE

CONTRACT NYH 83
HIGH   77.00:09/17/81
LOW   64.40:11/26/82
        RIG OF THURS

CENTS PER LB.
(GRID VALUE= 0.1)

79
78
76
75
74
73
72
71
70
69
68
67
66
65

31 7 14 21 28   5 12 19 28   2 9 16 23 30   6 13 20 27   4 11 18 25   1 8 15 22 29   6 13 20 27   3 10 17
JUN   JUL   AUG   SEP   OCT   NOV   DEC   JAN

32

SPIKE-35 TRADING RESULTS
83 Mar Cotton

Order	Entry and Exit Dates	Entry Rule	Entry and Exit Prices	Gain	Loss
Sell	6-14-82 6-18-82	REN	70.40 68.90	$ 750.00	
Buy	6-22-82 7- 1-82	TDR	71.20 74.90	1850.00	
Buy	7- 2-82 7- 6-82	REN	75.80 74.95		$ 450.00
Buy	7-13-82 7-15-82	REN	76.05 76.05	0	0
Buy	7-21-82 7-22-82	REN	75.80 75.40		200.00
Sell	7-26-82 7-29-82	CB2L	73.90 73.40	250.00	
Sell	8- 3-82 8- 5-82	REN	72.80 72.45	175.00	
Sell	8- 9-82 8-16-82	REN	71.90 69.90	1000.00	
Sell	8-16-82 8-18-82	REN	69.60 69.90		150.00
Sell	8-19-82 8-20-82	REN	69.10 69.90		400.00
Sell	8-26-82 8-30-82	REN	69.10 68.90	100.00	
Sell	9- 1-82 9- 2-82	REN	68.75 68.90		325.00
Buy	9- 2-82 9- 7-82	CA2H	70.50 69.10		700.00
Sell	9- 9-82 9-10-82	TDR	68.10 68.40		150.00
Sell	9-14-82 9-16-82	REN	68.00 67.60	200.00	

SPIKE-35 TRADING RESULTS
83 Mar Cotton (Cont'd)

Order	Entry and Exit Dates	Entry Rule	Entry and Exit Prices	Gain	Loss
Sell	9-17-82 9-22-82	REN	67.40 66.80	$ 300.00	
Sell	9-23-82 9-24-82	REN	66.65 66.65	0	0
Sell	9-27-82 9-28-82	REN	66.60 66.80		$ 100.00
Sell	9-29-82 10- 6-82	REN	66.50 65.15	675.00	
Buy	10-13-82 10-15-82	CA2H	67.45 67.45	0	0
Buy	10-19-82 10-20-82	REN	67.60 67.50		50.00
Buy	10-30-82 11- 3-82	REN	66.00 66.00	0	0
Sell	11- 3-82 11- 5-82	CB2L	65.35 65.60		125.00
Sell	11- 8-82 11- 8-82	REN	65.30 65.60		150.00
Sell	11-11-82 11-12-82	REN	65.30 65.40		50.00
Sell	11-18-82 11-19-82	REN	65.55 65.80		125.00
Sell	11-22-82 11-26-82	REN	65.55 64.55	500.00	
Sell	12- 8-82 12- 8-82	REN	64.90 65.20		150.00
Buy	12- 9-82 12-11-82	CA2H	67.50 66.55		525.00

COMMODITY PERSPECTIVE/CHICAGO, ILLINOIS 60604

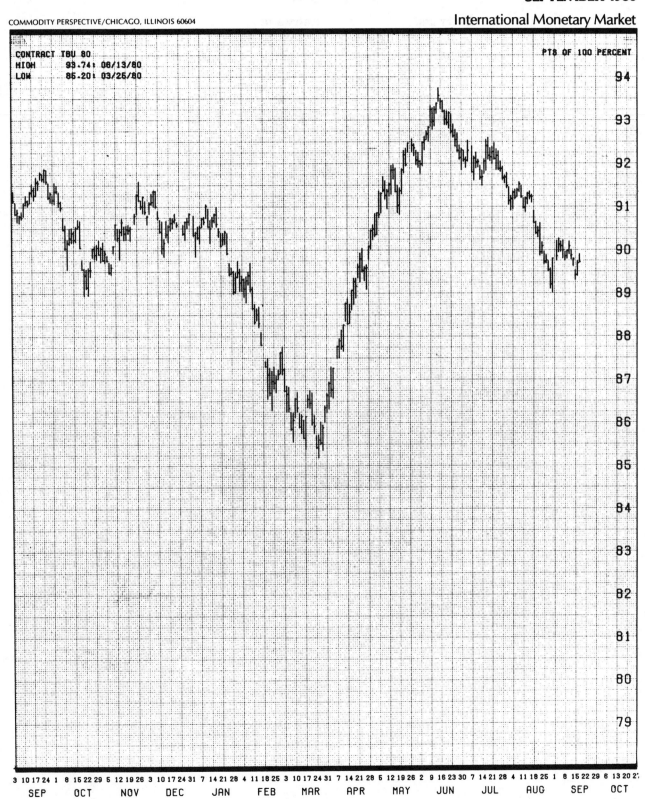

CONTRACT TBU 80
HIGH   93.74: 06/13/80
LOW   85.20: 03/26/80

PTS OF 100 PERCENT

SEP OCT NOV DEC JAN FEB MAR APR MAY JUN JUL AUG SEP OCT

SPIKE-35 TRADING RESULTS
80 Sept T-Bills

Order	Entry and Exit Dates	Entry Rule	Entry and Exit Prices	Gain	Loss
Sell	12-11-79	CB2L	90.42		
	12-13-79		90.30	$ 300.00	
Sell	12-20-79	REN	90.55		
	12-27-79		90.55	0	0
Sell	1- 2-80	REN	90.37		
	1- 3-80		90.40		$ 75.00
Sell	1- 7-80	REN	90.27		
	1- 7-80		90.40		325.00
Buy	1-10-80	CA2H	91.00		
	1-11-80		90.65		875.00
Buy	1-16-80	REN	90.82		
	1-17-80		90.67		375.00
Sell	1-21-80	CB2L	90.10		
	1-23-80		90.25		375.00
Sell	1-24-80	REN	90.10		
	1-29-80		89.50	1500.00	
Sell	1-29-80	REN	89.45		
	1-31-80		89.40	100.00	
Sell	2- 5-80	REN	89.22		
	2- 6-80		89.32		250.00
Sell	2- 8-80	REN	89.09		
	2-13-80		88.53	1400.00	
Sell	2-13-80	REN	88.32		
	2-22-80		87.11	3025.00	
Sell	3- 3-80	REN	87.00		
	3- 5-80		86.76	600.00	
Sell	3- 5-80	REN	86.65		
	3-10-80		86.12	1325.00	
Sell	3-13-80	REN	85.85		
	3-17-80		86.25		1000.00

SPIKE-35 TRADING RESULTS
80 Sept T-Bills (Cont'd)

Order	Entry and Exit Dates	Entry Rule	Entry and Exit Prices	Gain	Loss
Sell	3-21-80	REN	85.98		
	3-26-80		85.61	$ 925.00	
Sell	3-27-80	REN	85.43		
	3-27-80		85.60		425.00
Buy	4- 1-80	CA2H	86.90		
	4- 3-80		86.75		375.00
Buy	4- 3-80	REN	86.90		
	4- 9-80		87.74	2100.00	
Buy	4-10-80	REN	87.90		
	4-18-80		89.04	2850.00	
Buy	4-18-80	REN	89.27		
	4-23-80		89.60	825.00	
Buy	4-28-80	REN	89.81		
	5- 1-80		90.44	1575.00	

T. BILLS

MARCH 1981
International Monetary Market

COMMODITY PERSPECTIVE/CHICAGO, ILLINOIS 60604

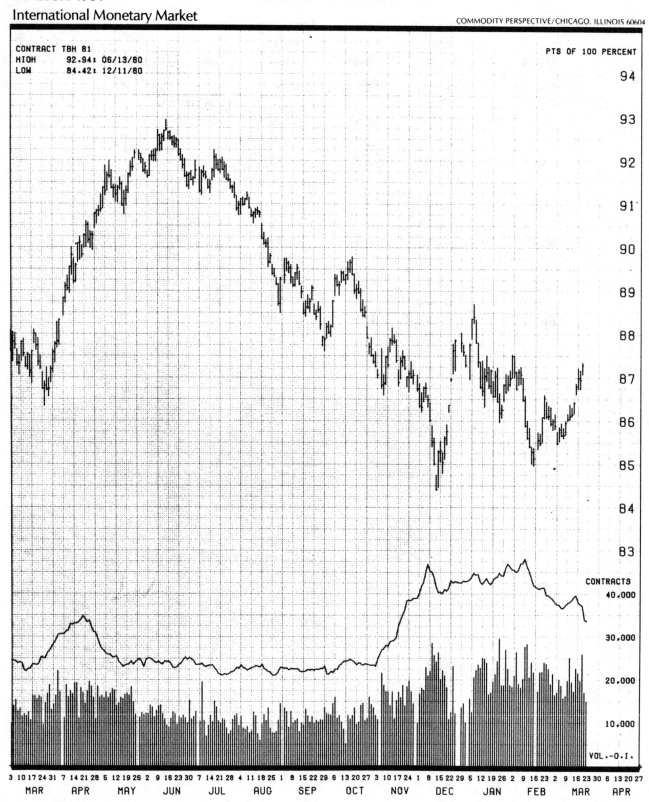

CONTRACT TBH 81
HIGH   92.94: 06/13/80
LOW   84.42: 12/11/80

PTS OF 100 PERCENT

SPIKE-35 TRADING RESULTS
81 Mar T-Bills

Order	Entry and Exit Dates	Entry Rule	Entry and Exit Prices	Gain	Loss
Buy	5- 1-80	REN	90.87		
	5- 7-80		91.62	$1875.00	
Buy	5-14-80	REN	91.35		
	5-15-80		91.35	0	0
Buy	5-20-80	REN	91.46		
	5-28-80		92.14	1700.00	
Buy	6- 2-80	REN	92.07		
	6- 4-80		92.07	0	0
Buy	6- 5-80	REN	92.15		
	6- 6-80		92.07		$200.00
Buy	6- 6-80	REN	92.15		
	6-11-80		92.37	550.00	
Buy	6-12-80	REN	92.58		
	6-16-80		92.63	125.00	
Sell	6-24-80	TDR	92.00		
	6-25-80		92.00	0	0
Sell	6-25-80	REN	91.85		
	6-30-80		91.68	425.00	
Sell	7- 7-80	REN	91.55		
	7- 9-80		91.73		450.00
Sell	7-14-80	REN	91.38		
	7-15-80		91.55		425.00
Buy	7-16-80	CA2H	92.07		
	7-18-80		91.71		400.00
Sell	7-30-80	CB2L	91.20		
	8- 4-80		90.98	550.00	
Sell	8- 8-80	REN	90.97		
	8-13-80		90.79	450.00	

SPIKE-35 TRADING RESULTS
81 Mar T-Bills (Cont'd)

Order	Entry and Exit Dates	Entry Rule	Entry and Exit Prices	Gain	Loss
Sell	8-15-80	REN	90.71		
	8-21-80		90.10	$1525.00	
Sell	8-21-80	REN	90.00		
	8-29-80		89.15	2125.00	
Sell	9- 5-80	REN	89.32		
	9- 9-80		89.32	0	0
Sell	9-12-80	REN	89.11		
	9-17-80		88.67	1300.00	
Sell	9-22-80	REN	88.60		
	9-24-80		88.51	225.00	
Sell	9-25-80	REN	88.37		
	9-30-80		87.95	1050.00	
Buy	10- 6-80	CA2H	89.30		
	10- 8-80		89.13		$425.00
Buy	10- 9-80	REN	89.32		
	10-13-80		89.25		175.00
Buy	10-14-80	REN	89.44		
	10-16-80		89.50	150.00	
Sell	10-22-80	CB2L	89.56		
	10-24-80		89.56	0	0
Sell	10-24-80	REN	88.42		
	10-29-80		87.90	1300.00	
Sell	10-29-80	REN	87.70		
	10-31-80		87.52	450.00	
Sell	10-31-80	REN	87.35		
	11- 5-80		87.25	250.00	
Sell	11- 5-80	REN	87.05		
	11- 7-80		86.90	375.00	

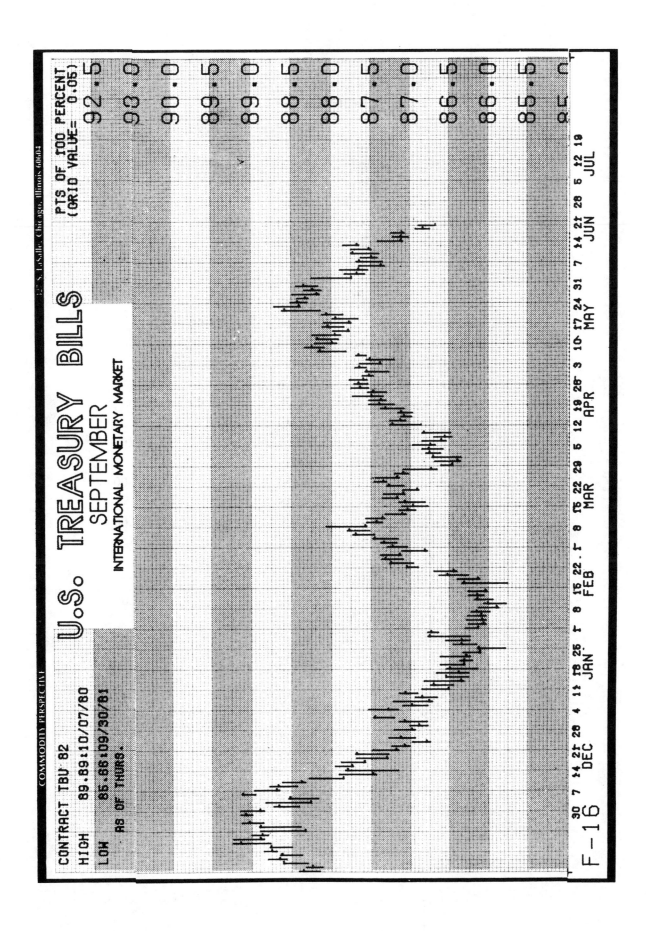

SPIKE-35 TRADING RESULTS
82 Sept T-Bills

Order	Entry and Exit Dates	Entry Rule	Entry and Exit Prices	Gain	Loss
Sell	12- 2-81 12- 3-81	CB2L	88.25 88.95		$1750.00
Sell	12- 8-81 12-15-81	REN	88.50 87.81	$1725.00	
Sell	12-17-81 12-18-81	REN	88.47 88.55		200.00
Sell	12-21-81 12-24-81	REN	87.30 87.07	575.00	
Sell	1- 5-82 1- 8-82	REN	86.90 86.90	0	0
Sell	1-11-82 1-13-82	REN	86.75 86.70	100.00	
Sell	1-13-82 1-15-82	REN	86.50 86.65		125.00
Sell	1-18-82 1-19-82	REN	86.35 86.52		425.00
Sell	1-19-82 1-21-82	REN	86.35 86.39		100.00
Sell	1-22-82 1-26-82	REN	86.34 86.15	475.00	
Buy	1-28-82 2- 1-82	TDR	86.75 86.30		1125.00
Sell	2- 2-82 2- 3-82	TDR	86.07 86.15		200.00
Sell	2- 8-82 2- 9-82	RR#2	86.02 86.02	0	0
Sell	2-16-82 2-16-82	REN	86.00 86.15		375.00
Buy	2-22-82 2-25-82	CA2H	87.04 87.24	500.00	

SPIKE-35 TRADING RESULTS
82 Sept T-Bills (Cont'd)

Order	Entry and Exit Dates	Entry Rule	Entry and Exit Prices	Gain	Loss
Buy	3- 2-82	REN	87.32		
	3- 3-82		87.22		$ 250.00
Buy	3- 3-82	REN	87.35		
	3- 8-82		87.69	$ 850.00	
Buy	3-17-82	REN	87.16		
	3-19-82		87.08		200.00
Buy	3-22-82	REN	87.17		
	3-24-82		87.26	225.00	
Sell	3-26-82	CB2L	86.74		
	3-31-82		86.42	800.00	
Sell	4- 6-82	RR#2	86.57		
	4- 8-82		86.61		100.00
Buy	4-16-82	CA2H	87.31		
	4-22-82		87.36	125.00	
Buy	4-22-82	REN	87.51		
	4-27-82		87.57	150.00	
Buy	4-30-82	REN	87.67		
	5- 3-82		87.54		325.00
Buy	5- 5-82	REN	87.65		
	5-10-82		88.14	1575.00	
Buy	5-19-82	REN	88.05		
	5-24-82		88.39	850.00	

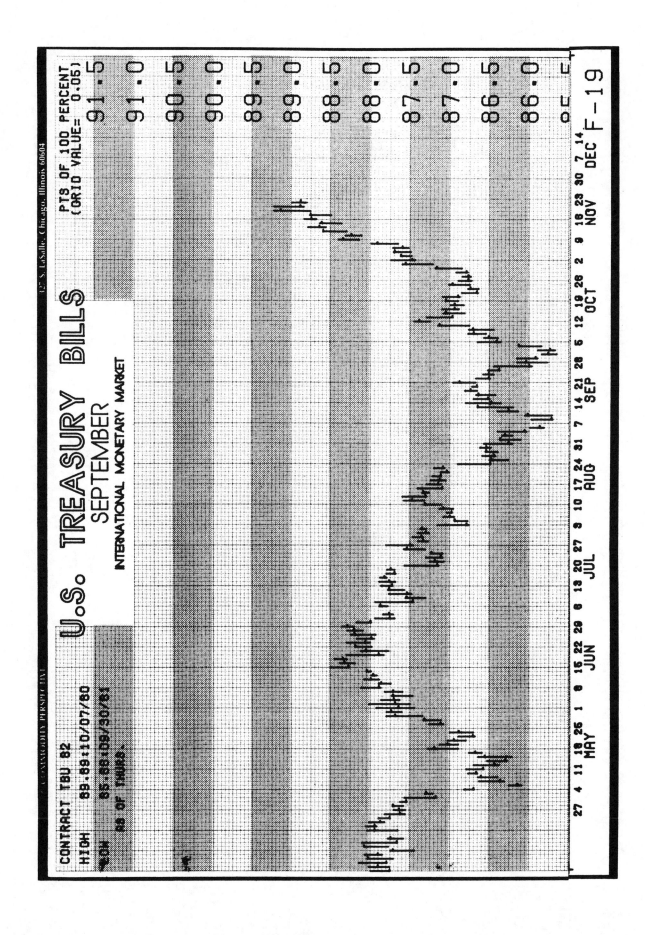

SPIKE-35 TRADING RESULTS
82 Sept T-Bills

Order	Entry and Exit Dates	Entry Rule	Entry and Exit Prices	Gain	Loss
Sell	5-13-81	REN	86.40		
	5-14-81		86.45		$125.00
Buy	5-27-81	CA2H	87.33		
	6- 1-81		87.69	$ 900.00	
Buy	6- 2-81	REN	87.75		
	6- 3-81		87.65		250.00
Buy	6- 5-81	REN	87.80		
	6-17-81		88.26	900.00	
Buy	6-25-81	REN	88.20		
	6-29-81		88.20	0	0
Sell	7- 1-81	CB2L	87.75		
	7- 6-81		87.78		75.00
Sell	7- 7-81	REN	87.75		
	7- 9-81		87.55	500.00	
Sell	7-16-81	REN	87.70		
	7-22-81		87.15	1050.00	
Sell	7-30-81	REN	87.30		
	7-31-81		87.30	0	0
Sell	8- 3-81	REN	87.15		
	8- 5-81		86.95	500.00	
Sell	8-14-81	REN	87.25		
	8-18-81		87.15	250.00	
Sell	8-19-81	REN	87.10		
	8-21-81		87.10	0	0
Sell	8-24-81	REN	86.90		
	8-26-81		86.50	1000.00	
Sell	8-27-81	REN	86.40		
	8-28-81		86.55		375.00
Sell	8-31-81	REN	86.40		
	9- 3-81		86.36	100.00	
Sell	9- 3-81	REN	86.22		
	9- 9-81		85.85	925.00	

SPIKE-35 TRADING RESULTS
82 Sept T-Bills (Cont'd)

Order	Entry and Exit Dates	Entry Rule	Entry and Exit Prices	Gain	Loss
Buy	9-11-81	TDR	86.65		
	9-16-81		86.50		$375.00
Buy	9-17-81	REN	86.65		
	9-22-81		86.65	0	0
Sell	9-29-81	TDR	85.92		
	10- 2-81		85.85	$ 175.00	
Buy	10- 9-81	CA2L	87.13		
	10-13-81		87.13	0	0
Buy	10-29-81	REN	87.50		
	11- 5-81		87.60	1500.00	
Buy	11- 6-81	REN	87.72		
	11-13-81		88.60	2200.00	

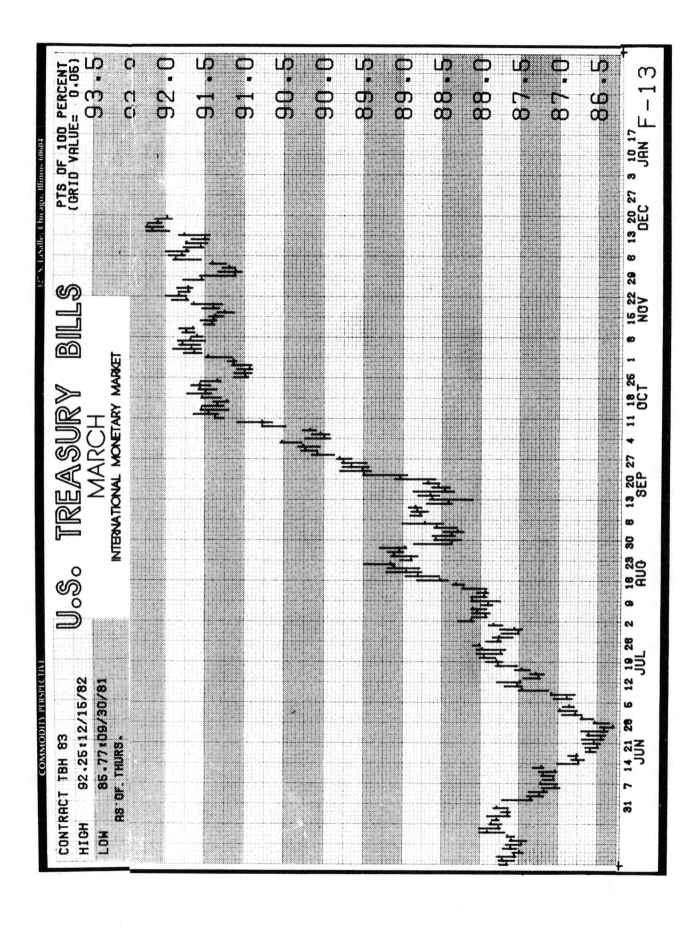

SPIKE-35 TRADING RESULTS
83 Mar T-Bills

Order	Entry and Exit Dates	Entry Rule	Entry and Exit Prices	Gain	Loss
Sell	6- 1-82	CB2L	87.35		
	6- 3-82		87.35	0	0
Sell	6- 3-82	REN	82.20		
	6- 7-82		87.20	0	0
Sell	6-10-82	REN	87.00		
	6-11-82		87.20		$ 500.00
Sell	6-14-82	REN	87.00		
	6-16-82		86.75	$ 625.00	
Sell	6-17-82	REN	86.65		
	6-21-82		86.65	0	0
Sell	6-21-82	REN	86.45		
	6-22-82		86.55		250.00
Sell	6-23-82	REN	86.45		
	6-23-82		86.55		250.00
Sell	6-24-82	REN	86.43		
	6-28-82		86.40	75.00	
Buy	7- 1-82	TDR	86.97		
	7- 6-82		86.85		300.00
Buy	7- 7-82	REN	86.98		
	7-13-82		87.45	1175.00	
Buy	7-16-82	REN	87.55		
	7-21-82		87.80	625.00	
Buy	7-22-82	REN	87.97		
	7-26-82		87.93		100.00
Buy	7-30-82	REN	87.77		
	8- 4-82		87.95	450.00	
Buy	8-12-82	REN	88.15		
	8-18-82		88.80	1625.00	
Buy	8-19-82	REN	88.97		
	8-23-82		89.02	125.00	

SPIKE-35 TRADING RESULTS
83 Mar T-Bills (Cont'd)

Order	Entry and Exit Dates	Entry Rule	Entry and Exit Prices	Gain	Loss
Buy	8-25-82	REN	89.15		
	8-26-82		89.05		$ 250.00
Sell	9- 1-82	TDR	88.30		
	9- 2-82		88.37		175.00
Sell	9-10-82	REN	88.70		
	9-14-82		88.65	$ 125.00	
Sell	9-15-82	REN	88.40		
	9-17-82		88.55		375.00
Buy	9-20-82	TDR	89.04		
	9-23-82		89.50	1150.00	
Buy	9-23-82	REN	89.67		
	9-24-82		89.50		425.00
Buy	9-24-82	REN	89.67		
	9-30-82		90.10	1075.00	
Buy	9-30-82	REN	90.25		
	10- 4-82		90.25	0	0
Buy	10- 7-82	REN	90.52		
	10-13-82		91.35	2075.00	
Buy	10-13-82	REN	91.47		
	10-14-82		91.44		75.00
Buy	10-19-82	REN	91.55		
	10-20-82		91.50		125.00
Buy	10-20-82	REN	91.57		
	10-21-82		91.50		175.00
Buy	10-29-82	REN	91.15		
	11- 4-82		91.62	1175.00	
Buy	11- 4-82	REN	91.70		
	11- 5-82		91.65		125.00
Buy	11-10-82	REN	91.80		
	11-11-80		91.50		750.00

SPIKE-35 TRADING RESULTS
83 Mar T-Bills (Cont'd)

Order	Entry and Exit Dates	Entry Rule	Entry and Exit Prices	Gain	Loss
Buy	11-17-82	REN	91.40		
	11-23-82		91.72	$ 800.00	
Sell	11-29-82	TDR	91.10		
	12- 1-82		91.12		$ 50.00
Buy	12- 3-82	TDR	91.87		
	12- 7-82		91.80		175.00
Buy	12-13-82	REN	91.75		
	12-16-82		92.15	1000.00	

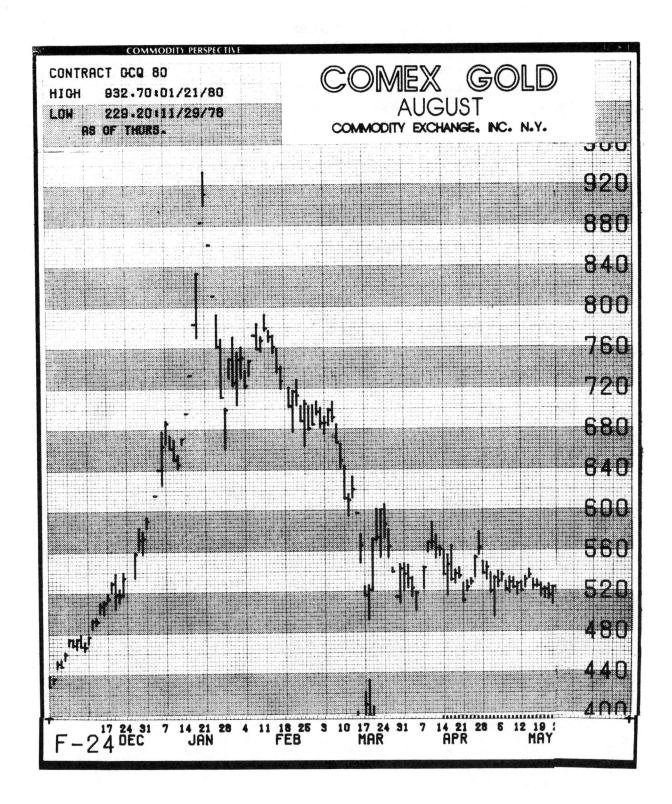

COMMODITY PERSPECTIVE

CONTRACT GCQ 80
HIGH   932.70:01/21/80
LOW   229.20:11/29/78
     AS OF THURS.

COMEX GOLD
AUGUST
COMMODITY EXCHANGE, INC. N.Y.

960
920
880
840
800
760
720
680
640
600
560
520
480
440
400

F-24 DEC 17 24 31 JAN 7 14 21 28 FEB 4 11 18 25 MAR 3 10 17 24 31 APR 7 14 21 28 MAY 5 12 19

SPIKE-35 TRADING RESULTS
80 Aug Gold

Order	Entry and Exit Dates	Entry Rule	Entry and Exit Prices	Gain	Loss
Buy	12-11-79 12-19-79	CA2H	492.00 510.00	$1800.00	
Buy	12-21-79 1- 8-80	REN	529.00 664.00	3500.00	
Buy	1-17-80 1-24-80	REN	782.00 782.00	0	0
Buy	1-30-80 1-31-80	REN	760.00 726.00		$3400.00
Buy	2- 1-80 2- 4-80	REN	750.00 726.00		2400.00
Buy	2- 7-80 2- 8-80	REN	770.00 760.00		1000.00
Buy	2-11-80 2-12-80	REN	780.00 770.00		1000.00
Sell	2-19-80 2-21-80	CB2L	703.00 718.00		1500.00
Sell	2-23-80 2-28-80	REN	702.00 702.00	0	0
Sell	3- 3-80 3- 5-80	REN	680.00 702.00		2000.00
Sell	3- 6-80 3-12-80	REN	684.00 612.00	7200.00	
Sell	3-14-80 3-19-80	REN	576.00 522.00	5400.00	
Sell	3-25-80 3-28-80	REN	570.00 539.00	3100.00	
Sell	4- 3-80 4- 7-80	REN	519.50 523.00		350.00
Sell	4-14-80 4-16-80	REN	560.00 546.00	1400.00	

SPIKE-35 TRADING RESULTS
80 Aug Gold (Cont'd)

Order	Entry and Exit Dates	Entry Rule	Entry and Exit Prices	Gain	Loss
Sell	4-16-80 4-18-80	REN	536.00 538.00		$ 200.00
Sell	4-21-80 4-23-80	REN	528.00 526.00	$ 200.00	
Sell	4-30-80 5- 2-80	REN	538.00 536.00	200.00	

GOLD (N.Y.)

DECEMBER 1980

Commodity Exchange, Inc. N.Y.

COMMODITY PERSPECTIVE/CHICAGO, ILLINOIS 60604

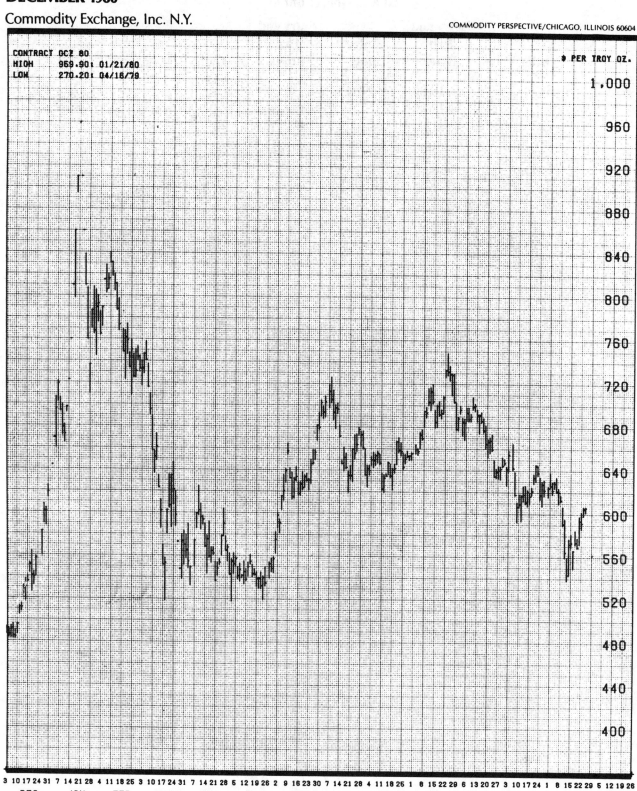

CONTRACT DCZ 80
HIGH   959.90: 01/21/80
LOW   270.20: 04/16/79

$ PER TROY OZ.

1,000
960
920
880
840
800
760
720
680
640
600
560
520
480
440
400

3 10 17 24 31 7 14 21 28 4 11 18 25 3 10 17 24 31 7 14 21 28 5 12 19 26 2 9 16 23 30 7 14 21 28 4 11 18 25 1 8 15 22 29 6 13 20 27 3 10 17 24 1 8 15 22 29 5 12 19 26

DEC   JAN   FEB   MAR   APR   MAY   JUN   JUL   AUG   SEP   OCT   NOV   DEC   JAN

SPIKE-35 TRADING RESULTS
80 Dec Gold

Order	Entry and Exit Dates	Entry Rule	Entry and Exit Prices	Gain	Loss
Sell	5- 6-80	REN	542.00		
	5- 9-80		548.00		$ 600.00
Sell	5-12-80	REN	541.00		
	5-13-80		546.00		500.00
Sell	5-19-80	REN	543.00		
	5-21-80		540.00	$ 300.00	
Sell	5-22-80	REN	532.00		
	5-22-80		540.00		800.00
Buy	5-29-80	TDR	558.00		
	6-10-80		640.00	8200.00	
Buy	6-18-80	REN	634.20		
	6-18-80		627.70		650.00
Buy	6-20-80	REN	634.20		
	6-23-80		630.00		420.00
Buy	6-24-80	REN	634.20		
	7- 2-80		693.80	5880.00	
Buy	7- 2-80	REN	703.00		
	7- 9-80		705.00	200.00	
Sell	7-14-80	CB2L	672.00		
	7-17-80		653.00	1900.00	
Sell	7-17-80	REN	646.00		
	7-21-80		644.00	200.00	
Sell	7-30-80	REN	660.00		
	8- 1-80		643.00	1700.00	
Sell	8- 8-80	REN	649.00		
	8-13-80		636.00	1300.00	
Sell	8-13-80	REN	633.00		
	8-18-80		642.00		900.00

SPIKE-35 TRADING RESULTS
80 Dec Gold (Cont'd)

Order	Entry and Exit Dates	Entry Rule	Entry and Exit Prices	Gain	Loss
Buy	8-20-80	CA2H	667.00		
	8-22-80		657.00		$1000.00
Buy	8-29-80	REN	655.00		
	9- 3-80		656.00	$ 100.00	
Buy	9- 4-80	REN	661.00		
	9-12-80		703.00	4200.00	
Buy	9-19-80	REN	701.00		
	9-24-80		731.00	3000.00	
Sell	9-29-80	TDR	679.00		
	10- 1-80		694.00		1500.00
Sell	10- 2-80	REN	674.00		
	10- 6-80		687.00		1300.00
Buy	10- 9-80	CB2H	700.00		
	10-13-80		695.00		500.00
Sell	10-16-80	TDR	678.00		
	10-21-80		668.00	1000.00	
Sell	10-22-80	REN	664.00		
	10-27-80		640.00	2400.00	
Sell	10-28-80	REN	635.00		
	10-28-80		641.00		600.00
Sell	10-31-80	REN	640.00		
	11- 3-80		648.00		800.00
Sell	11- 5-80	REN	641.00		
	11-11-80		611.00	3000.00	

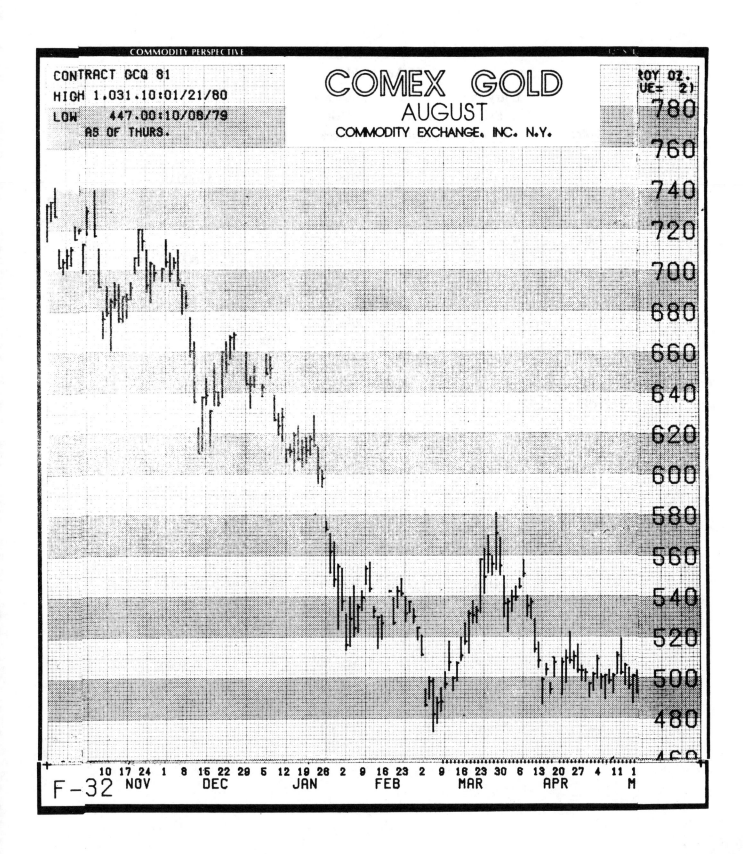

COMMODITY PERSPECTIVE

COMEX GOLD
AUGUST
COMMODITY EXCHANGE, INC. N.Y.

CONTRACT GCQ 81
HIGH 1,031.10:01/21/80
LOW   447.00:10/08/79
    AS OF THURS.

ROY OZ.
UE= 2)

780
760
740
720
700
680
660
640
620
600
580
560
540
520
500
480
460

F-32
10 17 24 1 8 15 22 29 5 12 19 26 2 9 16 23 2 9 16 23 30 6 13 20 27 4 11 1
NOV   DEC   JAN   FEB   MAR   APR   M

SPIKE-35 TRADING RESULTS
81 Aug Gold

Order	Entry and Exit Dates	Entry Rule	Entry and Exit Prices	Gain	Loss
Sell	11-13-80	REN	676.00		
	11-14-80		686.00		$1000.00
Sell	11-24-80	REN	692.00		
	12- 1-80		702.00		1000.00
Sell	12- 2-80	REN	698.00		
	12- 3-80		704.00		600.00
Sell	12- 4-80	REN	698.00		
	12-15-80		636.00	$6200.00	
Sell	12-29-80	REN	654.00		
	12-31-80		644.00	1000.00	
Sell	1- 2-81	REN	643.00		
	1- 5-81		649.00		900.00
Sell	1- 7-81	REN	638.00		
	1- 9-81		627.00	1100.00	
Sell	1-12-81	REN	612.00		
	1-14-81		612.00	0	0
Sell	1-15-81	REN	612.00		
	1-19-81		614.00		200.00
Sell	1-22-81	REN	611.00		
	2- 3-81		538.00	7300.00	
Sell	2-11-81	REN	534.00		
	2-18-81		539.00		500.00
Sell	2-25-81	REN	531.50		
	3- 4-81		498.00	3350.00	
Sell	3- 4-81	REN	486.00		
	3- 6-81		488.00		200.00
Buy	3-16-81	CA2H	518.00		
	3-19-81		530.00	1200.00	
Buy	3-19-81	REN	532.00		
	3-26-81		556.00	2400.00	

SPIKE-35 TRADING RESULTS
81 Aug Gold (Cont'd)

Order	Entry and Exit Dates	Entry Rule	Entry and Exit Prices	Gain	Loss
Buy	3-26-81	REN	560.00		
	3-27-81		556.00		$ 400.00
Buy	4- 3-81	REN	544.00		
	4- 7-81		540.00		400.00
Sell	4- 9-81	TDR	514.00		
	4-16-81		504.00	$1000.00	
Sell	4-20-81	REN	494.00		
	4-20-81		508.00		1400.00
Sell	4-24-81	RR#2	504.00		
	5- 1-81		502.00	200.00	

GOLD (N.Y.)

DECEMBER 1981

Commodity Exchange, Inc. N.Y.

COMMODITY PERSPECTIVE/CHICAGO, ILLINOIS 60604

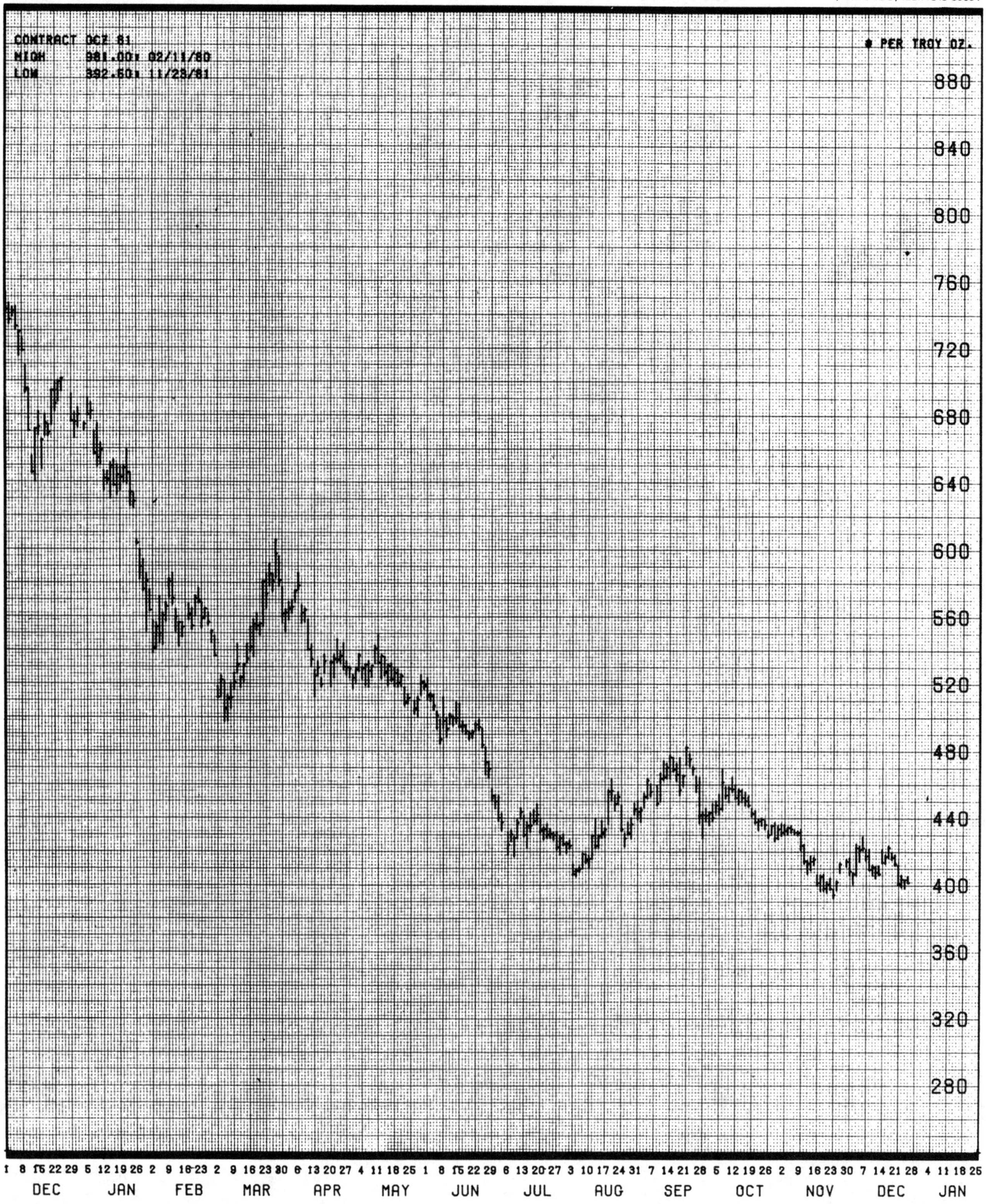

CONTRACT GCZ 81
HIGH 981.00: 02/11/80
LOW 392.60: 11/23/81
$ PER TROY OZ.
880
840
800
760
720
680
640
600
560
520
480
440
400
360
320
280
1 8 15 22 29 5 12 19 26 2 9 16 23 2 9 16 23 30 6 13 20 27 4 11 18 25 1 8 15 22 29 6 13 20 27 3 10 17 24 31 7 14 21 28 5 12 19 26 2 9 16 23 30 7 14 21 28 4 11 18 25
DEC JAN FEB MAR APR MAY JUN JUL AUG SEP OCT NOV DEC JAN

SPIKE-35 TRADING RESULTS
81 Dec Gold

Order	Entry and Exit Dates	Entry Rule	Entry and Exit Prices	Gain	Loss
Buy	5- 8-81 5-12-81	CA2H	540.00 532.00		$ 800.00
Sell	5-19-81 5-27-81	TDR	520.00 510.00	$1000.00	
Sell	6- 3-81 6- 8-81	REN	512.00 500.00	1200.00	
Sell	6-16-81 6-19-81	REN	494.00 492.00	200.00	
Sell	6-24-81 7- 1-81	REN	490.00 452.00	3800.00	
Sell	7- 1-81 7- 9-81	REN	449.00 430.00	1900.00	
Sell	7-14-81 7-15-81	REN	428.00 436.00		800.00
Sell	7-20-81 7-22-81	REN	432.00 432.00	0	0
Sell	7-22-81 7-24-81	REN	431.00 430.00	100.00	
Sell	7-27-81 7-29-81	REN	429.00 428.50	50.00	
Sell	7-30-81 7-31-81	REN	422.00 424.00		200.00
Sell	7-31-81 8- 5-81	REN	422.00 410.00	1200.00	
Buy	8-14-81 8-17-81	TDR	430.00 428.00		200.00
Buy	8-17-81 8-20-81	REN	430.00 453.00	2300.00	
Buy	8-28-81 9- 1-81	REN	442.00 442.00	0	0
Buy	9- 1-81 9- 8-81	REN	445.00 454.00	900.00	

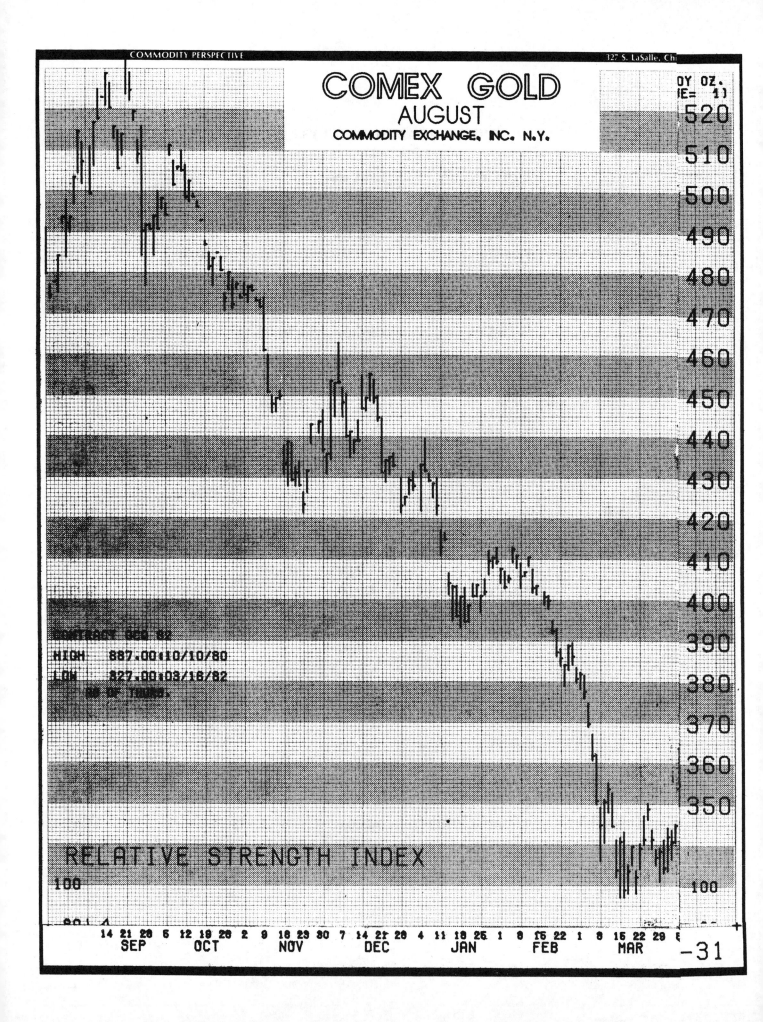

COMEX GOLD
AUGUST
COMMODITY EXCHANGE, INC. N.Y.

OY OZ.
IE= 1)

520

510

500

490

480

470

460

450

440

430

420

410

400

390

380

370

360

350

100

CONTRACT DEC 82
HIGH   887.00 10/10/80
LOW   327.00 03/16/82

RELATIVE STRENGTH INDEX

100

14 21 28   5 12 19 26   2 9 16 29 30   7 14 21 28   4 11 18 25   1 8 16 22   1 8 15 22 29 5
    SEP   OCT   NOV   DEC   JAN   FEB   MAR

-31

SPIKE-35 TRADING RESULTS
82 Aug Gold

Order	Entry and Exit Dates	Entry Rule	Entry and Exit Prices	Gain	Loss
Buy	9- 9-81	CA2H	517.00		
	9-15-81		523.00	$ 600.00	
Buy	9-21-81	REN	524.00		
	9-23-81		519.50		$ 450.00
Sell	9-25-81	CB2L	490.30		
	9-30-81		492.30		200.00
Sell	10-12-81	REN	501.50		
	10-23-81		484.00	1750.00	
Sell	10-23-81	REN	481.50		
	11- 2-81		477.50	400.00	
Sell	11- 5-81	REN	474.00		
	11- 9-81		474.00	0	0
Sell	11- 9-81	REN	471.50		
	11-13-81		449.50	2200.00	
Sell	11-16-81	REN	438.00		
	11-20-81		431.00	700.00	
Sell	11-20-81	REN	429.00		
	11-24-81		428.00	100.00	
Sell	12- 1-81	REN	432.00		
	12- 2-81		437.00		500.00
Buy	12- 2-81	TDR	453.70		
	12- 2-81		453.70	0	0
Buy	12-14-81	REN	447.00		
	12-17-81		449.50	250.00	
Sell	12-21-81	TDR	431.50		
	12-23-81		434.50		300.00
Sell	12-28-81	REN	430.00		
	12-30-81		426.00	400.00	

SPIKE-35 TRADING RESULTS
82 Aug Gold (Cont'd)

Order	Entry and Exit Dates	Entry Rule	Entry and Exit Prices	Gain	Loss
Sell	1- 4-82	REN	422.50		
	1- 4-82		429.50		$ 700.00
Sell	1- 8-82	REN	428.00		
	1-19-82		401.00	2700.00	
Sell	1-19-82	REN	395.50		
	1-21-82		401.00		$ 550.00
Sell	2- 2-82	REN	404.00		
	2- 2-82		410.00		600.00
Sell	2-11-82	REN	406.00		
	2-24-82		386.00	2000.00	
Sell	2-26-82	REN	383.50		
	3- 9-82		351.00	3250.00	
Sell	3-11-82	REN	344.50		
	3-15-82		341.00	350.00	
Sell	3-15-82	REN	333.50		
	3-17-82		335.00		150.00
Sell	3-19-82	REN	329.50		
	3-19-82		339.00		950.00
Sell	3-26-82	REN	339.00		
	3-30-82		339.00	0	0
Sell	3-30-82	REN	336.50		
	3-31-82		338.50		200.00

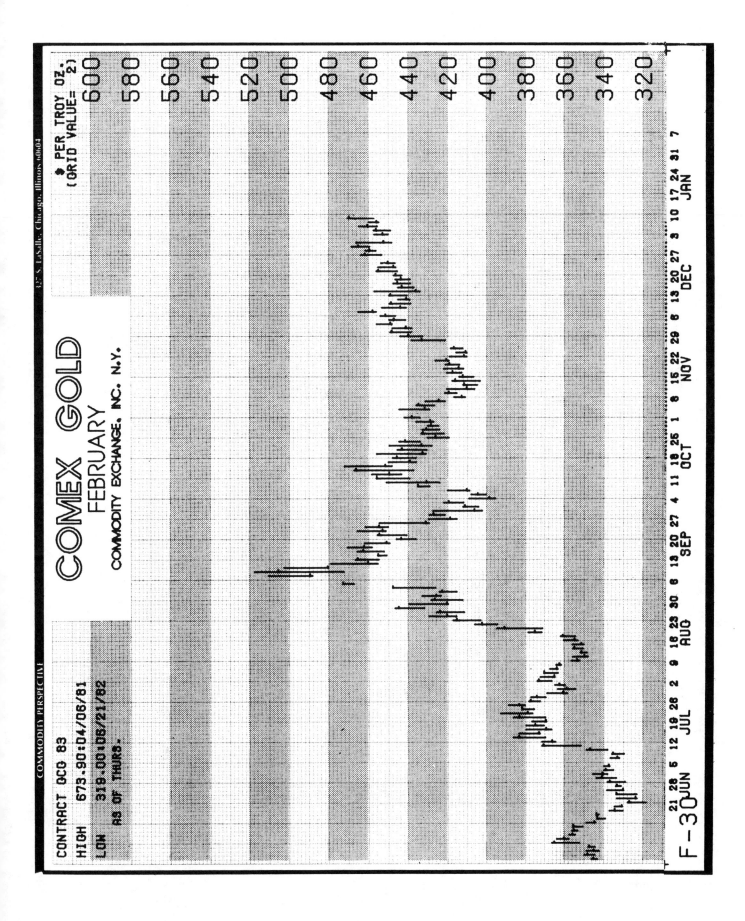

SPIKE-35 TRADING RESULTS
83 Feb Gold

Order	Entry and Exit Dates	Entry Rule	Entry and Exit Prices	Gain	Loss
Sell	6-17-82 6-22-82	CB2L	334.00 331.00	$ 300.00	
Sell	7- 2-82 7- 8-82	REN	337.50 338.00		50.00
Buy	7- 8-82 7-15-82	CA2H	347.00 373.00	$2600.00	
Buy	7-20-82 7-22-82	REN	375.00 378.00	300.00	
Buy	7-23-82 7-26-82	REN	383.00 378.00		500.00
Sell	7-28-82 7-30-82	TDR	360.00 360.00	0	0
Sell	8- 6-82 8-12-82	REN	363.50 352.00	1150.00	
Buy	8-18-82 8-25-82	CA2H	375.00 415.50	4050.00	
Buy	8-25-82 8-27-82	REN	421.00 424.00	300.00	
Buy	9- 2-82 9- 9-82	REN	428.00 489.50	6150.00	
Buy	9-16-82 9-17-82	REN	466.00 462.00		400.00
Sell	9-17-82 9-21-82	CB2L	451.00 451.00	0	0
Sell	9-24-82 10- 1-82	REN	444.00 412.00	3200.00	
Sell	10- 4-82 10- 6-82	REN	406.00 409.00		300.00
Buy	10-11-82 10-13-82	TDR	456.00 450.00		600.00

SPIKE-35 TRADING RESULTS
83 Feb Gold (Cont'd)

Order	Entry and Exit Dates	Entry Rule	Entry and Exit Prices	Gain	Loss
Buy	10-13-82 10-14-82	REN	456.00 450.00		600.00
Buy	10-21-82 10-21-82	REN	446.00 433.00		1300.00
Sell	10-25-82 10-27-82	CB2L	426.00 434.00		800.00
Sell	10-28-82 10-29-82	REN	426.00 432.00		600.00
Sell	11- 4-82 11-10-82	REN	428.00 420.00	$ 800.00	
Sell	11-10-82 11-12-82	REN	412.00 412.00	0	0
Sell	11-15-82 11-16-82	REN	430.00 436.00		600.00
Buy	11-19-82 11-22-82	CA2H	421.00 419.50		150.00
Buy	11-26-82 12- 1-82	REN	422.00 439.50	1750.00	
Buy	12- 2-82 12- 8-82	REN	449.00 452.00	300.00	
Buy	12-14-82 12-14-82	REN	449.00 441.00		800.00
Sell	12-14-82 12-16-82	CB2L	436.50 444.00		750.00
Buy	12-27-82 12-29-82	CA2H	462.00 460.00		200.00

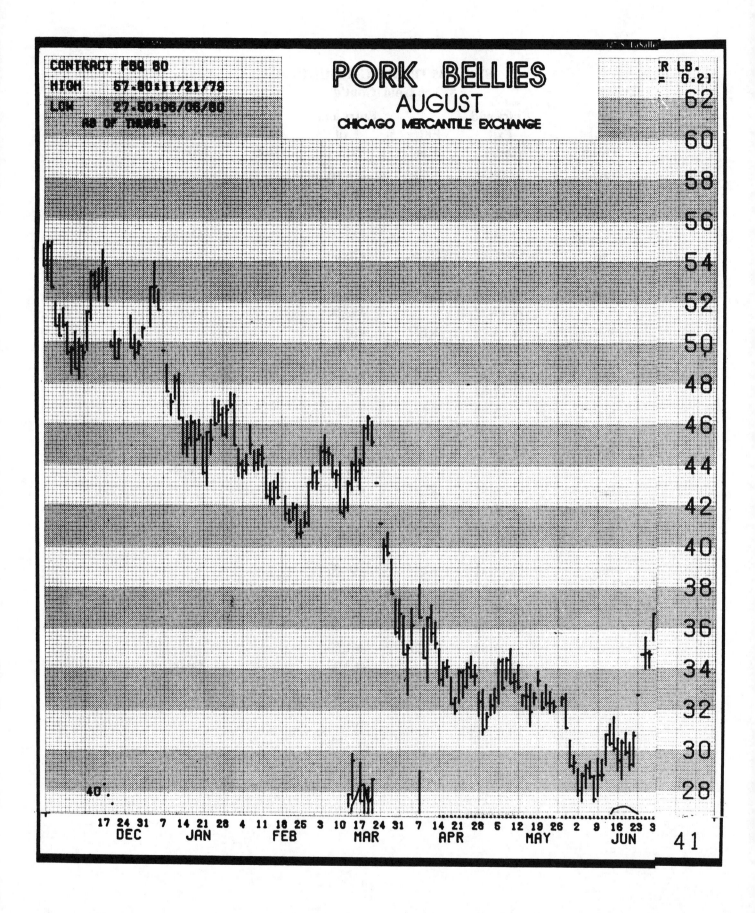

PORK BELLIES
AUGUST
CHICAGO MERCANTILE EXCHANGE

CONTRACT PBQ 80
HIGH   57.80×11/21/79
LOW   27.50×06/06/80
AS OF THURS.

R LB.
= 0.2)

41

SPIKE-35 TRADING RESULTS
80 Aug Pork Bellies

Order	Entry and Exit Dates	Entry Rule	Entry and Exit Prices	Gain	Loss
Buy	12-17-79 12-18-79	TDR	54.00 53.00		$ 375.00
Buy	12-27-79 12-28-79	REN	50.20 49.60		225.00
Buy	12-31-79 1- 4-80	REN	50.30 52.60	$ 862.50	
Sell	1- 8-80 1- 9-80	CB2L	47.60 47.60	0	0
Sell	1-11-80 1-16-80	REN	47.10 45.40	862.50	
Sell	1-17-80 1-18-80	REN	44.95 46.10		393.75
Sell	1-21-80 1-22-80	REN	45.20 45.50		112.50
Buy	1-30-80 1-31-80	TDR	47.00 46.75		93.75
Buy	2- 6-80 2- 7-80	REN	45.00 44.00		375.00
Sell	2-12-80 2-14-80	CB2L	42.40 42.40	0	0
Sell	2-19-80 2-21-80	REN	42.30 41.65	243.75	
Sell	2-22-80 2-26-80	REN	41.20 41.00	75.00	
Buy	2-28-80 2-29-80	CA2H	43.65 43.20		168.75
Buy	3- 3-80 3- 5-80	REN	43.70 44.60	337.50	
Buy	3-13-80 3-17-80	REN	43.65 43.70	18.75	

SPIKE-35 TRADING RESULTS
80 Aug Pork Bellies (Cont'd)

Order	Entry and Exit Dates	Entry Rule	Entry and Exit Prices	Gain	Loss
Buy	3-18-80	REN	44.10		
	3-21-80		45.80	$ 637.50	
Sell	3-25-80	CB2L	40.10		
	4- 3-80		35.20	1837.50	
Sell	4- 8-80	REN	34.70		
	4- 9-80		36.60		$ 712.50
Sell	4-14-80	REN	34.55		
	4-16-80		34.10	168.75	
Sell	4-17-80	REN	33.45		
	4-21-80		32.40	393.75	
Sell	4-28-80	REN	32.90		
	5- 1-80		31.75	431.25	
Buy	5- 5-80	TDR	34.40		
	5- 9-80		33.45		356.25
Buy	5-19-80	REN	33.20		
	5-20-80		32.60		150.00
Sell	5-28-80	CB2L	31.10		
	6- 4-80		28.85	843.75	
Sell	6- 6-80	REN	28.00		
	6- 9-80		28.80		300.00
Sell	6-17-80	REN	29.50		
	6-17-80		30.10		225.00

PORK BELLIES

JULY 1981

Chicago Mercantile Exchange

COMMODITY PERSPECTIVE/CHICAGO, ILLINOIS 60604

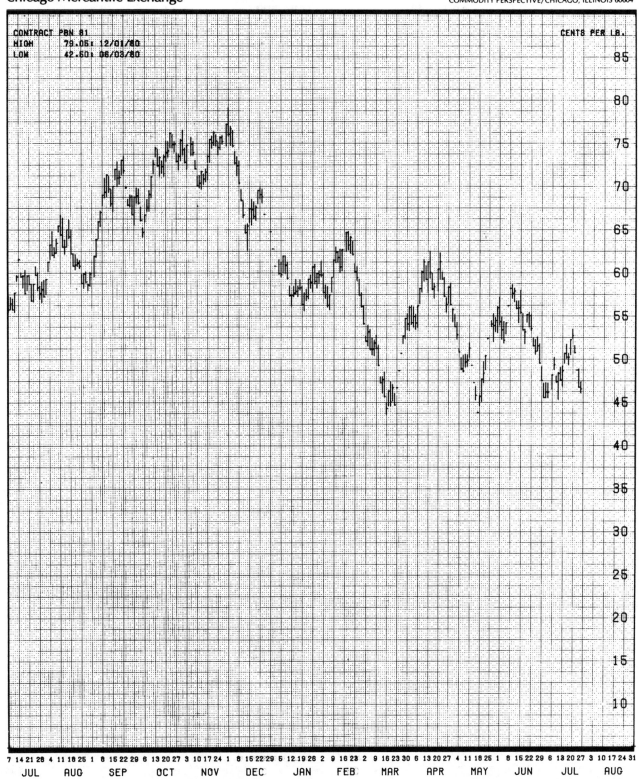

CONTRACT PBN 81
HIGH   79.05: 12/01/80
LOW   42.60: 06/03/80

CENTS PER LB.

JUL AUG SEP OCT NOV DEC JAN FEB MAR APR MAY JUN JUL AUG

SPIKE-35 TRADING RESULTS
81 July Pork Bellies

Order	Entry and Exit Dates	Entry Rule	Entry and Exit Prices	Gain	Loss
Sell	12- 4-80	CB2L	72.65		
	12-15-80		65.85	$2550.00	
Sell	1- 3-81	REN	60.80		
	1- 6-81		60.10	262.50	
Sell	1- 8-81	REN	59.80		
	1-13-81		57.50	862.50	
Sell	1-15-81	REN	57.40		
	1-15-80		57.90		$ 187.50
Sell	1-19-81	REN	57.60		
	1-21-81		57.60	0	0
Sell	1-28-81	REN	58.80		
	1-29-81		60.00		450.00
Sell	2- 2-81	REN	59.00		
	2- 4-81		57.80	450.00	
Sell	2- 4-81	REN	57.40		
	2- 4-81		57.40	0	0
Buy	2- 9-81	CA2H	61.40		
	2-11-81		61.40	0	0
Buy	2-13-81	REN	62.40		
	2-19-81		63.15	281.25	
Sell	2-26-81	TDR	56.10		
	3- 4-81		53.20	1087.50	
Sell	3- 4-81	REN	52.10		
	3- 6-81		51.20	337.50	
Sell	3-10-81	REN	51.10		
	3-13-81		47.65	1293.75	
Sell	3-13-81	REN	47.20		
	3-16-81		45.65	581.25	
Buy	3-26-81	CA2H	52.00		
	3-31-81		54.00	750.00	

SPIKE-35 TRADING RESULTS
81 July Pork Bellies (Cont'd)

Order	Entry and Exit Dates	Entry Rule	Entry and Exit Prices	Gain	Loss
Buy	3-31-81	REN	54.70		
	4- 2-81		54.00		$ 262.50
Buy	4- 6-81	REN	56.00		
	4-10-81		60.00	$1500.00	
Buy	4-14-81	REN	61.20		
	4-15-81		59.90		487.50
Buy	4-21-81	REN	60.40		
	4-22-81		60.00		150.00
Sell	4-29-81	TDR	55.80		
	5- 7-81		49.20	2475.00	
Sell	5-14-81	REN	46.60		
	5-19-81		45.85	281.25	
Buy	5-26-81	TDR	54.00		
	5-27-81		52.40		600.00
Buy	5-29-81	REN	54.45		
	6- 1-81		54.35		37.50

PORK BELLIES

FEBRUARY 1981

Chicago Mercantile Exchange

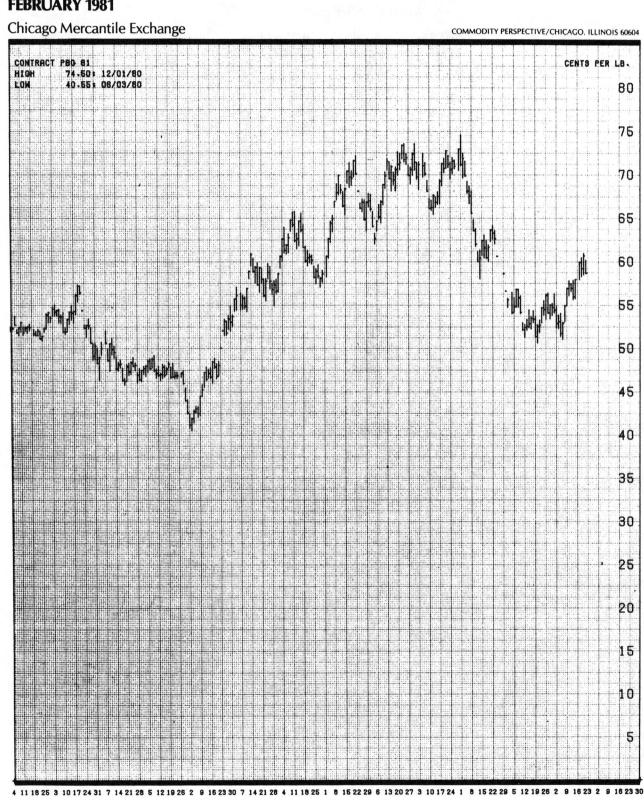

CONTRACT PBO 81

HIGH   74.50 : 12/01/80

LOW   40.55 : 06/03/80

CENTS PER LB.

FEB MAR APR MAY JUN JUL AUG SEP OCT NOV DEC JAN FEB MAR

SPIKE-35 TRADING RESULTS
81 Feb Pork Bellies

Order	Entry and Exit Dates	Entry Rule	Entry and Exit Prices	Gain	Loss
Buy	6-17-80	TDR	48.40		
	6-19-80		47.70		$ 266.00
Buy	6-20-80	REN	47.80		
	6-26-80		52.00	$1575.00	
Buy	6-27-80	REN	53.50		
	7- 1-80		52.97		202.00
Buy	7- 1-80	REN	53.40		
	7- 7-80		55.60	836.00	
Buy	7-10-80	REN	56.00		
	7-15-80		58.80	1050.00	
Buy	7-24-80	REN	59.30		
	7-25-80		57.70		608.00
Buy	7-31-80	REN	57.70		
	8- 6-80		61.20	1330.00	
Buy	8- 7-80	REN	62.60		
	8-12-80		64.10	570.00	
Buy	8-15-80	REN	64.60		
	8-18-80		63.50		418.00
Sell	8-25-80	TDR	58.10		
	8-27-80		58.85		244.00
Sell	8-28-80	REN	58.00		
	8-29-80		58.20		76.00
Buy	9- 4-80	TDR	64.50		
	9-11-80		65.90	532.00	
Buy	9-16-80	REN	69.90		
	9-18-80		69.50		152.00
Buy	9-19-80	REN	70.20		
	9-24-80		66.60		1368.00
Sell	9-26-80	TDR	64.85		
	9-29-80		66.85		760.00

SPIKE-35 TRADING RESULTS
81 Feb Pork Bellies (Cont'd)

Order	Entry and Exit Dates	Entry Rule	Entry and Exit Prices	Gain	Loss
Sell	10- 2-80	REN	64.70		
	10- 6-80		64.00	$ 266.00	
Buy	10-10-80	TDR	69.75		
	10-14-80		69.75	0	0
Buy	10-20-80	REN	70.85		
	10-24-80		71.60	285.00	
Buy	10-29-80	REN	71.85		
	10-31-80		71.30		$ 209.00
Sell	11- 7-80	TDR	68.00		
	11-12-80		66.10	722.00	
Buy	11-20-80	CA2H	72.60		
	11-22-80		71.10		570.00
Buy	11-28-80	REN	71.50		
	12- 2-80		70.95		209.00

PORK BELLIES

MARCH 1982

Chicago Mercantile Exchange

COMMODITY PERSPECTIVE/CHICAGO. ILLINOIS 60604

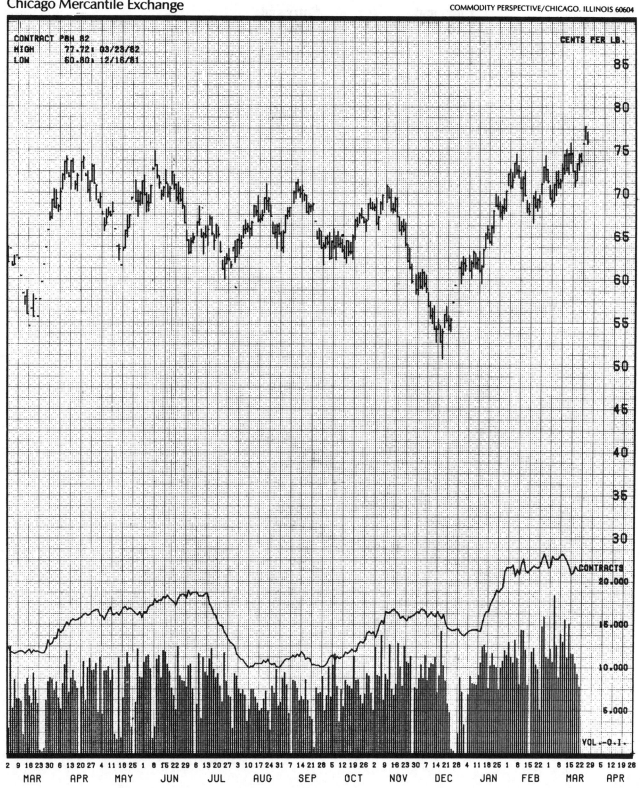

CONTRACT PBH 82
HIGH   77.72 x 03/23/82
LOW   60.80 x 12/16/81

CENTS PER LB.

SPIKE-35 TRADING RESULTS
82 Mar Pork Bellies

Order	Entry and Exit Dates	Entry Rule	Entry and Exit Prices	Gain	Loss
Sell	6-26-81	CB2L	68.40		
	7- 3-81		64.40	$1520.00	
Sell	7- 9-81	REN	64.55		
	7-10-81		65.25		$ 266.00
Sell	7-13-81	REN	64.90		
	7-13-81		65.25		133.00
Sell	7-16-81	REN	64.95		
	7-17-81		65.30		133.00
Sell	7-21-81	REN	64.30		
	7-24-81		61.85	931.00	
Buy	8- 5-81	CA2H	65.75		
	8- 7-81		65.75	0	0
Buy	8-11-81	REN	66.05		
	8-14-81		67.80	665.00	
Buy	8-19-81	REN	67.85		
	8-21-81		68.95	418.00	
Sell	8-25-81	TDR	65.20		
	8-27-81		65.40		76.00
Sell	8-28-81	REN	65.20		
	9- 1-81		65.20	0	0
Buy	9- 8-81	TDR	70.00		
	9-10-81		70.20	76.00	
Sell	9-23-81	TDR	64.70		
	9-29-81		63.85	323.00	
Sell	10- 1-81	REN	63.60		
	10- 2-81		64.25		247.00
Sell	10- 6-81	REN	62.35		
	10- 6-81		64.40		779.00
Sell	10- 9-81	REN	63.70		
	10-13-81		63.35	133.00	
Sell	10-16-81	REN	62.40		
	10-16-81		63.25		323.00

SPIKE-35 TRADING RESULTS
82 Mar Pork Bellies (Cont'd)

Order	Entry and Exit Dates	Entry Rule	Entry and Exit Prices	Gain	Loss
Buy	10-19-81 10-23-81	CA2H	66.80 67.10	$ 114.00	
Buy	10-27-81 10-29-81	REN	67.40 68.10	266.00	
Buy	11- 2-81 11- 2-81	REN	68.80 68.20		$ 225.00
Buy	11- 4-81 11-11-80	REN	68.80 69.40	225.00	
Sell	11-17-81 11-19-81	CB2L	65.70 66.20		190.00
Sell	11-20-81 11-30-81	REN	65.65 59.80	2223.00	
Sell	12- 4-81 12-10-81	REN	59.10 56.25	1083.00	
Sell	12-11-81 12-14-81	REN	55.70 54.25	551.00	
Sell	12-15-81 12-17-81	REN	54.15 54.40		95.00
Buy	12-29-81 1- 4-82	CA2H	60.60 61.50	342.00	
Buy	1- 5-82 1- 7-82	REN	61.80 61.80	0	0
Buy	1-11-82 1-11-82	REN	63.15 61.90		475.00
Buy	1-13-82 1-18-82	REN	62.25 65.20	1121.00	
Buy	1-19-82 1-25-82	REN	65.80 68.20	912.00	
Buy	1-27-82 1-28-82	REN	68.40 68.10		114.00
Buy	1-28-82 2- 5-82	REN	68.50 72.45	1501.00	

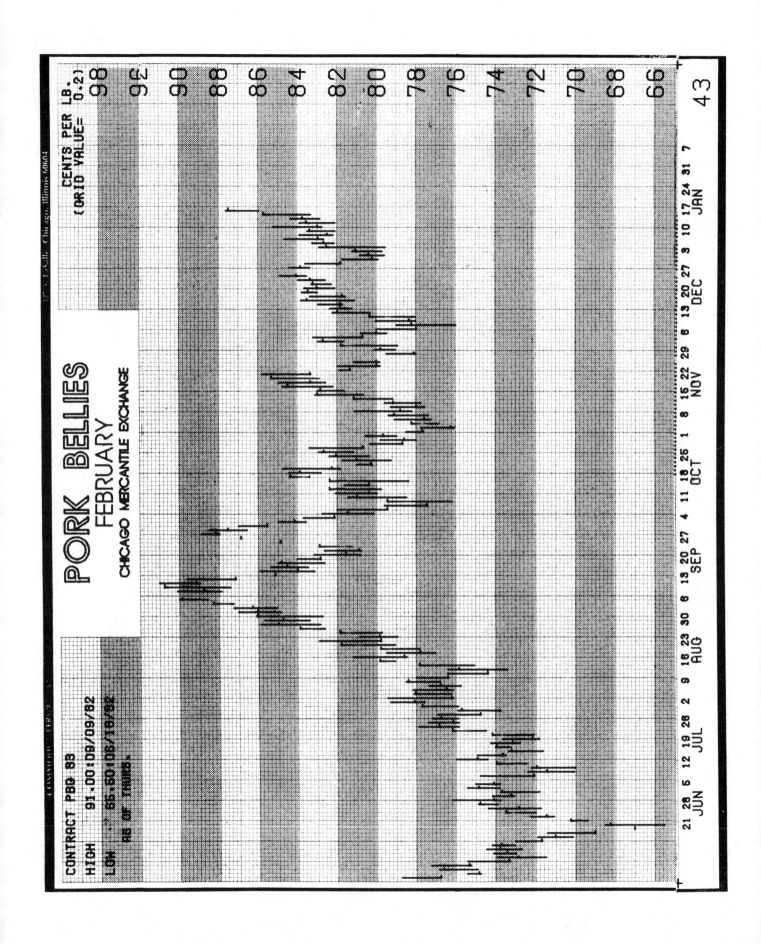

SPIKE-35 TRADING RESULTS
83 Feb Pork Bellies

Order	Entry and Exit Dates	Entry Rule	Entry and Exit Prices	Gain	Loss
Buy	6-25-82	TDR	74.80		
	6-29-82		74.00		$ 304.00
Buy	7- 1-82	REN	74.80		
	7- 6-82		74.00		304.00
Buy	7-12-82	REN	74.40		
	7-13-82		74.00		152.00
Buy	7-20-82	REN	74.20		
	7-23-82		76.15	$ 741.00	
Buy	7-26-82	REN	76.85		
	7-27-82		76.15		266.00
Buy	7-29-82	REN	76.80		
	8- 2-82		77.65	323.00	
Buy	8- 6-82	REN	78.15		
	8- 9-82		76.75		532.00
Sell	8-10-82	TDR	74.40		
	8-12-82		75.85		555.00
Buy	8-13-82	CA2H	79.80		
	8-17-82		78.60		456.00
Buy	8-18-82	REN	79.80		
	8-23-82		79.80	0	0
Buy	8-24-82	REN	79.80		
	8-27-82		83.90	1537.00	
Buy	8-30-82	REN	85.10		
	9- 1-82		85.95	323.00	
Buy	9- 1-82	REN	86.10		
	9- 7-82		88.30	825.00	
Buy	9- 8-82	REN	99.00		
	9-10-82		88.80		450.00
Sell	9-17-82	TDR	82.80		
	9-22-82		81.60	450.00	

SPIKE-35 TRADING RESULTS
83 Feb Pork Bellies (Cont'd)

Order	Entry and Exit Dates	Entry Rule	Entry and Exit Prices	Gain	Loss
Sell	9-30-82	REN	85.00		
	10-11-82		79.45	$2109.00	
Sell	10-14-82	REN	80.35		
	10-14-82		82.40		$ 779.00
Sell	10-20-82	REN	81.00		
	10-22-82		81.00	0	0
Sell	10-27-82	REN	80.35		
	10-29-82		79.00	513.00	
Sell	11- 1-82	REN	78.50		
	11- 3-82		77.80	266.00	
Buy	11-11-82	CA2H	81.20		
	11-16-82		82.75	589.00	
Buy	11-16-82	REN	83.10		
	11-17-82		82.80		114.00
Buy	11-18-82	REN	84.60		
	11-19-82		83.30		495.00
Buy	11-30-82	REN	80.10		
	12- 2-82		81.80	646.00	
Sell	12- 6-82	TDR	78.00		
	12- 8-82		78.25		95.00
Buy	12-15-82	TDR	83.50		
	12-16-82		81.80		646.00
Buy	12-17-82	REN	83.50		
	12-21-82		82.95		209.00
Buy	12-22-82	REN	83.50		
	12-28-82		83.60	38.00	
Sell	12-29-82	CB2L	80.20		
	12-31-82		80.40		76.00
Sell	1- 7-83	REN	82.50		
	1- 7-83		83.00		190.00
Sell	1-11-83	REN	82.45		
	1-11-83		83.40		361.00

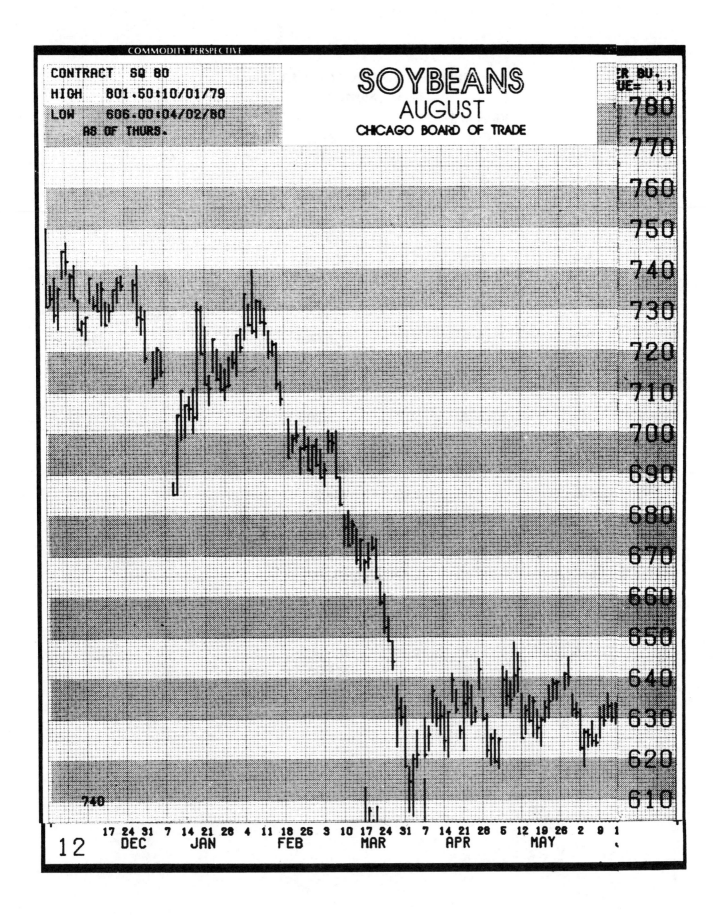

CONTRACT SQ 80
HIGH 801.50:10/01/79
LOW 606.00:04/02/80
AS OF THURS.

SOYBEANS
AUGUST
CHICAGO BOARD OF TRADE

ER BU.
UE= 1)

780
770
760
750
740
730
720
710
700
690
680
670
660
650
640
630
620
610

740

12

17 24 31 7 14 21 28 4 11 18 25 3 10 17 24 31 7 14 21 28 5 12 19 26 2 9 1
DEC   JAN   FEB   MAR   APR   MAY

SPIKE-35 TRADING RESULTS
80 Aug Soybeans

Order	Entry and Exit Dates	Entry Rule	Entry and Exit Prices	Gain	Loss
Sell	12-31-79	CB2L	718.00		
	1- 3-80		718.00	0	0
Sell	1- 9-80	REN	688.00		
	1-11-80		705.00		$ 850.00
Sell	1-16-80	REN	704.00		
	1-17-80		706.00		100.00
Buy	1-17-80	CA2H	730.00		
	1-21-80		719.00		550.00
Buy	1-30-80	REN	416.00		
	2- 6-80		426.00	$ 500.00	
Sell	2-14-80	CB2L	712.00		
	2-21-80		699.00	650.00	
Sell	2-22-80	REN	694.00		
	2-25-80		699.00		250.00
Sell	2-26-80	REN	696.00		
	2-27-80		697.00		50.00
Sell	2-29-80	REN	691.00		
	3- 3-80		692.00		50.00
Sell	3- 6-80	REN	689.00		
	3-12-80		678.00	550.00	
Sell	3-13-80	REN	674.00		
	3-19-80		672.00	100.00	
Sell	3-20-80	REN	668.00		
	3-31-80		632.00	1800.00	
Sell	3-31-80	REN	630.00		
	4- 2-80		618.00	600.00	
Sell	4-14-80	REN	626.00		
	4-15-80		631.00		250.00

SPIKE-35 TRADING RESULTS
80 Aug Soybeans (Cont'd)

Order	Entry and Exit Dates	Entry Rule	Entry and Exit Prices	Gain	Loss
Buy	4-16-80	TDR	637.00		
	4-17-80		631.00		$ 300.00
Buy	4-23-80	REN	635.00		
	4-23-80		634.00		50.00
Buy	4-25-80	REN	637.00		
	4-28-80		631.00		300.00
Sell	5- 1-80	CB2L	619.00		
	5- 2-80		625.00		300.00
Sell	5-12-80	REN	634.00		
	5-14-80		632.00	$ 100.00	
Sell	5-19-80	REN	627.00		
	5-20-80		630.00		150.00
Sell	5-29-80	REN	635.00		
	6- 5-80		627.00	400.00	

SOYBEANS

MAY 1981

Chicago Board of Trade

COMMODITY PERSPECTIVE/CHICAGO, ILLINOIS 60604

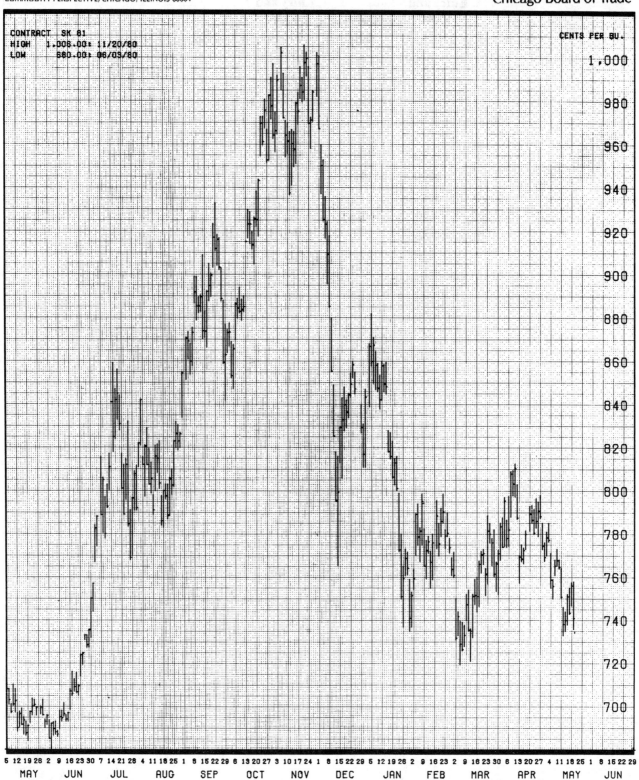

CONTRACT SK 81
HIGH   1,008.00: 11/20/80
LOW   680.00: 06/03/80

CENTS PER BU.

1,000
980
960
940
920
900
880
860
840
820
800
780
760
740
720
700

5 12 19 26   2 9 16 23 30   7 14 21 28   4 11 18 25   1 8 15 22 29   6 13 20 27   3 10 17 24 1   8 15 22 29   5 12 19 26   2 9 16 23   2 9 16 23 30   6 13 20 27   4 11 18 25   1 8 15 22 29

MAY   JUN   JUL   AUG   SEP   OCT   NOV   DEC   JAN   FEB   MAR   APR   MAY   JUN

SPIKE-35 TRADING RESULTS
81 May Soybeans

Order	Entry and Exit Dates	Entry Rule	Entry and Exit Prices	Gain	Loss
Buy	6-16-80	CA2H	706½		
	6-20-80		705½		$ 50.00
Buy	6-20-80	REN	710		
	6-27-80		727½	$ 375.00	
Buy	6-27-80	REN	732½		
	7- 8-80		788	2775.00	
Buy	7-11-80	REN	805		
	7-16-80		824	950.00	
Buy	7-17-80	REN	842		
	7-18-80		840		100.00
Sell	7-24-80	CB2L	784		
	7-28-80		788		200.00
Sell	7-25-80	REN	784		
	7-28-80		784	0	0
Sell	8- 7-80	REN	812		
	8- 8-80		812	0	0
Sell	8- 8-80	REN	802		
	8-12-80		805		150.00
Sell	8-15-80	REN	790½		
	8-19-80		800		475.00
Buy	8-25-80	TDR	822		
	8-27-80		821½		25.00
Buy	8-28-80	REN	826		
	9- 4-80		867	2050.00	
Buy	9- 5-80	REN	870½		
	9-10-80		884	675.00	
Buy	9-12-80	REN	892½		
	9-12-80		884½		400.00
Buy	9-16-80	REN	890		
	9-18-80		892	100.00	

SPIKE-35 TRADING RESULTS
81 May Soybeans (Cont'd)

Order	Entry and Exit Dates	Entry Rule	Entry and Exit Prices	Gain	Loss
Buy	9-18-80	REN	895		
	9-23-80		911	$ 800.00	
Sell	9-26-80	CB2L	858		
	9-30-80		863		$ 250.00
Sell	10- 2-80	REN	857½		
	10- 6-80		869		575.00
Buy	10-14-80	CA2H	923		
	10-15-80		913		500.00
Buy	10-17-80	REN	923		
	10-21-80		924	50.00	
Buy	10-21-80	REN	926		
	10-27-80		960	1700.00	
Buy	10-28-80	REN	975		
	10-30-80		977	100.00	
Buy	11- 3-80	REN	982		
	11- 6-80		988	300.00	
Sell	11-11-80	CB2L	937		
	11-13-80		960		1150.00
Sell	11-24-80	REN	983		
	11-26-80		972	550.00	
Sell	12- 1-80	REN	969		
	12-15-80		812	7850.00	
Sell	12-29-80	REN	940		
	12-31-80		930	500.00	
Buy	1- 2-81	TDR	866½		
	1- 5-81		859		375.00

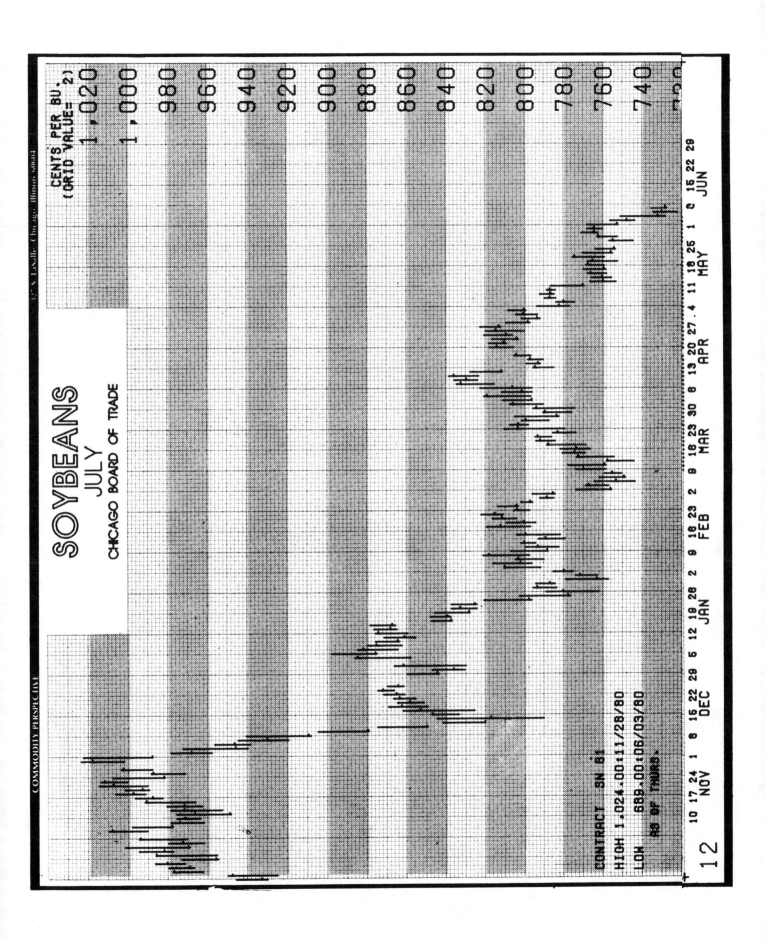

SOYBEANS
JULY
CHICAGO BOARD OF TRADE

CENTS PER BU.
(GRID VALUE= 2)

1,020
1,000
980
960
940
920
900
880
860
840
820
800
780
760
740

CONTRACT SN 81
HIGH 1,024.00:11/28/80
LOW 689.00:06/03/80
AS OF THURS.

10 17 24 1 8 15 22 29 5 12 19 28 2 9 16 23 2 9 16 23 30 6 13 20 27 4 11 18 25 1 8 15 22 28
NOV   DEC   JAN   FEB   MAR   APR   MAY   JUN

12

COMMODITY PERSPECTIVE

LFS LaSalle Chicago, Illinois 60604

SPIKE-35 TRADING RESULTS
81 July Soybeans

Order	Entry and Exit Dates	Entry Rule	Entry and Exit Prices	Gain	Loss
Buy	1-13-81	REN	876.00		
	1-14-81		868.00		$ 400.00
Sell	1-19-81	CB2L	828.00		
	1-21-81		833.00		250.00
Sell	1-21-81	REN	828.00		
	1-27-81		784.00	$2200.00	
Sell	1-29-81	REN	778.00		
	2- 2-81		776.00	100.00	
Buy	2- 6-81	CA2H	818.00		
	2- 9-81		803.00		750.00
Buy	2-13-81	REN	800.00		
	2-18-81		800.00	0	0
Buy	2-19-81	REN	813.00		
	2-23-81		806.00		350.00
Sell	2-26-81	CB2L	788.00		
	3- 6-81		754.00	1700.00	
Sell	3-11-81	REN	749.00		
	3-12-81		759.00		500.00
Buy	3-18-81	TDR	792.00		
	3-19-81		788.00		200.00
Buy	3-23-81	REN	794.00		
	3-25-81		802.00	400.00	
Buy	3-26-81	REN	804.00		
	3-30-81		800.00		200.00
Buy	3-31-81	REN	801.00		
	4- 6-81		801.00	0	0
Buy	4- 6-81	REN	820.00		
	4- 9-81		829.00	450.00	
Buy	4- 9-81	REN	833.00		
	4-10-81		828.00		250.00

SPIKE-35 TRADING RESULTS
81 July Soybeans (Cont'd)

Order	Entry and Exit Dates	Entry Rule	Entry and Exit Prices	Gain	Loss
Buy	4-20-81	REN	806.00		
	4-22-81		810.00	$ 200.00	
Buy	4-23-81	REN	815.00		
	4-24-81		809.00		$ 300.00
Buy	4-24-81	REN	815.00		
	4-28-81		809.00		300.00
Sell	5- 4-81	CB2L	782.00		
	5- 6-81		784.00		100.00
Sell	5-11-81	REN	780.00		
	5-14-81		761.00	950.00	
Sell	5-19-81	REN	759.00		
	5-19-81		768.00		450.00
Sell	5-21-81	REN	760.00		
	5-26-81		756.00	200.00	
Sell	6- 1-81	REN	755.00		
	6- 5-81		732.00	1150.00	

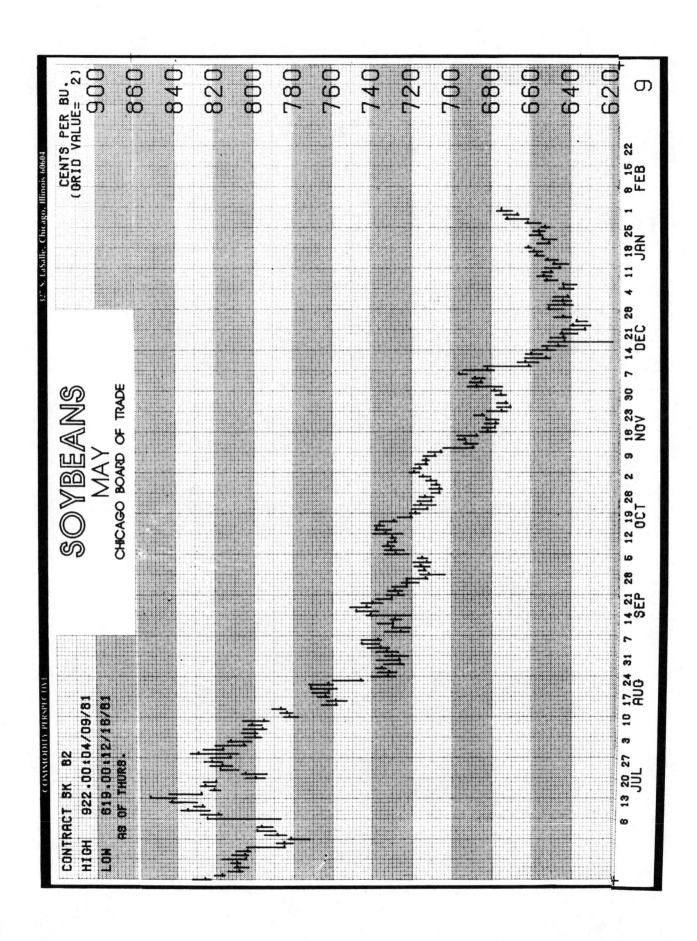

SOYBEANS
MAY
CHICAGO BOARD OF TRADE

CONTRACT 5K B2
HIGH 922.00:04/09/81
LOW   619.00:12/16/81
AS OF THURS.

CENTS PER BU.
(GRID VALUE= 2)

900
860
840
820
800
780
760
740
720
700
680
660
640
620
9

6 13 20 27 3 10 17 24 31 7 14 21 28 5 12 19 26 2 9 16 23 30 7 14 21 28 4 11 18 25 1 8 15 22
JUL   AUG   SEP   OCT   NOV   DEC   JAN   FEB

SPIKE-35 TRADING RESULTS
82 May Soybeans

Order	Entry and Exit Dates	Entry Rule	Entry and Exit Prices	Gain	Loss
Buy	6-30-81	TDR	824		
	7- 7-81		841	$ 850.00	
Buy	7-17-81	REN	818		
	7-20-81		817		$ 50.00
Buy	7-21-81	REN	822		
	7-23-81		816		300.00
Sell	7-29-81	TDR	796		
	7-30-81		800		200.00
Sell	7-31-81	REN	795		
	8- 5-81		785	500.00	
Sell	8- 6-81	REN	765		
	8-10-81		762	150.00	
Sell	8-14-81	REN	761		
	8-19-81		733	1400.00	
Sell	8-20-81	REN	731		
	8-21-81		735		200.00
Sell	8-24-81	REN	725		
	8-24-81		726½		75.00
Sell	9- 1-81	REN	733		
	9- 3-81		730	150.00	
Sell	9- 7-81	REN	726		
	9- 7-81		730		200.00
Buy	9- 8-81	CA2H	748		
	9-10-81		742		300.00
Sell	9-16-81	TDR	722		
	9-22-81		713	450.00	
Sell	9-24-81	REN	711		
	9-25-81		716		300.00
Buy	9-30-81	TDR	732		
	10- 1-81		729½		125.00
Buy	10- 5-81	REN	733		
	10- 8-81		736	300.00	

SPIKE-35 TRADING RESULTS
82 May Soybeans (Cont'd)

Order	Entry and Exit Dates	Entry Rule	Entry and Exit Prices	Gain	Loss
Sell	10-15-81 10-16-81	TDR	710 715		$ 250.00
Sell	10-19-81 10-21-81	REN	709½ 707	$ 125.00	
Sell	10-29-81 11- 5-81	REN	713 693	1000.00	
Sell	11- 6-81 11-11-81	REN	688 683	250.00	
Sell	11-11-81 11-12-81	REN	677 678½		75.00
Sell	11-16-81 11-18-81	REN	677 675	100.00	
Buy	11-27-81 11-30-81	CA2H	696 688		400.00
Sell	12- 1-81 12- 4-81	CB2L	661 662		50.00
Sell	12- 7-81 12-10-81	REN	652 646	300.00	
Sell	12-11-81 12-17-81	REN	642 639½	125.00	
Sell	12-24-81 12-28-81	REN	644 644	0	0
Sell	12-29-81 12-30-81	REN	640 646		300.00
Buy	12-30-81 1- 1-82	TDR	651 651	0	0
Buy	1- 6-82 1-12-82	REN	653 656½	325.00	
Buy	1-19-82 1-27-82	REN	657 674	850.00	

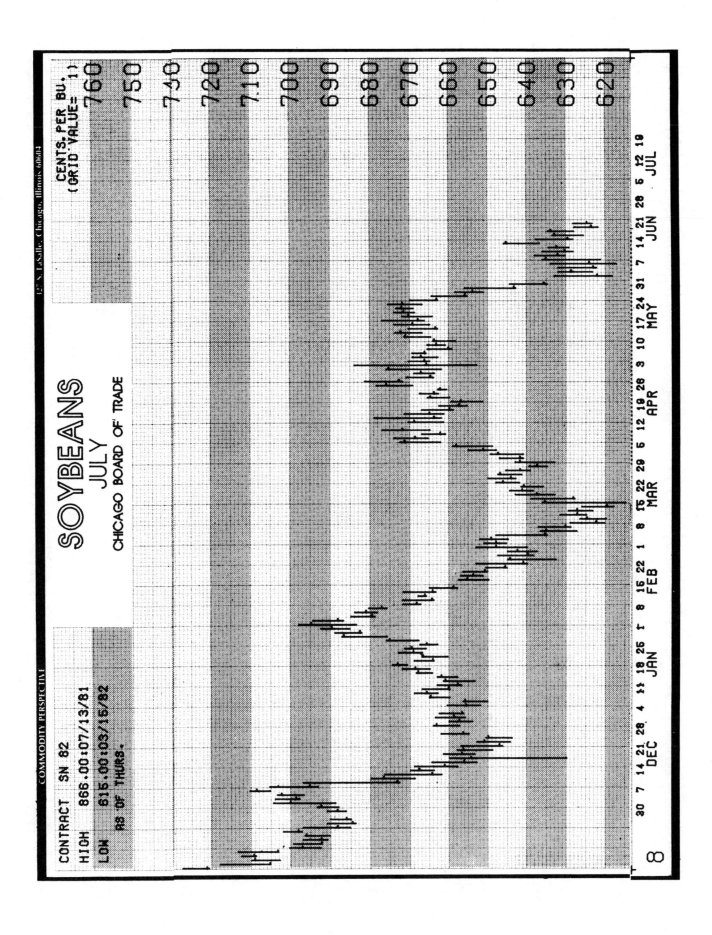

SOYBEANS
JULY
CHICAGO BOARD OF TRADE

COMMODITY PERSPECTIVE

CONTRACT SN 82
HIGH   866.00:07/13/81
LOW   615.00:03/16/82
       AS OF THURS.

CENTS PER BU.
(GRID VALUE= 1)

760
750
730
720
710
700
690
680
670
660
650
640
630
620

30 7 14 21 28 4 11 18 25 1 8 15 22 1 8 15 22 29 5 12 19 26 3 10 17 24 31 7 14 21 28 5 12 19
DEC   JAN   FEB   MAR   APR   MAY   JUN   JUL

8

SPIKE-35 TRADING RESULTS
82 July Soybeans

Order	Entry and Exit Dates	Entry Rule	Entry and Exit Prices	Gain	Loss
Buy	1-26-82	REN	670.00		
	2- 2-82		690.00	$1000.00	
Sell	2- 9-82	TDR	664.00		
	2-11-82		666.00		$ 100.00
Sell	2-12-82	REN	664.00		
	2-18-82		655.00	450.00	
Sell	2-18-82	REN	654.00		
	2-22-82		651.00	150.00	
Sell	2-22-82	REN	645.00		
	2-24-82		645.00	0	0
Sell	2-25-82	REN	640.00		
	2-26-82		643.00		150.00
Sell	3- 3-82	REN	643.00		
	3- 5-82		635.00	400.00	
Sell	3- 5-82	REN	634.00		
	3-10-82		625.00	450.00	
Sell	3-12-82	REN	622.00		
	3-15-82		627.00		250.00
Buy	3-22-82	CA2H	646.00		
	3-24-82		644.00		100.00
Buy	3-31-82	REN	642.00		
	4- 7-82		667.00	1250.00	
Buy	4- 8-82	REN	671.00		
	4-12-82		662.00		450.00
Buy	4-13-82	REN	671.00		
	4-14-82		663.00		400.00
Buy	4-20-82	REN	665.00		
	4-22-82		662.00		150.00
Buy	4-22-82	REN	669.00		
	4-27-82		671.00	150.00	

SPIKE-35 TRADING RESULTS
82 July Soybeand (Cont'd)

Order	Entry and Exit Dates	Entry Rule	Entry and Exit Prices	Gain	Loss
Buy	4-30-82	REN	675.00		
	4-30-82		667.00		$ 400.00
Buy	5-11-82	REN	666.00		
	5-13-82		670.00	$ 200.00	
Buy	5-14-82	REN	672.00		
	5-18-82		669.00		150.00
Buy	5-19-82	REN	672.00		
	5-20-82		670.00		100.00
Buy	5-20-82	REN	672.00		
	5-21-82		671.00		50.00
Sell	5-24-82	CB2L	663.00		
	6- 3-82		629.00	1700.00	
Sell	6- 4-82	REN	622.00		
	6- 7-82		624.00		100.00
Sell	6-14-82	REN	629.00		
	6-16-82		633.00		200.00

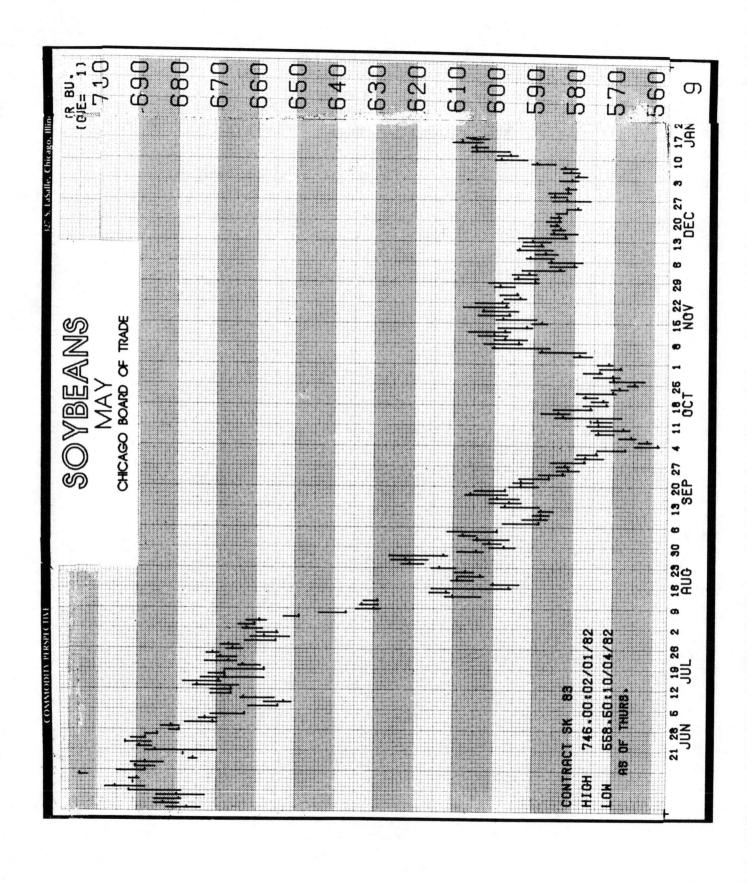

SPIKE-35 TRADING RESULTS
83 May Soybeans

Order	Entry and Exit Dates	Entry Rule	Entry and Exit Prices	Gain	Loss
Sell	6-30-82 7- 8-82	TDR	671 655½	$ 775.00	
Sell	7-15-82 7-16-82	REN	666 669		$ 150.00
Sell	7-19-82 7-21-82	REN	666 665	50.00	
Sell	7-27-82 7-29-82	REN	665 658	350.00	
Sell	8- 5-82 8-16-82	REN	653 612	2050.00	
Sell	8-16-82 8-18-82	REN	609 605	200.00	
Sell	8-27-82 9- 1-82	REN	609 601	350.00	
Sell	9- 7-82 9- 9-82	REN	597 589	400.00	
Sell	9-10-82 9-13-82	REN	587 588½		75.00
Sell	9-20-82 9-22-82	REN	596 593½	125.00	
Sell	9-22-82 9-27-82	REN	592½ 582½	500.00	
Sell	9-28-82 9-30-82	REN	581 577½	175.00	
Sell	9-30-82 10- 6-82	REN	576½ 564	625.00	
Buy	10-13-82 10-15-82	TDR	582½ 582½	0	0
Buy	10-21-82 10-21-82	REN	577½ 572		275.00

SPIKE-35 TRADING RESULTS
83 May Soybeans (Cont'd)

Order	Entry and Exit Dates	Entry Rule	Entry and Exit Prices	Gain	Loss
Sell	10-25-82	CB2L	565		
	10-27-82		570		$ 250.00
Buy	11- 4-82	CA2H	588		
	11- 9-82		594	$ 300.00	
Buy	11-10-82	REN	600½		
	11-11-82		597		175.00
Buy	11-17-82	REN	598		
	11-18-82		596		100.00
Buy	11-18-82	REN	598		
	11-22-82		597		50.00
Buy	11-26-82	REN	599		
	11-29-82		594		250.00
Sell	12- 2-82	CB2L	583½		
	12- 6-82		583½	0	0
Sell	12-13-82	REN	585		
	12-14-82		591		300.00
Sell	12-14-82	REN	587		
	12-17-82		585½	75.00	
Sell	12-22-82	REN	583		
	12-27-82		582	50.00	
Sell	1- 3-83	REN	581		
	1- 5-83		581½		25.00
Buy	1- 7-83	CA2H	589½		
	1-14-83		604½	750.00	
Buy	1-14-83	REN	605½		
	1-18-83		605½	0	0

COMMODITY PERSPECTIVE/CHICAGO, ILLINOIS 60604

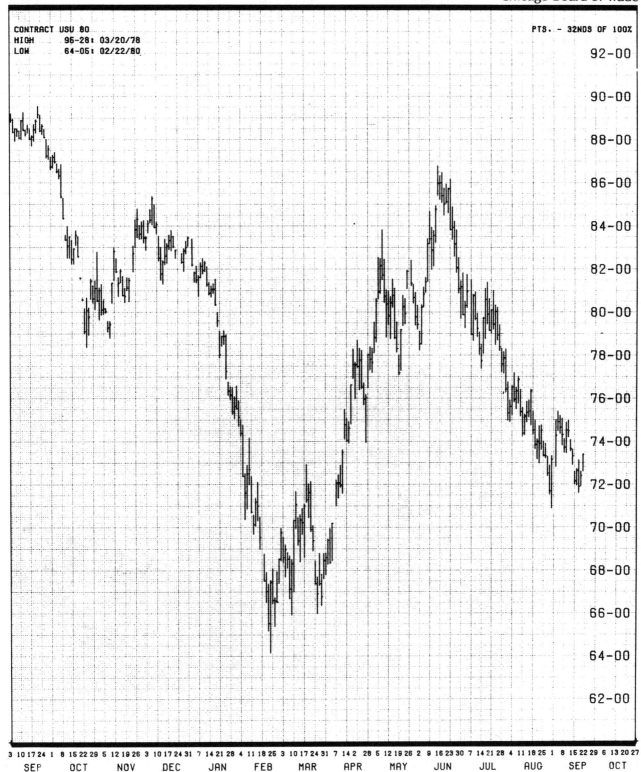

CONTRACT USU 80
HIGH   96-28: 03/20/78
LOW   64-05: 02/22/80

PTS. - 32NDS OF 100%

92-00
90-00
88-00
86-00
84-00
82-00
80-00
78-00
76-00
74-00
72-00
70-00
68-00
66-00
64-00
62-00

3 10 17 24 1 8 15 22 29 5 12 19 26 3 10 17 24 31 7 14 21 28 4 11 18 25 3 10 17 24 31 7 14 21 28 5 12 19 26 2 9 16 23 30 7 14 21 28 4 11 18 25 1 8 15 22 29 6 13 20 27

SEP   OCT   NOV   DEC   JAN   FEB   MAR   APR   MAY   JUN   JUL   AUG   SEP   OCT

SPIKE-35 TRADING RESULTS
80 Sept T-Bonds

Order	Entry and Exit Dates	Entry Rule	Entry and Exit Prices	Gain	Loss
Sell	12-11-79	CB2L	82.16		
	12-14-79		82.10	$ 187.50	
Sell	12-21-79	REN	82.30		
	12-27-79		82.30	0	0
Sell	1- 2-80	REN	82.08		
	1- 8-80		81.24	500.00	
Sell	1-11-80	REN	81.20		
	1-16-80		81.04	500.00	
Sell	1-17-80	REN	80.26		
	1-23-80		78.28	1937.50	
Sell	1-24-80	REN	78.00		
	1-29-80		76.12	1593.75	
Sell	1-29-80	REN	76.04		
	1-31-80		75.20	500.00	
Sell	2- 1-80	REN	75.12		
	2- 7-80		72.15	2906.25	
Sell	2-11-80	REN	71.20		
	2-13-80		70.24	875.00	
Sell	2-15-80	REN	70.04		
	2-22-80		67.04	3000.00	
Sell	2-26-80	REN	65.18		
	2-27-80		66.18		$1000.00
Sell	3- 5-80	REN	68.16		
	3-10-80		68.12	125.00	
Buy	3-10-80	CA2H	70.12		
	3-12-80		70.12	0	0
Buy	3-18-80	REN	71.08		
	3-20-80		71.08	0	0

SPIKE-35 TRADING RESULTS
80 Sept T-Bonds (Cont'd)

Order	Entry and Exit Dates	Entry Rule	Entry and Exit Prices	Gain	Loss
Sell	3-25-80	TDR	67.00		
	3-26-80		67.12		$ 437.50
Sell	3-27-80	REN	67.00		
	3-28-80		67.12		375.00
Buy	4- 7-80	TDR	72.04		
	4- 9-80		72.04	0	0
Buy	4-10-80	REN	72.08		
	4-15-80		74.02	$1781.25	
Buy	4-16-80	REN	74.26		
	4-18-80		76.22	1875.00	
Buy	4-21-80	REN	77.20		
	4-22-80		77.16		125.00
Buy	4-23-80	REN	77.26		
	4-23-80		77.16		312.50
Buy	4-28-80	REN	77.26		
	4-30-80		77.26	0	0
Buy	5- 1-80	REN	78.04		
	5- 8-80		81.24	3625.00	
Buy	5-14-80	REN	80.24		
	5-15-80		80.16		250.00
Sell	5-19-80	TDR	77.08		
	5-20-80		78.12		1125.00
Sell	5-29-80	REN	79.24		
	6- 3-80		79.16	250.00	
Buy	6- 6-80	CA2H	83.08		
	6-10-80		83.08	0	0
Buy	6-10-80	REN	83.16		
	6-17-80		86.00	3000.00	

T-BONDS

JUNE 1981
Chicago Board of Trade

COMMODITY PERSPECTIVE/CHICAGO, ILLINOIS 60604

USM 81
94-20: 11/20/78
59-11: 06/06/81

PTS. - 32NDS OF 100%

84-00
82-00
80-00
78-00
76-00
74-00
72-00
70-00
68-00
66-00
64-00
62-00
60-00
58-00
56-00
54-00

2 9 16 23 30 7 14 21 28 4 11 18 25 1 8 15 22 29 6 13 20 27 3 10 17 24 1 8 15 22 29 5 12 19 26 2 9 16 23 2 9 16 23 30 6 13 20 27 4 11 18 25 1 8 15 22 29 6 13 20 27

JUN JUL AUG SEP OCT NOV DEC JAN FEB MAR APR MAY JUN JUL

SPIKE-35 TRADING RESULTS
81 June T-Bonds

Order	Entry and Exit Dates	Entry Rule	Entry and Exit Prices	Gain	Loss
Sell	6-26-80 7- 1-80	TDR	81.20 80.23	$ 960.25	
Sell	7- 1-80 7- 3-80	REN	80.18 79.23	843.75	
Sell	7- 7-80 7- 9-80	REN	79.15 80.13		$ 937.50
Sell	7-11-80 7-15-80	REN	78.13 78.02	343.75	
Sell	7-23-80 7-24-80	REN	78.20 79.24		1125.00
Sell	7-24-80 7-30-80	REN	78.20 77.22	937.50	
Sell	7-30-80 8- 4-80	REN	77.08 75.16	1750.00	
Sell	8- 8-80 8-14-80	REN	75.16 75.01	468.75	
Sell	8-18-80 8-21-80	REN	75.01 74.01	1000.00	
Sell	8-25-80 8-29-80	REN	73.20 72.28	750.00	
Sell	9- 8-80 9- 9-80	REN	74.18 74.19		31.25
Sell	9-11-80 9-17-80	REN	73.30 73.03	843.75	
Sell	9-17-80 9-19-80	REN	72.18 73.06		625.00
Sell	9-22-80 9-24-80	REN	72.12 71.30	687.50	

SPIKE-35 TRADING RESULTS
81 June T-Bonds (Cont'd)

Order	Entry and Exit Dates	Entry Rule	Entry and Exit Prices	Gain	Loss
Sell	9-25-80 9-30-80	REN	71.10 70.10	$1000.00	
Buy	10- 9-80 10-13-80	CA2H	74.18 74.00		$ 562.50
Buy	10-14-80 10-16-80	REN	74.18 74.13		156.25
Sell	10-21-80 10-24-80	CB2L	71.31 71.10	656.25	
Sell	10-27-80 10-31-80	REN	70.31 68.09	2687.50	
Sell	11- 3-80 11- 3-80	REN	68.07 68.17		315.00
Sell	11- 5-80 11- 7-80	REN	68.07 67.22	531.25	
Buy	11-18-80 11-21-80	TDR	70.07 70.04		94.00
Buy	11-25-80 11-26-80	REN	71.02 70.02		1000.00
Buy	11-26-80 11-28-80	REN	70.17 70.02		468.75
Buy	12- 5-80 12- 9-80	REN	70.01 69.30		94.00
Sell	12- 9-80 12-12-80	CB2L	68.16 68.08	250.00	
Buy	12-22-80 12-24-80	TDR	73.00 72.16		500.00
Buy	12-29-80 12-30-80	REN	73.01 72.26		218.75
Buy	1- 5-81 1- 7-81	REN	73.01 73.16	500.00	

T-BONDS

SEPTEMBER 1981

Chicago Board of Trade

COMMODITY PERSPECTIVE/CHICAGO, ILLINOIS 60604

CONTRACT USU 81
HIGH   92-16: 02/02/79
LOW   56-12: 09/09/81

PTS. - 32NDS OF 100%

84-00
82-00
80-00
78-00
76-00
74-00
72-00
70-00
68-00
66-00
64-00
62-00
60-00
58-00
56-00
54-00

1 8 15 22 29 6 13 20 27 3 10 17 24 1 8 15 22 29 5 12 19 26 2 9 16 23 2 9 16 23 30 6 13 20 27 4 11 18 25 1 8 15 22 29 6 13 20 27 3 10 17 24 31 7 14 21 28 5 12 19 26

SEP   OCT   NOV   DEC   JAN   FEB   MAR   APR   MAY   JUN   JUL   AUG   SEP   OCT

SPIKE-35 TRADING RESULTS
81 Sept T-Bonds

Order	Entry and Exit Dates	Entry Rule	Entry and Exit Prices	Gain	Loss
Sell	1-15-81	TDR	71.08		
	1-16-81		71.24		$ 500.00
Sell	1-19-81	REN	71.08		
	1-20-81		71.24		500.00
Sell	1-21-81	REN	71.08		
	1-23-81		70.20	$ 625.00	
Sell	1-29-81	REN	70.16		
	1-30-81		70.16	0	0
Sell	2- 2-81	REN	70.04		
	2- 4-81		69.15	656.25	
Sell	2- 5-81	REN	68.24		
	2- 9-81		68.24	0	0
Sell	2- 9-81	REN	68.12		
	2-17-81		66.08	2125.00	
Sell	2-24-81	REN	67.10		
	2-25-81		67.15		150.25
Sell	2-25-81	REN	67.10		
	2-27-81		67.00	312.50	
Sell	2-27-81	REN	66.18		
	3- 3-81		66.20		62.50
Buy	3-12-81	TDR	68.20		
	3-17-81		69.12	750.00	
Buy	3-17-81	REN	69.16		
	3-19-81		70.04	625.00	
Sell	3-24-81	TDR	66.18		
	3-30-81		66.10	250.00	
Sell	4- 3-81	REN	66.02		
	4- 8-81		65.30	125.00	
Sell	4-13-81	REN	64.30		
	4-14-81		65.04		187.50

SPIKE-35 TRADING RESULTS
81 Sept T-Bonds (Cont'd)

Order	Entry and Exit Dates	Entry Rule	Entry and Exit Prices	Gain	Loss
Sell	4-15-81 4-20-81	REN	64.28 64.16	$ 375.00	
Sell	4-24-81 4-27-81	REN	64.18 64.20		$ 62.50
Sell	4-27-81 5- 6-81	REN	64.08 61.13	4843.75	
Sell	5-13-81 5-14-81	REN	61.24 61.24	0	0
Buy	5-18-81 5-20-81	TDR	64.30 64.04		750.00
Buy	5-26-81 6- 1-81	REN	65.08 65.26	562.50	

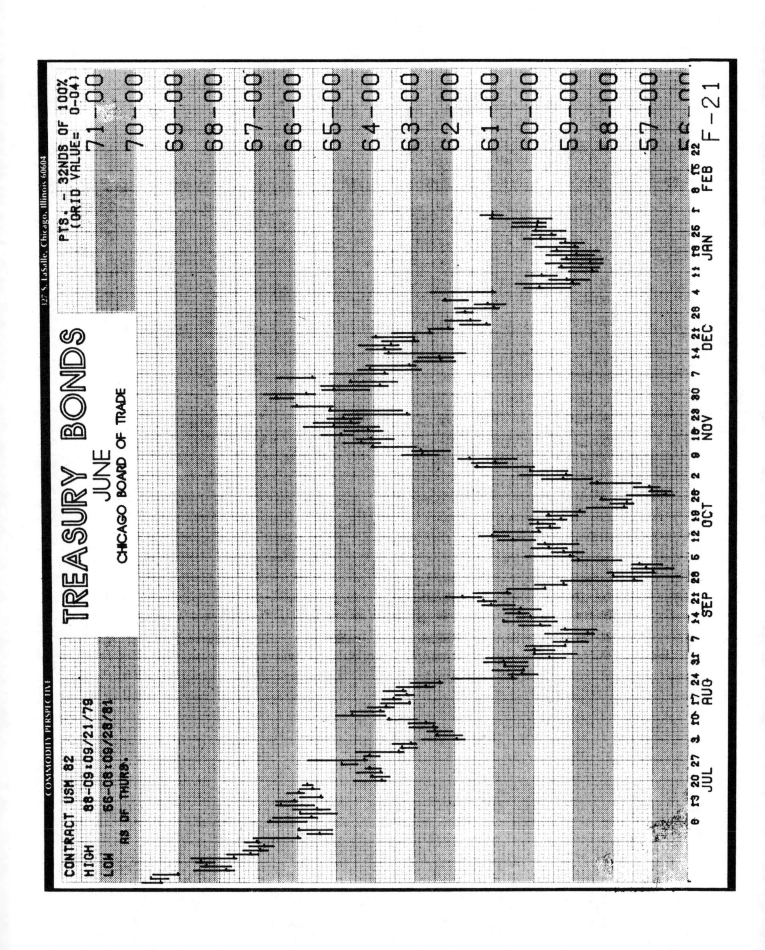

127 S. LaSalle, Chicago, Illinois 60604

TREASURY BONDS
JUNE
CHICAGO BOARD OF TRADE

CONTRACT USM 82

HIGH   88-09:09/21/79

LOW   56-06:09/28/81
        AS OF THURS.

PTS. - 32NDS OF 100%
(GRID VALUE= 0-04)

71-00
70-00
69-00
68-00
67-00
66-00
65-00
64-00
63-00
62-00
61-00
60-00
59-00
58-00
57-00

F-21

JUL   AUG   SEP   OCT   NOV   DEC   JAN   FEB
6 13 20 27 3 10 17 24 31 7 14 21 28 5 12 19 26 2 9 16 23 30 7 14 21 28 4 11 18 25 1 8 15 22

SPIKE-35 TRADING RESULTS
82 June T-Bonds

Order	Entry and Exit Dates	Entry Rule	Entry and Exit Prices	Gain	Loss
Sell	6-30-81 7- 2-81	CB2L	66.00 66.00	0	0
Sell	7- 9-81 7-10-81	REN	65.16 65.32		$ 500.00
Sell	7-14-81 7-15-81	REN	65.16 66.03		593.75
Sell	7-20-81 7-22-81	REN	64.17 64.04	$ 406.25	
Sell	7-29-81 7-31-81	REN	64.03 63.13	687.50	
Sell	7-31-81 8- 5-81	REN	63.10 62.16	812.50	
Sell	8-14-81 8-17-81	REN	63.20 63.20	0	0
Sell	8-18-81 8-19-81	REN	63.04 63.16		375.00
Sell	8-20-81 8-26-81	REN	63.03 60.17	2562.50	
Sell	8-27-81 8-28-81	REN	60.07 60.24		531.25
Sell	8-31-81 9- 2-81	REN	60.07 60.00	218.75	
Sell	9- 3-81 9- 8-81	REN	59.18 59.06	375.00	
Sell	9- 8-81 9- 9-81	REN	59.05 59.05	0	0
Buy	9-11-81 9-12-81	CA2H	60.24 59.24		1000.00
Buy	9-17-81 9-22-81	REN	60.24 61.07	468.75	

SPIKE-35 TRADING RESULTS
82 June T-Bonds (Cont'd)

Order	Entry and Exit Dates	Entry Rule	Entry and Exit Prices	Gain	Loss
Sell	9-25-81 9-29-81	CB2L	57.15 58.00		$ 531.25
Sell	9-29-81 10- 1-81	REN	57.15 57.06	$ 281.25	
Buy	10-12-81 10-13-81	TDR	61.00 60.16		500.00
Buy	10-20-81 10-20-81	REN	59.28 59.09		593.75
Sell	10-21-81 10-23-81	TDR	57.22 57.22	0	0
Sell	10-23-81 10-28-81	REN	57.19 57.01	562.50	
Buy	11- 3-81 11- 6-81	CA2H	60.02 60.29	843.75	
Buy	11- 6-81 11-13-81	REN	61.13 64.00	2593.75	
Buy	11-13-81 11-17-81	REN	64.10 64.02		250.00
Buy	11-18-81 11-20-81	REN	64.28 64.18		312.50
Buy	11-24-81 11-30-81	REN	65.01 65.31	937.50	
Buy	12- 4-81 12- 7-81	REN	65.07 64.19		625.00
Sell	12- 9-81 12-14-81	CB2L	63.03 62.12	718.75	
Sell	12-21-81 12-24-81	REN	62.31 62.04	843.75	
Sell	1- 4-82 1- 8-82	REN	60.30 59.12	1562.50	

SPIKE-35 TRADING RESULTS
82 June T-Bonds (Cont'd)

Order	Entry and Exit Dates	Entry Rule	Entry and Exit Prices	Gain	Loss
Sell	1-11-82	REN	58.31		
	1-13-82		59.08		$ 281.25
Sell	1-13-82	REN	58.15		
	1-15-82		59.08		790.00
Sell	1-18-82	REN	58.15		
	1-19-82		59.12		843.75
Sell	1-20-82	REN	58.28		
	1-21-82		59.12		500.00
Buy	1-25-82	CA2H	59.29		
	1-27-82		59.27		62.50

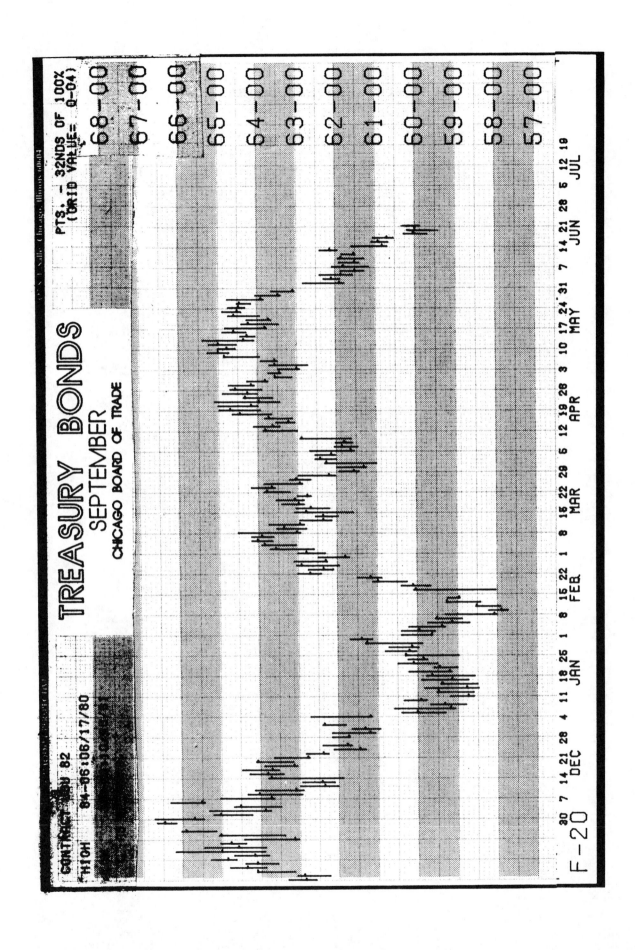

TREASURY BONDS
SEPTEMBER
CHICAGO BOARD OF TRADE

PTS. — 32NDS OF 100%
(GRID VALUE= 0-04)

CONTRACT: SEPTEMBER 82
HIGH   64-06:06/17/80

F-20

SPIKE-35 TRADING RESULTS
82 Sept T-Bonds

Order	Entry and Exit Dates	Entry Rule	Entry and Exit Prices	Gain	Loss
Buy	1-27-82 2- 1-82	REN	60.11 60.12	$ 31.25	
Sell	2- 4-82 2- 5-82	TDR	59.04 59.17		$ 250.00
Sell	2- 8-82 2-10-82	REN	59.04 58.04	1000.00	
Buy	2-19-82 2-24-82	TDR	61.06 62.10	1125.00	
Buy	2-25-82 2-26-82	REN	62.22 62.12		312.50
Buy	3- 2-82 3- 5-82	REN	62.29 63.28	968.75	
Buy	3- 8-82 3- 8-82	REN	64.00 63.28		125.00
Buy	3-17-82 3-19-82	REN	62.23 63.00	281.25	
Buy	3-22-82 3-24-82	REN	63.06 63.20	437.50	
Sell	3-29-82 3-31-82	CB2H	61.18 61.18	0	0
Sell	4- 6-82 4- 7-82	REN	61.20 61.28		250.00
Buy	4-12-82 4-14-82	TDR	63.26 63.18		250.00
Buy	4-16-82 4-20-82	REN	63.28 64.14	437.50	
Buy	4-21-82 4-21-82	REN	64.24 64.06		562.50
Buy	4-26-82 4-27-82	REN	64.10 64.10	0	0

SPIKE-35 TRADING RESULTS
82 Sept T-Bonds (Cont'd)

Order	Entry and Exit Dates	Entry Rule	Entry and Exit Prices	Gain	Loss
Sell	5- 3-82 5- 4-82	CB2L	63.00 63.16		$ 500.00
Buy	5- 6-82 5-10-82	TDR	63.26 63.26	0	0
Buy	5-11-82 5-12-82	REN	65.00 64.24		250.00
Buy	5-20-82 5-24-82	REN	64.19 64.16		93.75
Buy	5-26-82 5-26-82	REN	64.20 64.15		156.25
Sell	5-27-82 6- 3-82	CB2L	63.16 62.04	$1250.00	
Sell	6- 3-82 6- 7-82	REN	61.28 61.28	0	0
Sell	6- 8-82 6- 9-82	REN	61.16 61.27		343.75
Sell	6-14-82 6-16-82	REN	61.12 60.30	437.50	
Sell	6-20-82 6-21-82	REN	60.27 60.02	781.25	

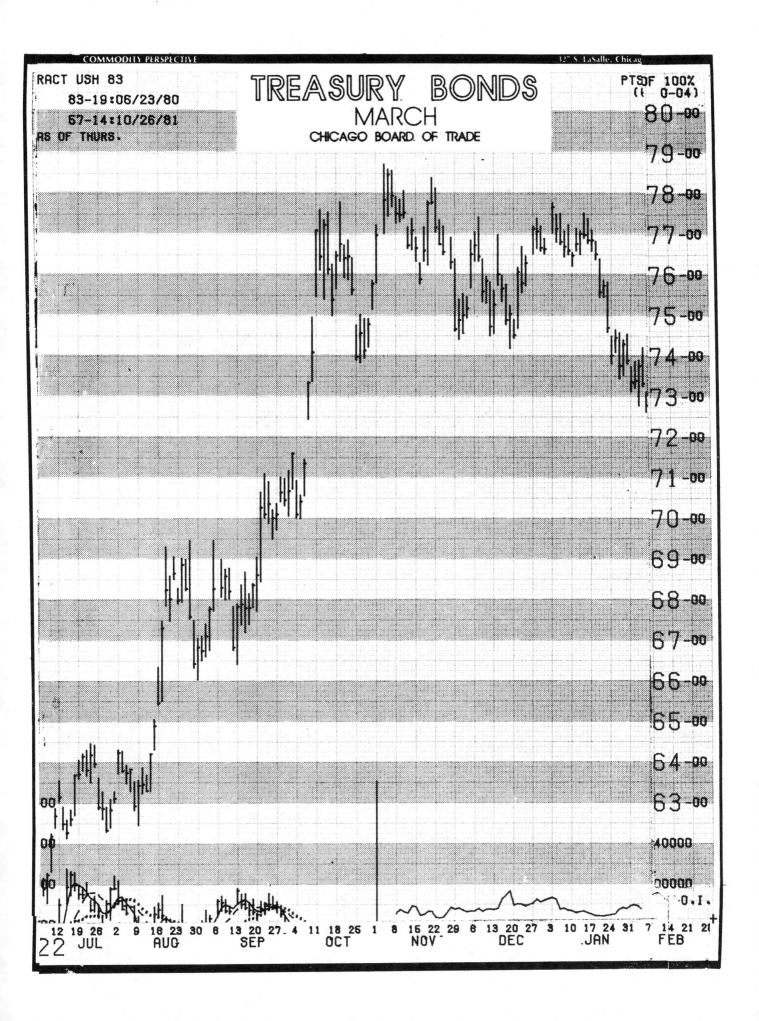

SPIKE-35 TRADING RESULTS
83 Mar T-Bonds

Order	Entry and Exit Dates	Entry Rule	Entry and Exit Prices	Gain	Loss
Buy	7-16-82	CA2H	58.21		
	7-21-82		58.21	0	0
Buy	7-22-82	REN	59.05		
	7-26-82		58.20		$ 531.25
Buy	7-30-82	REN	57.28		
	8- 4-82		58.24	$ 875.00	
Buy	8-10-82	REN	58.24		
	8-10-82		58.13		343.75
Buy	8-12-82	REN	58.16		
	8-23-82		62.31	3500.00	
Buy	8-24-82	REN	63.20		
	8-26-82		63.08		375.00
Buy	9- 2-82	REN	62.04		
	9- 8-82		63.04	1000.00	
Buy	9- 9-82	REN	63.18		
	9- 9-82		63.04		375.00
Buy	9-14-82	REN	63.08		
	9-15-82		62.25		468.75
Buy	9-16-82	REN	62.24		
	9-20-82		62.20		125.00
Buy	9-20-82	REN	63.12		
	9-23-82		65.02	1678.50	
Buy	9-28-82	REN	65.12		
	9-30-82		65.12	0	0
Buy	9-30-82	REN	65.20		
	10 -1-82		65.20	0	0
Buy	10- 7-82	REN	67.15		
	10-13-82		71.14	3968.75	
Buy	10-13-82	REN	72.03		
	10-14-82		71.18		531.25

SPIKE-35 TRADING RESULTS
83 Mar T-Bonds (Cont'd)

Order	Entry and Exit Dates	Entry Rule	Entry and Exit Prices	Gain	Loss
Buy	10-19-82 10-20-82	REN	72.07 71.12		$ 843.75
Buy	10-21-82 10-23-82	REN	71.22 71.12		312.50
Buy	10-29-82 11- 5-82	REN	70.05 72.27	$2687.50	
Buy	11-17-82 11-22-82	REN	72.03 72.23	625.00	
Sell	11-29-82 12- 1-82	TDR	69.20 69.25		156.25
Sell	12- 9-82 12-14-82	REN	70.18 70.23		156.25
Sell	12-17-82 12-21-82	REN	69.27 70.01		125.00
Buy	12-27-82 12-29-82	REN	72.03 72.00		93.75
Buy	1- 3-83 1- 5-83	REN	72.04 72.03		31.25
Buy	1-11-83 1-14-83	REN	71.25 71.31	187.50	
Sell	1-18-83 1-21-83	TDR	71.15 70.24	718.75	
Sell	1-21-83 1-26-83	REN	70.16 69.16	1000.00	
Sell	1-26-83 1-28-83	REN	68.31 69.10		375.00
Sell	1-31-83 2- 2-83	REN	68.24 68.12	375.00	
Sell	2- 4-83 2- 7-83	REN	68.04 68.12		250.00
Sell	2- 9-83 2-10-83	REN	67.24 68.02		312.50

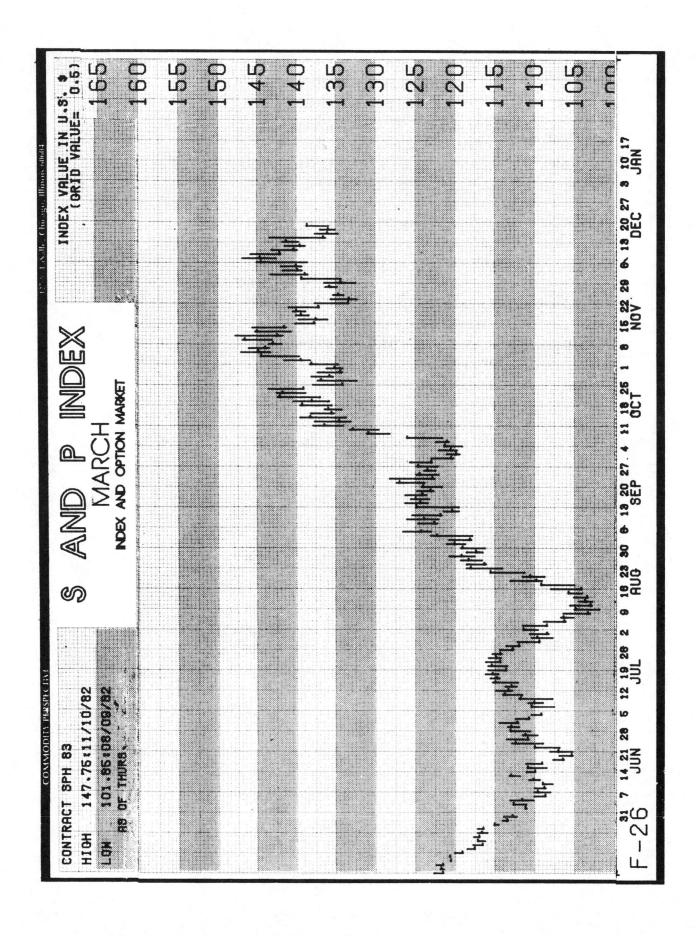

SPIKE-35 TRADING RESULTS
83 Mar S & P Index

Order	Entry and Exit Dates	Entry Rule	Entry and Exit Prices	Gain	Loss
Sell	5-27-82 6- 3-82	TDR	113.50 112.70	$ 400.00	
Sell	6- 3-82 6- 8-82	REN	111.00 110.00	500.00	
Sell	6- 9-82 6-10-82	REN	108.50 109.00		$ 250.00
Sell	6-15-82 6-16-82	REN	109.50 111.00		750.00
Sell	6-17-82 6-21-82	REN	107.50 106.50	500.00	
Sell	7- 1-82 7- 7-82	REN	111.00 110.50	250.00	
Sell	7- 8-82 7- 8-82	REN	109.00 110.50		750.00
Buy	7- 9-82 7-13-82	TDR	113.75 113.00		375.00
Buy	7-14-82 7-19-82	REN	114.00 114.50	250.00	
Buy	7-20-82 7-22-82	REN	115.50 114.30		600.00
Sell	7-28-82 7-30-82	CB2L	109.50 109.70		100.00
Sell	7-30-82 8- 2-82	REN	109.40 109.60		100.00
Sell	8- 3-82 8-10-82	REN	108.40 105.00	1700.00	
Sell	8-10-82 8-12-82	REN	103.20 104.20		500.00
Buy	8-20-82 8-27-82	CA2H	115.50 118.00	1250.00	

SPIKE-35 TRADING RESULTS
83 Mar S & P Index (Cont'd)

Order	Entry and Exit Dates	Entry Rule	Entry and Exit Prices	Gain	Loss
Buy	8-31-82	REN	120.00		
	9- 1-82		119.00		$ 500.00
Buy	9- 2-82	REN	120.07		
	9- 7-82		122.50	$1250.00	
Buy	9- 8-82	REN	124.50		
	9- 9-82		122.50		1000.00
Buy	9-13-82	REN	124.50		
	9-15-82		124.00		250.00
Buy	9-15-82	REN	125.00		
	9-17-82		124.50		250.00
Buy	9-21-82	REN	125.00		
	9-22-82		124.00		500.00
Buy	9-28-82	REN	124.50		
	9-28-82		123.50		500.00
Sell	9-30-82	CB2L	120.00		
	10- 4-82		120.50		250.00
Sell	10- 4-82	REN	120.00		
	10- 5-82		121.50		750.00
Buy	10- 7-82	CA2H	131.00		
	10-13-82		134.50	1750.00	
Buy	10-13-82	REN	136.70		
	10-15-82		135.50		600.00
Buy	10-18-82	REN	138.30		
	10-20-82		138.00		150.00
Buy	10-20-82	REN	139.50		
	10-22-82		142.00	1250.00	
Buy	11- 1-82	REN	137.00		
	11- 5-82		144.40	3700.00	
Buy	11- 9-82	REN	145.00		
	11-10-82		143.00		1000.00

SPIKE-35 TRADING RESULTS
83 Mar S & P Index (Cont'd)

Order	Entry and Exit Dates	Entry Rule	Entry and Exit Prices	Gain	Loss
Sell	11-19-82	TDR	137.40		
	11-24-82		134.00	$1700.00	
Sell	11-29-82	REN	133.50		
	11-30-82		135.50		$1000.00
Buy	12- 6-82	TDR	144.40		
	12- 8-82		144.40	0	0
Buy	12-14-82	REN	142.20		
	12-14-82		139.50		1350.00
Sell	12-14-82	CB2L	136.50		
	12-16-82		136.50	0	0

COMMODITY PERSPECTIVE/CHICAGO, ILLINOIS 60604

CONTRACT CU 80
HIGH   363.00: 09/02/80
LOW   280.00: 04/01/80

CENTS PER BU.

410
400
390
380
370
360
350
340
330
320
310
300
290
280
270
260

3 10 17 24 1 8 15 22 29 5 12 19 26 3 10 17 24 31 7 14 21 28 4 11 18 25 3 10 17 24 31 7 14 21 28 5 12 19 26 2 9 16 23 30 7 14 21 28 4 11 18 25 1 8 15 22 29 6 13 20 27

SEP   OCT   NOV   DEC   JAN   FEB   MAR   APR   MAY   JUN   JUL   AUG   SEP   OCT

SPIKE-35 TRADING RESULTS
80 Sept Corn

Order	Entry and Exit Dates	Entry Rule	Entry and Exit Prices	Gain	Loss
Sell	12-17-79 12-19-79	CB2L	305.50 305.50	0	0
Buy	12-26-79 1- 2-80	CA2H	317.00 314.75		$ 125.00
Sell	1-10-80 1-16-80	CB2L	295.50 299.50		200.00
Buy	1-30-80 2- 1-80	CA2H	305.50 304.75		75.00
Buy	2- 1-80 2- 6-80	REN	305.50 307.00	$ 125.00	
Buy	2-13-80 2-14-80	REN	305.50 304.50		50.00
Buy	2-21-80 2-22-80	REN	303.50 303.00		25.00
Buy	2-25-80 2-27-80	REN	303.75 303.00		37.50
Sell	2-27-80 3- 4-80	CB2L	302.00 296.00	300.00	
Sell	3-10-80 3-12-80	REN	293.75 294.50		75.00
Sell	3-17-80 3-19-80	REN	294.00 295.75		137.50
Sell	3-20-80 3-26-80	REN	294.00 290.50	175.00	
Sell	3-26-80 3-31-80	REN	289.75 284.75	250.00	
Sell	3-31-80 4- 1-80	REN	283.00 284.50		75.00
Buy	4- 9-80 4-10-80	TDR	295.50 294.00		75.00

SPIKE-35 TRADING RESULTS
80 Sept Corn (Cont'd)

Order	Entry and Exit Dates	Entry Rule	Entry and Exit Prices	Gain	Loss
Buy	4-16-80	REN	292.00		
	4-17-80		291.00		$ 50.00
Buy	4-25-80	REN	292.50		
	4-28-80		290.00		125.00
Buy	5- 2-80	REN	289.00		
	5- 7-80		293.00	$ 200.00	

CORN

MARCH 1981

Chicago Board of Trade

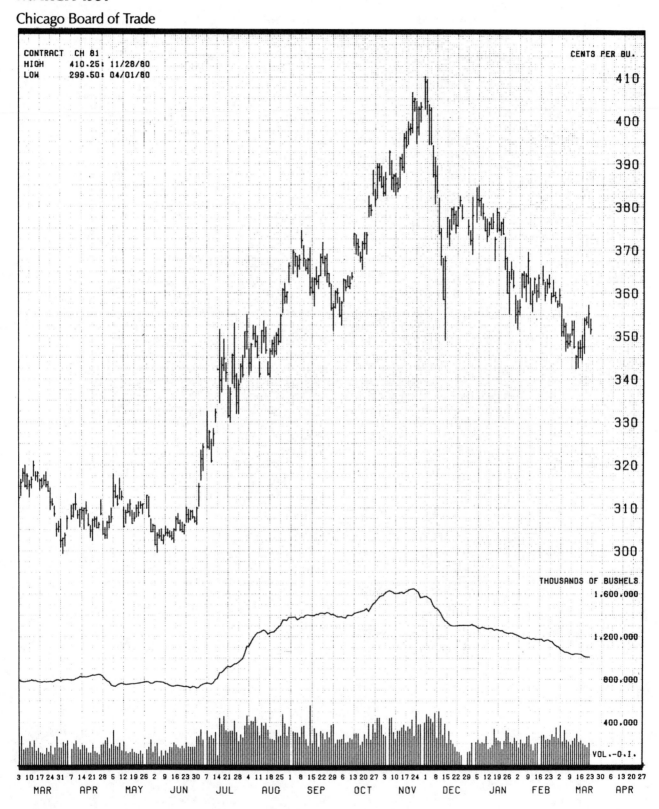

SPIKE-35 TRADING RESULTS
81 Mar Corn

Order	Entry and Exit Dates	Entry Rule	Entry and Exit Prices	Gain	Loss
Buy	5- 8-80	REN	314		
	5-12-80		310		$ 200.00
Buy	5-21-80	REN	311		
	5-23-80		310		50.00
Buy	5-27-80	REN	311		
	5-28-80		309½		75.00
Sell	5-29-80	CB2L	304½		
	6- 2-80		306		75.00
Sell	6- 2-80	REN	304		
	6- 4-80		303½	$ 25.00	
Sell	6-12-80	REN	303		
	6-13-80		304		50.00
Buy	6-16-80	CA2H	307½		
	6-18-80		306		75.00
Buy	6-23-80	REN	308		
	6-25-80		307½		25.00
Buy	6-30-80	REN	310		
	7- 8-80		324	700.00	
Buy	7- 8-80	REN	325		
	7- 9-80		324		50.00
Buy	7-10-80	REN	328		
	7-16-80		339	575.00	
Buy	7-16-80	REN	343		
	7-18-80		343	0	0
Buy	7-23-80	REN	344		
	7-25-80		341		150.00
Buy	7-30-80	REN	343½		
	8- 4-80		347	175.00	
Buy	8- 6-80	REN	351½		
	8- 8-80		348½		150.00

SPIKE-35 TRADING RESULTS
81 Mar Corn (Cont'd)

Order	Entry and Exit Dates	Entry Rule	Entry and Exit Prices	Gain	Loss
Buy	8-12-80 8-14-80	REN	351 350		$ 50.00
Buy	8-20-80 8-20-80	REN	349 346½		125.00
Buy	8-21-80 8-28-80	REN	348½ 357½	$ 450.00	
Buy	8-29-80 9- 4-80	REN	362½ 368	275.00	
Buy	9- 8-80 9- 9-80	REN	370½ 368		125.00
Buy	9-18-80 9-23-80	REN	364 367	150.00	
Buy	9-24-80 9-24-80	REN	368 367		50.00
Sell	9-26-80 9-30-80	CB2L	356 357		25.00
Sell	10- 2-80 10- 6-80	REN	356 358		100.00
Buy	10-13-80 10-15-80	CA2H	374 371½		125.00
Buy	10-20-80 10-21-80	REN	372 371		50.00
Buy	10-21-80 10-30-80	REN	372 387	750.00	
Buy	11- 5-80 11- 7-80	REN	387½ 386½		50.00

CORN

JULY 1981

Chicago Board of Trade

COMMODITY PERSPECTIVE/CHICAGO, ILLINOIS 60604

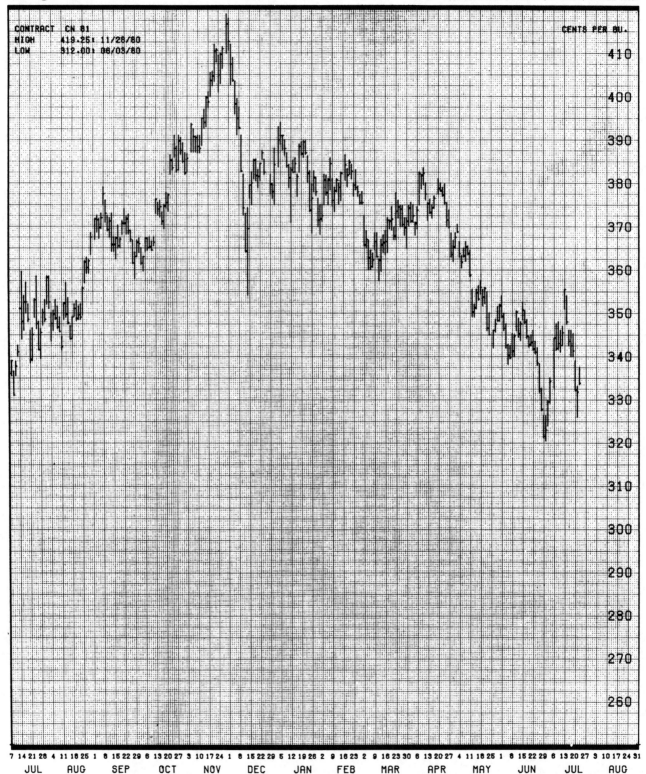

CONTRACT CN 81
HIGH   419.25: 11/28/80
LOW   312.00: 06/05/80

CENTS PER BU.

SPIKE-35 TRADING RESULTS
81 July Corn

Order	Entry and Exit Dates	Entry Rule	Entry and Exit Prices	Gain	Loss
Buy	11-12-80 11-14-80	REN	391.00 393.75	$ 137.50	
Buy	11-14-80 11-24-80	REN	395.00 410.00	750.00	
Buy	11-25-80 12- 2-80	REN	411.00 412.00	50.00	
Sell	12- 4-80 12-12-80	TDR	398.25 374.50	1187.50	
Sell	12-19-80 12-22-80	REN	379.50 381.75		$ 112.50
Sell	12-29-80 12-31-80	REN	381.50 379.50	100.00	
Buy	1- 2-81 1- 6-81	CA2H	390.00 390.00	0	0
Buy	1-14-81 1-15-81	REN	384.00 382.00		100.00
Buy	1-16-80 1-20-81	REN	384.00 386.50	125.00	
Buy	1-21-81 1-22-81	REN	389.50 386.00		175.00
Sell	1-23-81 1-27-81	TDR	373.75 378.00		212.50
Sell	1-29-81 2- 2-81	REN	373.50 372.00	75.00	
Buy	2- 6-81 2- 9-81	CA2H	384.50 380.50		200.00
Buy	2-13-81 2-17-81	REN	381.00 382.00	50.00	

SPIKE-35 TRADING RESULTS
81 July Corn (Cont'd)

Order	Entry and Exit Dates	Entry Rule	Entry and Exit Prices	Gain	Loss
Buy	2-19-81 2-20-81	REN	384.50 381.50		$ 150.00
Sell	2-26-81 3- 6-81	TDR	375.50 363.00	$ 625.00	
Sell	3-11-81 3-12-81	REN	360.50 363.50		150.00
Buy	3-19-81 3-20-81	TDR	371.50 369.50		100.00
Buy	3-23-81 3-25-81	REN	372.00 373.00	50.00	
Buy	3-26-81 3-26-81	REN	372.50 372.00		25.00
Buy	3-31-81 4- 1-81	REN	374.00 371.50		125.00
Buy	4- 6-81 4- 9-81	REN	374.50 381.50	350.00	
Buy	4-20-81 4-22-81	REN	377.50 378.00	50.00	

CORN

MARCH 1982

Chicago Board of Trade

COMMODITY PERSPECTIVE/CHICAGO, ILLINOIS 60604

CONTRACT CH 82
HIGH 406.60: 04/09/81
LOW 253.00: 12/16/81

CENTS PER BU.

THOUSANDS OF BUSHELS

VOL.-O.I.

MAR APR MAY JUN JUL AUG SEP OCT NOV DEC JAN FEB MAR APR

SPIKE-35 TRADING RESULTS
82 Mar Corn

Order	Entry and Exit Dates	Entry Rule	Entry and Exit Prices	Gain	Loss
Sell	4-23-81 4-30-81	CB2L	392.00 383.50	$ 425.00	
Sell	5- 4-81 5- 6-81	REN	383.00 388.00		$ 250.00
Sell	5-11-81 5-14-81	REN	386.00 379.00	350.00	
Sell	5-19-81 5-27-81	REN	381.00 373.00	400.00	
Sell	6- 1-81 6- 5-81	REN	371.50 363.50	400.00	
Buy	6-15-81 6-17-81	TDR	378.00 375.00		150.00
Buy	6-22-81 6-22-81	REN	376.50 372.50		200.00
Sell	6-25-81 6-30-81	TDR	362.00 358.00	700.00	
Buy	7- 6-81 7- 9-81	TDR	377.50 374.00		175.00
Buy	7-10-81 7-14-81	REN	379.00 380.00	50.00	
Buy	7-24-81 7-24-81	REN	367.00 366.00		50.00
Sell	7-30-81 7-31-81	TDR	356.50 361.00		225.00
Sell	8- 3-81 8- 7-81	REN	357.00 350.00	350.00	
Sell	8- 7-81 8-12-81	REN	348.00 341.00	350.00	
Sell	8-13-81 8-17-81	REN	331.00 330.00	50.00	

SPIKE-35 TRADING RESULTS
82 Mar Corn (Cont'd)

Order	Entry and Exit Dates	Entry Rule	Entry and Exit Prices	Gain	Loss
Sell	8-18-81 8-20-81	REN	327.00 330.00		$ 150.00
Sell	8-21-81 8-26-81	REN	327.00 316.00	550.00	
Sell	8-27-81 8-28-81	REN	312.50 318.00		275.00
Sell	9- 4-81 9-10-81	REN	323.00 314.00	$ 450.00	
Sell	9-11-81 9-14-81	REN	313.00 316.00		150.00
Sell	9-18-81 9-25-81	REN	314.50 307.50	350.00	
Sell	9-25-81 9-29-81	REN	306.00 305.00	50.00	
Sell	10- 9-81 10-12-81	REN	309.00 310.00		50.00
Buy	10-13-81 10-15-81	TDR	316.50 315.00		75.00
Sell	10-22-81 10-23-81	TDR	305.50 307.50		100.00
Sell	10-26-81 10-28-81	REN	306.50 305.00	75.00	
Sell	11- 3-81 11-12-81	REN	306.00 299.00	350.00	

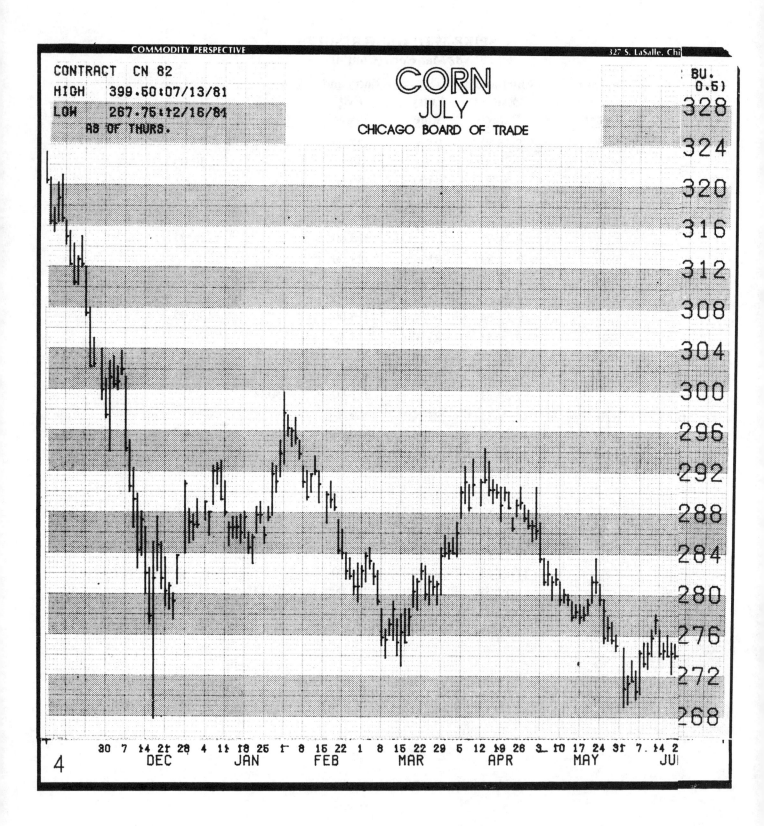

327 S. LaSalle, Chi

CORN
JULY
CHICAGO BOARD OF TRADE

CONTRACT CN 82

HIGH   399.50:07/13/81

LOW   267.75:12/16/81

AS OF THURS.

BU.
0.5)

328
324
320
316
312
308
304
300
296
292
288
284
280
276
272
268

4   30 7 14 21 28 4 11 18 25 1 8 15 22 1 8 15 22 29 5 12 19 26 3 10 17 24 31 7 14 2

DEC   JAN   FEB   MAR   APR   MAY   JUL

SPIKE-35 TRADING RESULTS
82 July Corn

Order	Entry and Exit Dates	Entry Rule	Entry and Exit Prices	Gain	Loss
Sell	11-16-81 11-19-81	CB2L	315.00 312.50	$ 125.00	
Sell	11-23-81 11-27-81	REN	310.50 302.50	400.00	
Sell	11-27-81 12- 1-81	REN	302.00 300.50	75.00	
Sell	12- 7-81 12-16-81	REN	300.50 282.00	900.25	
Sell	12-22-81 12-24-81	REN	280.00 281.00		$ 50.00
Buy	12-28-81 12-30-81	TDR	290.75 286.00		237.50
Buy	1- 6-82 1- 8-82	REN	289.00 292.00	150.00	
Sell	1-15-82 1-18-82	TDR	286.00 286.50		25.00
Sell	1-19-82 1-21-82	REN	286.00 286.00	0	0
Buy	1-27-82 2- 3-82	CA2H	292.00 295.75	187.50	
Sell	2-17-82 2-25-82	TDR	289.00 282.20	340.00	
Sell	2-25-82 2-26-82	REN	281.70 282.00		15.00
Sell	3- 5-82 3-10-82	REN	281.50 276.00	550.00	
Sell	3-12-82 3-16-82	REN	275.00 276.50		75.00
Sell	3-24-82 3-25-82	REN	279.50 281.50		150.00
Sell	3-26-82 3-29-82	REN	279.50 281.00		75.00

SPIKE-35 TRADING RESULTS
82 July Corn (Cont'd)

Order	Entry and Exit Dates	Entry Rule	Entry and Exit Prices	Gain	Loss
Buy	3-29-82	CA2H	284.00		
	3-31-82		283.50		$ 25.00
Buy	4- 2-82	RR#2	286.00		
	4- 7-82		289.50	$ 175.00	
Buy	4- 8-82	REN	291.50		
	4-14-82		291.00		25.00
Sell	4-22-82	CB2L	286.50		
	4-23-82		288.50		100.00
Sell	4-29-82	REN	286.75		
	4-30-82		286.75	0	0
Sell	4-30-82	REN	286.50		
	5- 7-82		282.00	225.00	
Sell	5-10-82	REN	281.00		
	5-17-82		278.50	125.00	
Sell	5-25-82	REN	279.00		
	5-27-82		277.00	100.00	
Sell	5-27-82	REN	275.50		
	6- 3-82		271.50	200.00	
Sell	6- 4-82	REN	270.50		
	6- 7-82		271.50		50.00
Sell	6-15-82	REN	274.00		
	6-16-82		275.00		50.00

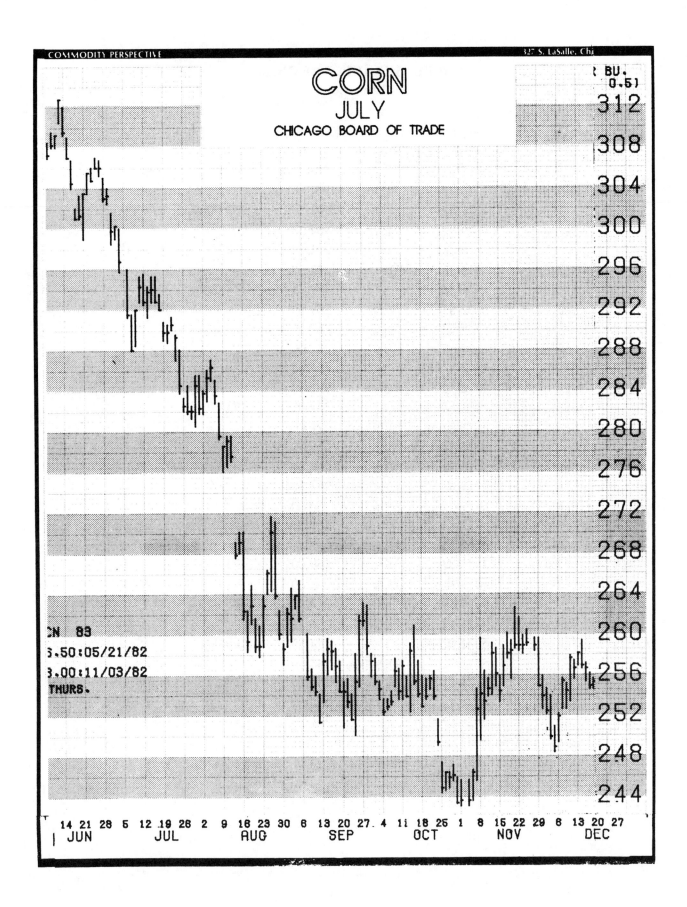

CORN
JULY
CHICAGO BOARD OF TRADE

SPIKE-35 TRADING RESULTS
83 July Corn

Order	Entry and Exit Dates	Entry Rule	Entry and Exit Prices	Gain	Loss
Sell	6-16-82	CB2L	304.50		
	6-21-82		301.50	$ 150.00	
Sell	6-28-82	REN	304.50		
	7- 8-82		291.50	650.00	
Sell	7-16-82	REN	292.50		
	7-21-82		290.25	112.50	
Sell	7-22-82	REN	289.50		
	7-29-82		282.50	362.00	
Sell	7-30-82	REN	282.00		
	8- 2-82		284.00		$ 100.00
Sell	8- 6-82	REN	282.50		
	8-11-82		279.00	175.00	
Sell	8-11-82	REN	278.00		
	8-16-82		269.00	450.00	
Sell	8-16-82	REN	267.00		
	8-18-82		262.50	325.00	
Sell	8-19-82	REN	259.00		
	8-23-82		260.00		50.00
Sell	8-27-82	REN	262.50		
	8-31-82		260.00	125.00	
Sell	9- 7-82	REN	260.00		
	9-13-82		254.50	275.00	
Sell	9-17-82	REN	256.50		
	9-21-82		254.50	100.00	
Sell	9-21-82	REN	254.00		
	9-23-82		253.00	50.00	
Buy	9-24-82	TDR	261.50		
	9-28-82		261.50	0	0

SPIKE-35 TRADING RESULTS
83 July Corn (Cont'd)

Order	Entry and Exit Dates	Entry Rule	Entry and Exit Prices	Gain	Loss
Buy	10- 7-82 10-11-82	REN	255.00 254.00		$ 50.00
Buy	10-11-82 10-12-82	REN	257.00 254.50		125.00
Buy	10-13-82 10-15-82	REN	257.00 255.00		100.00
Buy	10-21-82 10-21-82	REN	256.00 254.00		100.00
Sell	10-22-82 10-28-82	CB2L	249.50 246.50	$ 150.00	
Sell	10-29-82 11- 3-82	REN	244.75 243.75	50.00	
Buy	11-11-82 11-15-82	TDR	258.00 256.00		100.00
Buy	11-16-82 11-18-82	REN	258.00 257.00		50.00
Buy	11-19-82 11-23-82	REN	258.50 258.50	0	0

(Variance non-trade-re-enter rule #2).
For next two days

Order	Entry and Exit Dates	Entry Rule	Entry and Exit Prices	Gain	Loss
Sell	11-30-82 12- 6-82	TDR	254.00 250.00	200.00	

SWISS FRANC

SEPTEMBER 1980

International Monetary Market

COMMODITY PERSPECTIVE/CHICAGO, ILLINOIS 60604

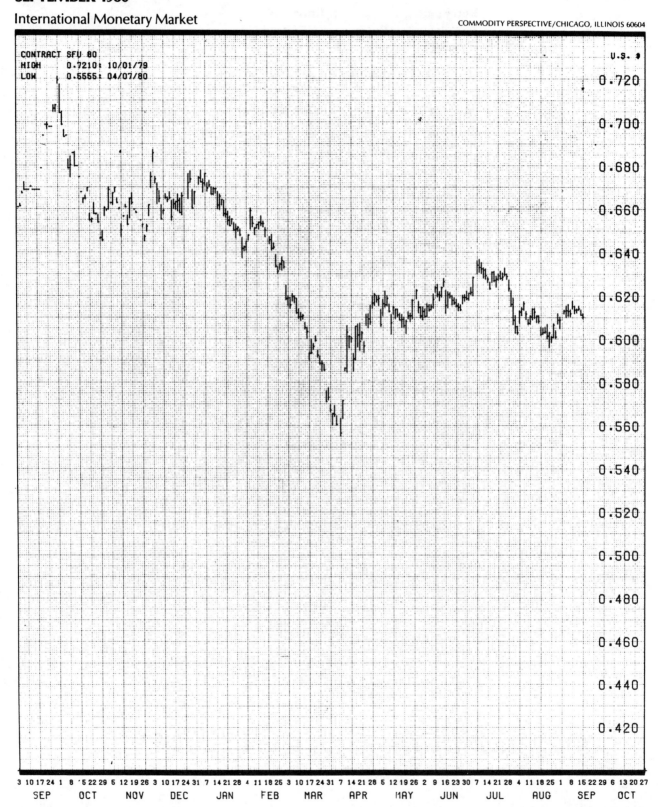

CONTRACT SFU 80
HIGH   0.7210: 10/01/79
LOW   0.5555: 04/07/80

U.S. $

0.720
0.700
0.680
0.660
0.640
0.620
0.600
0.580
0.560
0.540
0.520
0.500
0.480
0.460
0.440
0.420

3 10 17 24 1 8 15 22 29 5 12 19 26 3 10 17 24 31 7 14 21 28 4 11 18 25 3 10 17 24 31 7 14 21 28 5 12 19 26 9 16 23 30 7 14 21 28 4 11 18 25 1 8 15 22 29 6 13 20 27

SEP   OCT   NOV   DEC   JAN   FEB   MAR   APR   MAY   JUN   JUL   AUG   SEP   OCT

SPIKE-35 TRADING RESULTS
80 Sept Swiss Franc

Order	Entry and Exit Dates	Entry Rule	Entry and Exit Prices	Gain	Loss
Buy	12-26-79	CA2H	67.20		
	12-28-79		66.95		$ 312.50
Buy	1- 2-80	REN	67.40		
	1- 4-80		67.25		187.50
Buy	1- 7-80	REN	67.47		
	1- 8-80		67.20		337.50
Sell	1-18-80	CB2L	65.80		
	1-22-80		65.80	0	0
Sell	1-22-80	REN	65.78		
	1-24-80		65.50	$ 350.00	
Sell	1-25-80	REN	65.12		
	1-29-80		65.05	87.50	
Sell	1-30-80	REN	65.01		
	2- 4-80		64.30	887.50	
Buy	2- 6-80	TDR	65.95		
	2- 8-80		65.17		975.00
Buy	2-13-80	REN	65.47		
	2-15-80		65.20		300.00
Sell	2-20-80	TDR	64.20		
	2-26-80		63.40	1000.00	
Sell	2-29-80	REN	62.25		
	3- 4-80		61.95	375.00	
Sell	3- 4-80	REN	61.92		
	3- 5-80		61.98		75.00
Sell	3- 7-80	REN	61.60		
	3-12-80		61.10	625.00	
Sell	3-13-80	REN	60.80		
	3-19-80		59.57	1537.50	
Sell	3-21-80	REN	59.38		
	4- 2-80		56.80	3225.00	

SPIKE-35 TRADING RESULTS
80 Sept Swiss Franc (Cont'd)

Order	Entry and Exit Dates	Entry Rule	Entry and Exit Prices	Gain	Loss
Sell	4- 3-80 4- 8-80	REN	56.45 56.40	$ 50.00	
Buy	4-10-80 4-14-80	CA2H	60.37 60.15		$ 275.00
Buy	4-16-80 4-18-80	REN	60.40 60.20		125.00
Buy	4-23-80 4-25-80	REN	60.65 60.95	375.00	
Buy	4-28-80 5- 1-80	REN	61.50 61.80	375.00	
Buy	5- 6-80 5- 7-80	REN	61.90 61.60		375.00
Sell	5-19-80 5-21-80	REN	60.60 61.00		500.00
Buy	5-27-80 5-28-80	CA2H	62.30 61.79		637.50
Buy	6- 3-80 6- 5-80	REN	61.52 61.40		150.00
Buy	6- 6-80 6-11-80	REN	61.60 62.10	625.00	
Buy	6-13-80 6-16-80	REN	62.49 62.30		237.50
Sell	6-24-80 6-26-80	TDR	61.50 61.70		250.00

SWISS FRANC

MARCH 1981

International Monetary Market

COMMODITY PERSPECTIVE/CHICAGO, ILLINOIS 60604

```
CONTRACT SFH 81
HIGH    0.6700: 02/21/80
LOW     0.4984: 02/13/81
```

U.S. $

0.720
0.700
0.680
0.660
0.640
0.620
0.600
0.580
0.560
0.540
0.520
0.500

CONTRACTS
16,000
12,000
8,000
4,000
VOL.-O.I.

3 10 17 24 31 7 14 21 28 5 12 19 26 2 9 16 23 30 7 14 21 28 4 11 18 25 1 8 15 22 29 6 13 20 27 3 10 17 24 1 8 15 22 29 5 12 19 26 2 9 16 23 2 9 16 23 30 6 13 20 27

MAR   APR   MAY   JUN   JUL   AUG   SEP   OCT   NOV   DEC   JAN   FEB   MAR   APR

SPIKE-35 TRADING RESULTS
81 Mar Swiss Franc

Order	Entry and Exit Dates	Entry Rule	Entry and Exit Prices	Gain	Loss
Buy	7- 3-80 7- 9-80	TDR	64.16 64.65	$ 612.50	
Buy	7-17-80 7-18-80	REN	64.35 63.45		$1125.00
Buy	7-22-80 7-25-80	REN	64.35 64.50	187.50	
Sell	7-28-80 8- 4-80	CB2L	63.73 62.35	1725.00	
Sell	8- 8-80 8-11-80	REN	62.45 62.74		375.00
Sell	8-15-80 8-20-80	REN	62.75 62.25	625.00	
Sell	8-22-80 8-26-80	REN	62.10 62.27		212.50
Buy	8-28-80 9- 4-80	CA2H	62.73 63.35	775.00	
Buy	9- 8-80 9-10-80	REN	63.40 63.30		125.00
Buy	9-11-80 9-12-80	REN	63.50 63.30		250.00
Sell	9-18-80 9-24-80	CB2L	62.70 62.43	337.50	
Buy	10- 3-80 10- 7-80	CA2H	63.50 63.03		587.50
Sell	10-13-80 10-15-80	CB2L	62.70 62.70	0	0
Sell	10-16-80 10-20-80	REN	62.45 62.30	187.50	
Sell	10-22-80 10-29-80	REN	61.90 60.63	1587.50	

SPIKE-35 TRADING RESULTS
81 Mar Swiss Franc (Cont'd)

Order	Entry and Exit Dates	Entry Rule	Entry and Exit Prices	Gain	Loss
Sell	10-30-80 11- 3-80	REN	60.50 60.26	$ 300.00	
Sell	11- 5-80 11-10-80	REN	59.90 59.70	250.00	
Buy	11-10-80 11-12-80	CA2H	60.98 60.90		$ 100.00
Buy	11-19-80 11-20-80	REN	60.35 60.05		375.00

SWISS FRANC

SEPTEMBER 1981

International Monetary Market

COMMODITY PERSPECTIVE/CHICAGO, ILLINOIS 60604

SPIKE-35 TRADING RESULTS
81 Sept Swiss Franc

Order	Entry and Exit Dates	Entry Rule	Entry and Exit Prices	Gain	Loss
Sell	11-28-80 12- 2-80	CB2L	62.00 62.00	0	0
Sell	12- 4-80 12-12-80	REN	61.85 59.85	$2500.00	
Sell	12-16-80 12-17-80	REN	59.47 59.61		$ 175.00
Sell	12-29-80 12-30-80	REN	60.15 60.20		62.50
Sell	12-30-80 1- 2-81	REN	59.95 50.92	37.50	
Sell	1- 9-81 1-14-81	REN	60.07 59.30	962.50	
Sell	1-15-81 1-19-81	REN	58.95 58.90	62.50	
Sell	1-22-81 2- 3-81	REN	58.50 55.05	4312.50	
Sell	2- 4-80 2-17-80	REN	54.75 52.85	2375.00	
Buy	2-20-81 2-24-80	TDR	55.63 54.50		1412.50
Sell	3- 2-81 3- 3-81	TDR	51.90 52.50		750.00
Buy	3-17-81 3-20-81	TDR	54.40 54.70	375.00	
Sell	3-26-81 3-30-81	TDR	53.23 53.35		150.00
Sell	4- 3-81 4- 7-81	REN	53.25 52.95	375.00	

SPIKE-35 TRADING RESULTS
81 Sept Swiss Franc (Cont'd)

Order	Entry and Exit Dates	Entry Rule	Entry and Exit Prices	Gain	Loss
Sell	4-10-81	REN	52.45		
	4-14-81		52.35	$ 125.00	
Sell	4-14-81	REN	52.15		
	4-20-81		51.60	687.50	
Sell	4-24-81	REN	51.75		
	4-28-81		51.45	375.00	
Sell	4-29-81	REN	51.05		
	5- 1-81		50.95	125.00	
Sell	5- 4-81	REN	50.50		
	5- 6-81		50.25	312.50	
Sell	5- 7-81	REN	50.00		
	5- 8-81		50.30		375.00
Sell	5-11-81	REN	50.00		
	5-13-81		49.90	125.00	
Sell	5-14-81	REN	49.65		
	5-14-81		49.90		$ 312.50
Sell	5-21-81	REN	49.50		
	5-28-81		49.30	250.00	

SWISS FRANC

MARCH 1982

International Monetary Market

COMMODITY PERSPECTIVE/CHICAGO, ILLINOIS 60604

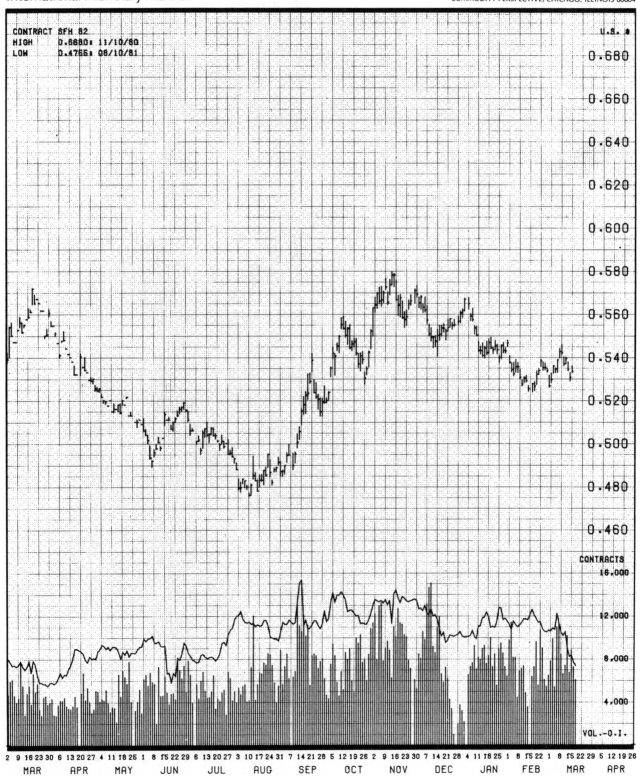

SPIKE-35 TRADING RESULTS
82 Mar Swiss Franc

Order	Entry and Exit Dates	Entry Rule	Entry and Exit Prices	Gain	Loss
Sell	7-27-81	CB2L	49.50		
	7-29-81		49.60		$ 125.00
Sell	7-29-81	REN	49.40		
	8- 5-81		48.15	$1562.00	
Sell	8- 7-81	REN	47.95		
	8-11-81		48.00		62.50
Buy	8-21-81	CA2H	49.50		
	8-24-81		48.50		1250.00
Buy	8-28-81	REN	49.00		
	8-31-81		48.90		125.00
Buy	9- 3-81	REN	49.10		
	9- 8-81		49.45	437.50	
Buy	9- 9-81	REN	49.51		
	9-16-81		51.50	2487.50	
Buy	9-16-81	REN	51.82		
	9-22-81		52.97	1437.50	
Buy	9-29-81	REN	52.10		
	10- 6-81		53.50	1750.00	
Buy	10- 7-81	REN	54.30		
	10-13-81		55.30	1250.00	
Sell	10-20-81	CB2L	54.20		
	10-22-81		54.20	0	0
Sell	10-26-81	REN	53.30		
	10-28-81		53.53		287.50
Buy	10-29-81	CA2H	55.22		
	11- 5-81		56.57	1687.50	
Buy	11- 6-81	REN	57.00		
	11- 9-81		57.00	0	0
Buy	11-11-81	REN	57.30		
	11-13-81		57.47	212.50	
Sell	11-17-81	CB2L	56.40		
	11-18-81		56.65		312.50

SPIKE-35 TRADING RESULTS
82 Mar Swiss Franc (Cont'd)

Order	Entry and Exit Dates	Entry Rule	Entry and Exit Prices	Gain	Loss
Sell	11-19-81	REN	56.40		
	11-23-81		55.85	$ 687.50	
Sell	11-30-81	REN	56.50		
	12- 4-81		56.80		$ 375.00
Sell	12- 4-81	REN	56.25		
	12- 7-81		56.35		125.00
Sell	12- 7-81	REN	56.15		
	12-11-81		54.95	1500.00	
Sell	12-14-81	REN	54.70		
	12-14-81		54.95		312.50
Sell	12-18-81	REN	55.00		
	12-21-81		55.30		375.00
Buy	12-28-81	CA2H	56.00		
	1- 5-82		55.97		37.50
Sell	1- 8-82	TDR	55.00		
	1-13-82		54.35	812.50	

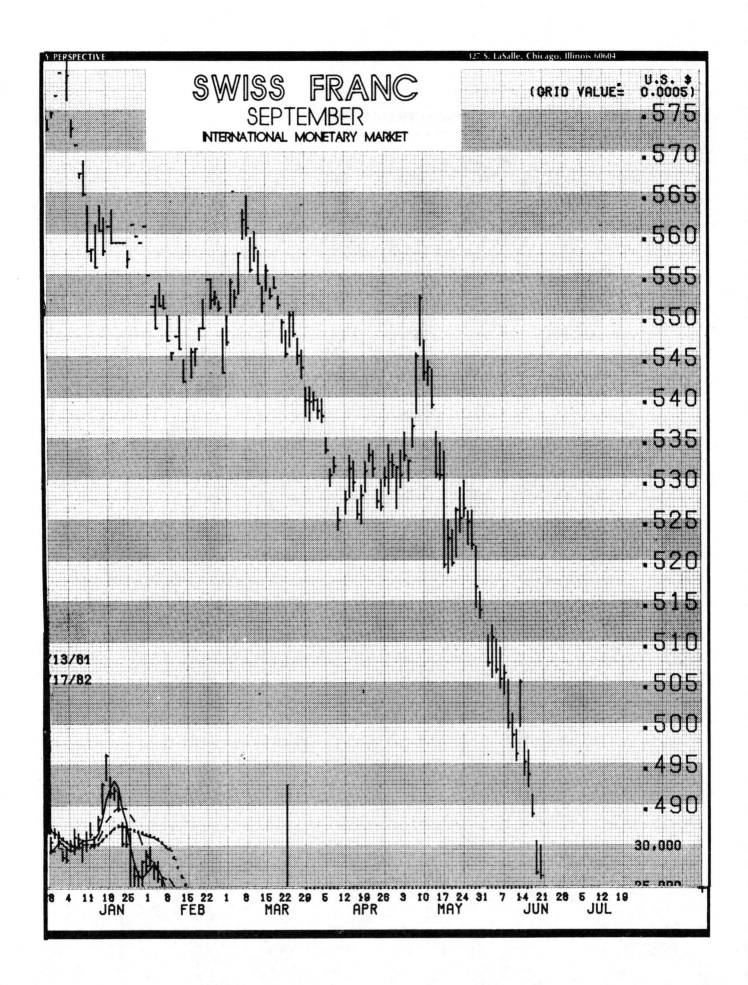

SPIKE-35 TRADING RESULTS
82 Sept Swiss Franc

Order	Entry and Exit Dates	Entry Rule	Entry and Exit Prices	Gain	Loss
Sell	1-11-82	TDR	55.77		
	1-13-82		55.81		$ 50.00
Sell	1-25-82	REN	55.80		
	2- 4-82		55.15	$ 812.50	
Sell	2- 8-82	REN	54.84		
	2-11-82		54.75	112.50	
Sell	2-12-82	REN	54.45		
	2-17-82		54.55		112.50

Since a dot (or one trade situation) for the day of the 22nd we can only enter on the open, the next day of the 23rd. We have always assumed the open on these charts to be the high (or low) nearest previous close or as near previous close as possible.

Order	Entry and Exit Dates	Entry Rule	Entry and Exit Prices	Gain	Loss
Buy	2-23-82	CA2H	55.45		
	2-24-82		55.20		312.50
Buy	3- 2-82	REN	55.24		
	3- 9-82		55.95	887.50	
Sell	3-19-82	CB2L	54.94		
	3-23-82		54.90	50.00	
Sell	3-25-82	REN	54.50		
	3-31-82		53.97	662.50	
Sell	4- 1-82	REN	53.85		
	4-13-82		52.76	1362.50	
Sell	4-15-82	REN	52.74		
	4-19-82		52.84		125.00
Sell	4-22-82	REN	52.80		
	4-26-82		53.00		250.00
Sell	4-29-82	REN	52.65		
	4-30-82		53.15		625.00
Sell	5- 4-82	REN	53.05		
	5- 5-82		53.40		437.50

SPIKE-35 TRADING RESULTS
82 Sept Swiss Franc (Cont'd)

Order	Entry and Exit Dates	Entry Rule	Entry and Exit Prices	Gain	Loss
Buy	5- 5-82	CA2H	53.65		
	5-10-82		54.50	$1062.50	
Sell	5-17-82	CB2L	51.95		
	5-19-82		52.26		$ 387.50
Sell	5-26-82	REN	52.45		
	6- 7-82		50.65	2250.00	
Sell	6- 8-82	REN	50.50		
	6-11-82		50.07	537.50	

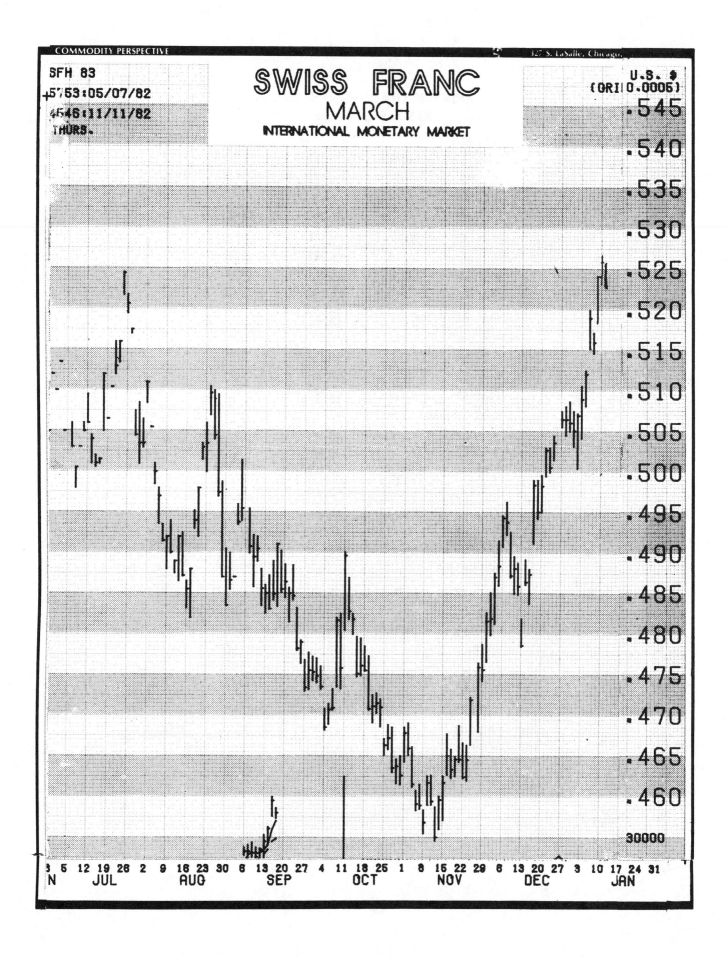

SWISS FRANC
MARCH
INTERNATIONAL MONETARY MARKET

SFH 83
+5753:05/07/82
4646:11/11/82
THURS.

U.S. $
(ORI 0.0005)

.545
.540
.535
.530
.525
.520
.515
.510
.505
.500
.495
.490
.485
.480
.475
.470
.465
.460

30000

3 5 12 19 26 2 9 16 23 30 6 13 20 27 4 11 18 25 1 8 15 22 29 6 13 20 27 3 10 17 24 31
N JUL AUG SEP OCT NOV DEC JAN

SPIKE-35 TRADING RESULTS
83 Mar Swiss Franc

Order	Entry and Exit Dates	Entry Rule	Entry and Exit Prices	Gain	Loss
Buy	7-22-82 7-27-82	CA2H	51.60 51.75	$ 187.50	
Sell	8- 4-82 8-10-82	CB2L	50.00 49.20	1000.00	
Sell	8-10-82 8-12-82	REN	49.13 49.00	162.50	
Sell	8-13-82 8-17-82	REN	48.80 48.75	62.50	
Buy	8-23-82 8-26-82	TDR	50.35 50.45	125.00	
Sell	8-30-82 8-31-82	TDR	48.35 48.70		$ 437.50
Sell	9- 9-82 9- 9-82	REN	48.95 49.10		187.50
Sell	9-10-82 9-14-82	REN	48.80 48.55	312.50	
Sell	9-14-82 9-15-82	REN	48.45 48.50		62.50
Sell	9-21-82 9-22-82	REN	48.50 48.55		62.50
Sell	9-22-82 9-29-82	REN	48.45 47.55	1125.00	
Sell	10- 1-82 10- 6-82	REN	47.35 47.10	312.50	
Buy	10-11-82 10-13-82	CA2H	48.96 48.25		887.50
Sell	10-25-82 10-27-82	CB2L	46.64 46.72		100.00
Sell	10-27-82 10-29-82	REN	46.60 46.37	287.50	

SPIKE-35 TRADING RESULTS
83 Mar Swiss Franc (Cont'd)

Order	Entry and Exit Dates	Entry Rule	Entry and Exit Prices	Gain	Loss
Sell	10-29-82	REN	46.35		
	11- 1-82		46.45		$ 125.00
Sell	11- 3-82	REN	46.25		
	11- 9-82		45.90	$ 437.50	
Sell	11-11-82	REN	45.70		
	11-12-82		45.95		312.50
Sell	11-22-82	REN	46.32		
	11-23-82		46.47		187.50
Buy	11-24-82	CA2H	47.20		
	12- 2-82		48.15	1187.50	
Buy	12- 2-82	REN	48.25		
	12- 8-82		49.25	1250.00	
Buy	12-14-82	REN	48.80		
	12-29-82		50.60	2250.00	
Buy	12-30-82	REN	50.65		
	12-30-82		50.60		62.50
Buy	12-31-82	REN	50.65		
	1- 1-83		50.49		200.00
Buy	1- 1-83	REN	50.70		
	1-11-83		52.40	2125.00	

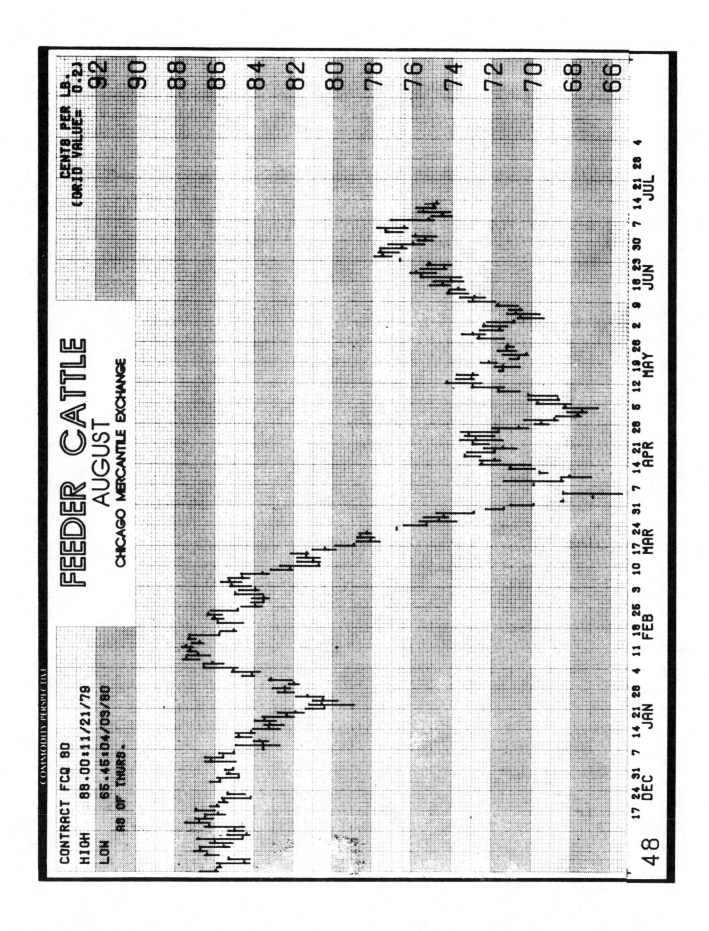

COMMODITY PERSPECTIVE

FEEDER CATTLE
AUGUST
CHICAGO MERCANTILE EXCHANGE

CONTRACT FCQ 80
HIGH   88.00±11/21/79
LOW   65.45±04/03/80
        AS OF THURS.

CENTS PER LB.
(GRID VALUE=   0.2)

92
90
88
86
84
82
80
78
76
74
72
70
68
66

48

17 24 31 7 14 21 28 4 11 18 26 3 10 17 24 31 7 14 21 28 5 12 19 26 2 9 16 23 30 7 14 21 28 4
DEC   JAN   FEB   MAR   APR   MAY   JUN   JUL

SPIKE-35 TRADING RESULTS
80 Aug Feeder Cattle

(It changed sometime from 4.2
I am using 4.4 per point for all of these).

Order	Entry and Exit Dates	Entry Rule	Entry and Exit Prices	Gain	Loss
Sell	1- 8-80 1- 9-80	CB2L	83.55 83.55	0	0
Sell	1-14-80 1-16-80	REN	83.55 83.25	$ 120.00	
Sell	1-17-80 1-23-80	REN	83.15 80.55	1144.00	
Buy	1-31-80 2-12-80	CA2H	84.10 86.85	1210.00	
Sell	2-14-80 2-19-80	CB2L	85.80 85.80	0	0
Sell	2-22-80 2-27-80	REN	85.00 84.00	440.00	
Sell	3- 6-80 3-12-80	REN	84.00 81.00	1320.00	
Sell	3-15-80 3-26-80	REN	80.60 75.30	2332.00	
Sell	3-26-80 3-27-80	REN	74.60 74.70		$ 44.00
Sell	3-27-80 4- 3-80	REN	74.40 68.40	2640.00	
Buy	4-16-80 4-17-80	TDR	73.35 71.80		682.00
Buy	4-22-80 4-23-80	REN	73.35 72.75		240.00
Buy	4-24-80 4-24-80	REN	73.20 72.80		176.00
Sell	4-29-80 5- 2-80	TDR	68.85 67.65	528.00	
Buy	5-12-80 5-14-80	CA2H	74.30 72.95		595.00
Buy	5-27-80 5-29-80	REN	71.35 72.60	550.00	
Buy	6- 6-80 6-16-80	RÉN	70.95 73.60	726.00	
Buy	6-17-80 6-19-80	REN	74.45 75.45	440.00	

FEEDER CATTLE

MARCH 1981

Chicago Mercantile Exchange

COMMODITY PERSPECTIVE/CHICAGO, ILLINOIS 60604

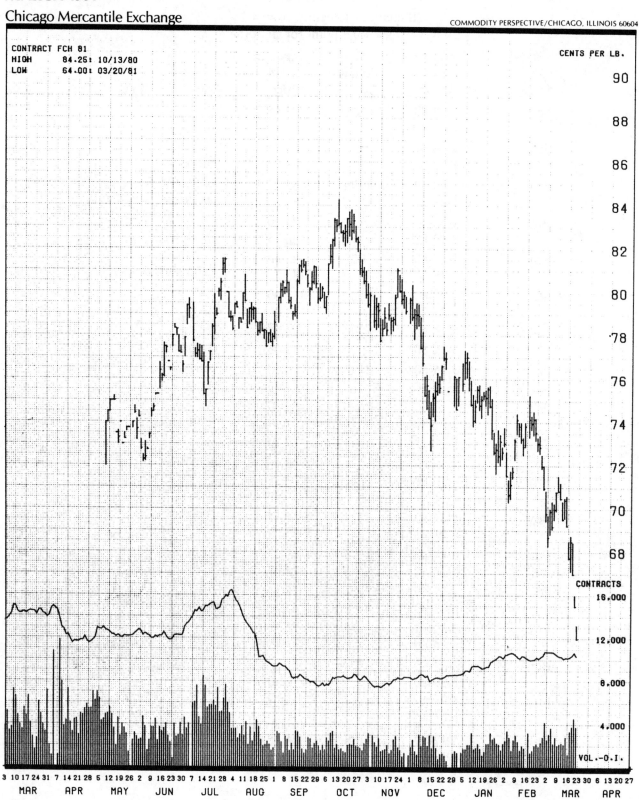

CONTRACT FCH 81
HIGH   84.25: 10/13/80
LOW   64.00: 03/20/81

CENTS PER LB.

90
88
86
84
82
80
'78
76
74
72
70
68

CONTRACTS
16,000
12,000
8,000
4,000

VOL.-O.I.

3 10 17 24 31 7 14 21 28 5 12 19 26 2 9 16 23 30 7 14 21 28 4 11 18 25 1 8 15 22 29 6 13 20 27 3 10 17 24 1 8 15 22 29 5 12 19 26 2 9 16 23 2 9 16 23 30 6 13 20 27

MAR   APR   MAY   JUN   JUL   AUG   SEP   OCT   NOV   DEC   JAN   FEB   MAR   APR

SPIKE-35 TRADING RESULTS
81 Mar Feeder Cattle

Order	Entry and Exit Dates	Entry Rule	Entry and Exit Prices	Gain	Loss
Buy	6-23-80 6-25-80	CA2H	78.00 77.98		$ 10.00
Buy	7- 2-80 7- 7-80	REN	78.50 79.15	$ 285.00	
Sell	7-14-80 7-16-80	CB2L	75.30 75.70		176.00
Buy	7-23-80 7-30-80	CA2H	80.00 79.95		22.00
Buy	8- 5-80 8- 6-80	REN	79.45 78.75		308.00
Buy	8- 8-80 8-12-80	REN	79.92 79.25		294.80
Sell	8-19-80 8-21-80	CB2L	78.20 78.60		176.00
Sell	8-22-80 8-27-80	REN	78.15 78.10	22.00	
Buy	9- 2-80 9- 5-80	CA2H	79.70 80.05	154.00	
Buy	9- 8-80 9- 9-80	REN	80.45 80.15		132.00
Buy	9-15-80 9-19-80	REN	79.60 80.95	594.00	
Buy	9-25-80 9-26-80	REN	80.95 80.40		242.00
Sell	10- 2-80 10- 6-80	CB2L	79.30 80.20		395.00
Buy	10- 6-80 10- 8-80	CA2H	81.25 81.25	0	0

SPIKE-35 TRADING RESULTS
81 Mar Feeder Cattle (Cont'd)

Order	Entry and Exit Dates	Entry Rule	Entry and Exit Prices	Gain	Loss
Buy	10- 8-80 10-14-80	REN	81.65 83.00	$ 595.00	
Buy	10-17-80 10-20-80	REN	83.25 82.75		$ 220.00
Buy	10-21-80 10-21-80	REN	83.40 83.20		88.00
Buy	10-22-80 10-23-80	REN	83.40 82.80		264.00
Sell	10-27-80 11- 3-80	CB2L	81.05 79.90	506.00	

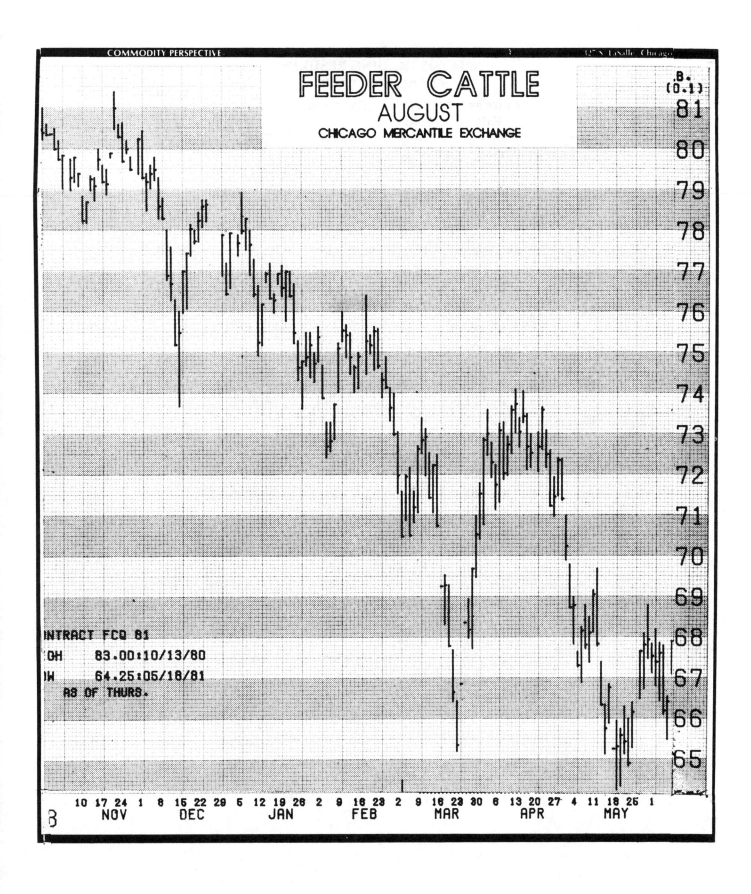

FEEDER CATTLE
AUGUST
CHICAGO MERCANTILE EXCHANGE

B.
(0.1)

INTRACT FCQ 81
OH   83.00:10/13/80
OW   64.25:05/18/81
AS OF THURS.

81
80
79
78
77
76
75
74
73
72
71
70
69
68
67
66
65

10 17 24 1 8 15 22 29 5 12 19 26 2 9 16 23 2 9 16 23 30 6 13 20 27 4 11 18 25 1
   NOV   DEC   JAN   FEB   MAR   APR   MAY

B

SPIKE-35 TRADING RESULTS
81 Aug Feeder Cattle

Order	Entry and Exit Dates	Entry Rule	Entry and Exit Prices	Gain	Loss
Sell	10-29-80 11-12-80	TDR	79.70 78.95	$ 330.00	
Sell	11-18-80 11-19-80	REN	79.10 79.80		$ 308.00
Buy	11-20-80 11-24-80	TDR	81.00 80.25		330.00
Buy	12- 1-80 12- 1-80	REN	80.30 79.45		374.00
Sell	12- 5-80 12-15-80	TDR	78.55 76.00	1122.00	
Sell	12-29-80 12-31-80	REN	77.10 77.90		352.00
Sell	1- 7-81 1-13-81	REN	77.65 76.70	418.00	
Sell	1-20-81 1-20-81	REN	76.25 76.95		308.00
Sell	1-21-81 1-27-81	REN	76.35 74.80	682.00	
Sell	1-28-81 1-30-81	REN	74.60 75.20		264.00
Sell	2- 2-81 2- 5-81	REN	74.65 72.85	792.00	
Sell	2-12-81 2-13-81	REN	74.65 74.85		88.00
Sell	2-17-81 2-17-81	REN	74.60 74.80		88.00
Sell	2-20-81 2-24-81	REN	74.80 74.65	66.00	
Sell	2-24-81 3- 4-81	REN	74.25 72.00	990.00	

SPIKE-35 TRADING RESULTS
81 Aug Feeder Cattle (Cont'd)

Order	Entry and Exit Dates	Entry Rule	Entry and Exit Prices	Gain	Loss
Sell	3-12-81 3-13-81	REN	71.35 72.25		$ 395.00
Sell	3-13-81 3-26-81	REN	71.40 68.40	$1320.00	
Buy	3-31-81 4- 2-81	TDR	72.85 72.80		22.00
Buy	4- 6-81 4- 8-81	REN	73.00 72.00		440.00
Buy	4- 9-81 4-13-81	REN	73.10 73.35	110.00	
Buy	4-14-81 4-15-81	REN	73.70 73.00		308.00
Buy	4-21-81 4-22-81	REN	73.45 72.65		352.00
Sell	4-23-81 4-27-81	CB2L	71.20 71.50		132.00
Sell	4-29-81 5- 6-81	REN	71.00 68.20	1232.00	
Sell	5-12-81 5-14-81	REN	67.40 66.40	440.00	
Sell	5-18-81 5-19-81	REN	65.70 65.40	132.00	
Sell	5-21-81 5-22-81	REN	65.20 65.45		110.00
Buy	5-26-81 5-28-81	CA2H	67.65 67.75	44.00	
Buy	6- 1-81 6- 1-81	REN	68.00 67.50		220.00

FEEDER CATTLE

MARCH 1982

Chicago Mercantile Exchange

COMMODITY PERSPECTIVE/CHICAGO, ILLINOIS 60604

CONTRACT FCH 82
HIGH   74.25: 04/23/81
LOW   54.45: 12/31/81

CENTS PER LB.

CONTRACTS
16,000

VOL.-O.I.

| MAR | APR | MAY | JUN | JUL | AUG | SEP | OCT | NOV | DEC | JAN | FEB | MAR | APR |

SPIKE-35 TRADING RESULTS
82 Mar Feeder Cattle

Order	Entry and Exit Dates	Entry Rule	Entry and Exit Prices	Gain	Loss
Sell	7- 7-81 7-10-81	TDR	67.20 66.90	$ 132.00	
Sell	7-15-81 7-23-81	REN	66.30 64.65	725.00	
Buy	7,31-81 8- 4-81	TDR	67.00 66.65		$ 154.00
Buy	8- 5-81 8- 7-81	REN	67.00 66.95		22.00
Buy	8-11-81 8-17-81	REN	67.30 67.90	396.00	
Sell	8-24-81 8-26-81	CB2L	66.50 67.00		220.00
Buy	9- 1-81 9- 3-81	CA2H	68.60 68.25		154.00
Buy	9- 3-81 9-14-81	REN	68.60 69.90	572.00	
Sell	9-23-81 9-29-81	TDR	68.35 67.90	198.00	
Sell	10- 1-81 10- 2-81	REN	67.50 67.85		154.00
Sell	10- 6-81 10- 8-81	REN	67.65 67.25	175.00	
Buy	10-19-81 10-20-81	TDR	68.80 68.50		132.00
Sell	10-23-81 10-27-81	CB2L	66.20 66.20	0	0
Sell	11- 2-81 11- 4-81	REN	66.15 66.15	0	0
Buy	11- 9-81 11-11-81	TDR	67.50 67.50	0	0

SPIKE-35 TRADING RESULTS
82 Mar Feeder Cattle (Cont'd)

Order	Entry and Exit Dates	Entry Rule	Entry and Exit Prices	Gain	Loss
Buy	11-16-81	REN	68.00		
	11-16-81		67.50		$ 220.00
Sell	11-18-81	TDR	65.82		
	11-24-81		64.85	$ 426.80	
Sell	12- 4-81	REN	64.95		
	12- 9-81		62.30	1166.00	
Sell	12- 9-81	REN	61.75		
	12-15-81		59.80	858.00	
Sell	12-15-81	REN	59.30		
	12-17-81		58.30	440.00	
Sell	12-21-81	REN	57.80		
	12-24-81		58.50		308.00
Sell	12-30-81	REN	56.20		
	1- 4-82		55.40	352.00	
Buy	1- 8-82	TDR	59.10		
	1-12-82		59.95	374.00	
Buy	1-14-82	REN	60.15		
	1-19-82		61.55	616.00	
Buy	1-21-82	REN	62.25		
	1-25-82		61.75		220.00
Buy	1-29-82	REN	61.90		
	2- 5-82		64.80	1276.00	

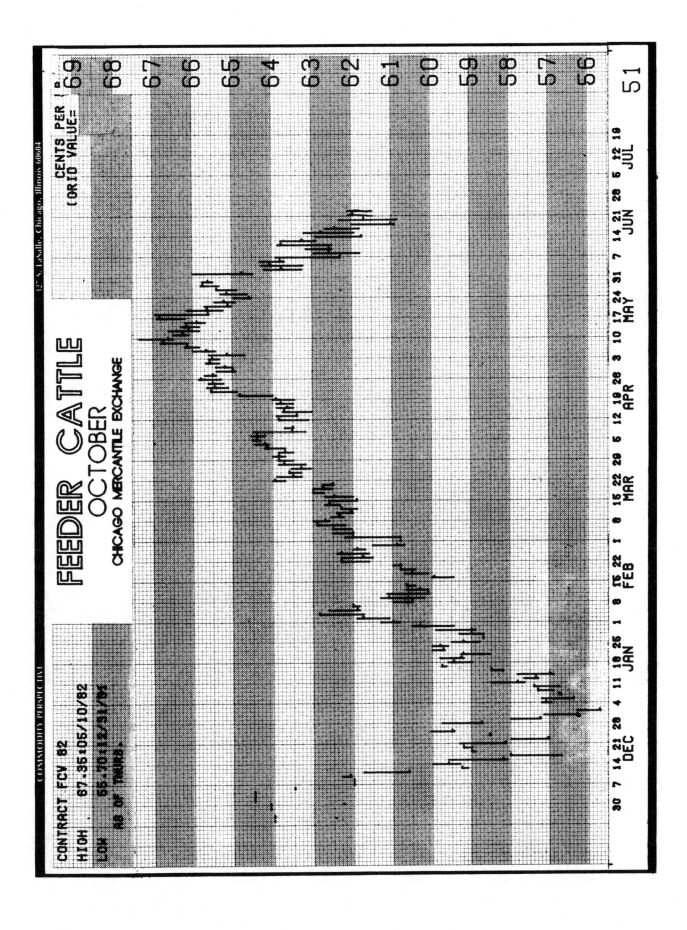

125 S. LaSalle, Chicago, Illinois 60604

CENTS PER lb.
(ORIG VALUE=

FEEDER CATTLE
OCTOBER
CHICAGO MERCANTILE EXCHANGE

CONTRACT FCV 82
HIGH   67.35:05/10/82
LOW   55.70:12/31/81
NO OF TRDES.

69
68
67
66
65
64
63
62
61
60
59
58
57
56

51

30 7 14 21 28   4 11 18 25   1 8 15 22 29   1 8 15 22 29   3 10 17 24 31   7 14 21 28 5 12 19
DEC   JAN   FEB   MAR   APR   MAY   JUN   JUL

SPIKE-35 TRADING RESULTS
82 Oct Feeder Cattle

Order	Entry and Exit Dates	Entry Rule	Entry and Exit Prices	Gain	Loss
Buy	2-18-82	REN	60.65		
	2-24-82		61.70	$ 462.00	
Buy	3- 4-82	REN	62.05		
	3- 9-82		62.55	220.00	
Buy	3-16-82	REN	62.65		
	3-19-82		62.70	22.00	
Buy	3-22-82	REN	63.70		
	3-24-82		63.45		$ 132.00
Buy	3-29-82	REN	63.75		
	3-31-82		63.70		22.00
Buy	4- 1-82	REN	63.75		
	4- 7-82		64.35	264.00	
Buy	4-19-82	REN	63.85		
	4-23-82		65.40	682.00	
Buy	4-28-82	REN	65.55		
	4-30-82		65.40		66.00
Buy	5- 5-82	REN	65.60		
	5-11-82		66.45	374.00	
Buy	5-17-82	REN	66.30		
	5-18-82		65.90		176.00
Sell	5-20-82	TDR	65.10		
	5-25-82		65.10	0	0
Sell	6- 1-82	REN	65.10		
	6- 4-82		64.10	440.00	
Sell	6- 7-82	REN	63.70		
	6- 9-82		62.65	462.00	
Sell	6-14-82	REN	62.50		
	6-21-82		61.80	308.00	

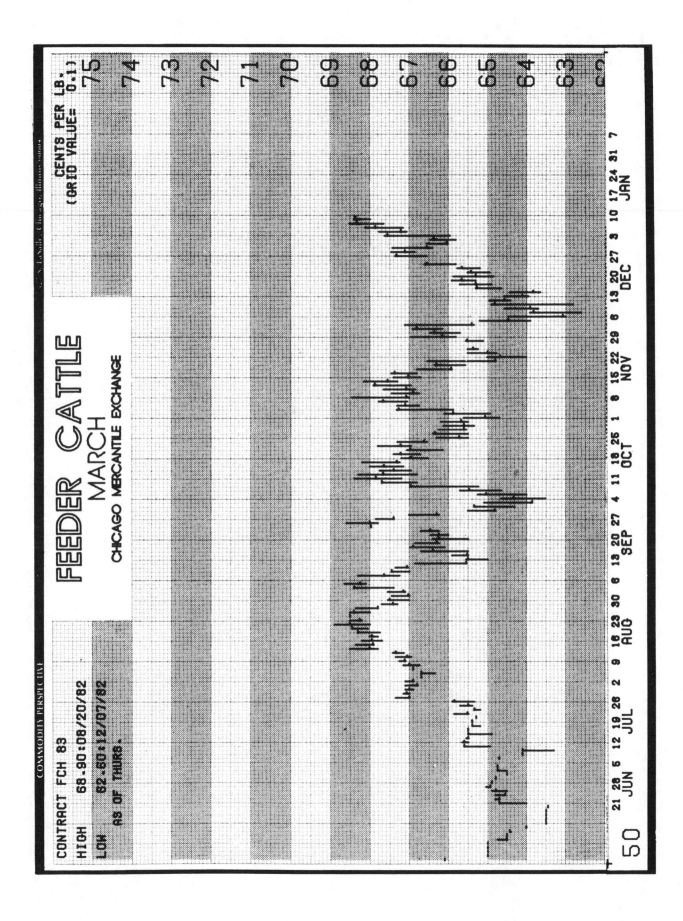

COMMODITY PERSPECTIVE

FEEDER CATTLE
MARCH
CHICAGO MERCANTILE EXCHANGE

CONTRACT FCH 83
HIGH 68.90:08/20/82
LOW 62.60:12/07/82
AS OF THURS.

CENTS PER LB.
(GRID VALUE= 0.1)

75 74 73 72 71 70 69 68 67 66 65 64 63

50

21 28 5 12 19 26 2 9 16 23 30 6 13 20 27 4 11 18 25 1 8 15 22 29 6 13 20 27 3 10 17 24 31 7
JUN   JUL   AUG   SEP   OCT   NOV   DEC   JAN

SPIKE-35 TRADING RESULTS
83 Mar Feeder Cattle

Order	Entry and Exit Dates	Entry Rule	Entry and Exit Prices	Gain	Loss
Buy	7-26-82 7-29-82	CA2H	65.85 66.95	$ 484.00	
Buy	8- 6-82 8-10-82	REN	66.95 66.95	0	0
Buy	8-11-82 8-16-82	REN	67.10 67.90	352.00	
Buy	8-18-82 8-20-82	REN	68.05 68.30	110.00	
Sell	8-31-82 9- 1-82	TDR	67.00 67.50		$ 220.00
Sell	9- 9-82 9-14-82	REN	67.40 65.60	792.00	
Sell	9-21-82 9-22-82	REN	66.20 66.30		44.00
Buy	9-24-82 9-27-82	CA2H	68.00 67.85		66.00
Sell	9-30-82 10- 5-82	CB2L	64.80 64.35	198.00	
Sell	10-14-82 10-15-82	REN	67.30 67.70		176.00
Sell	10-15-82 10-19-82	REN	67.30 67.30	0	0
Sell	10-20-82 10-22-82	REN	66.95 67.25		132.00
Sell	10-22-82 10-29-82	REN	66.90 65.65	550.00	
Sell	11- 1-82 11- 2-82	REN	65.55 65.65		44.00
Buy	11- 5-82 11- 8-82	TDR	67.65 67.10		242.00

SPIKE-35 TRADING RESULTS
83 Mar Feeder Cattle (Cont'd)

Order	Entry and Exit Dates	Entry Rule	Entry and Exit Prices	Gain	Loss
Buy	11-11-82 11-15-82	REN	67.65 67.40		$ 110.00
Sell	11-19-82 11-23-82	TDR	64.80 64.85		22.00
Sell	12- 2-82 12- 8-82	REN	65.50 63.85	$ 726.00	
Sell	12- 9-82 12- 9-82	REN	63.05 63.95		396.00
Sell	12-14-82 12-15-82	REN	63.90 64.70		352.00
Sell	12-21-82 12-22-82	REN	65.30 65.40		44.00
Buy	12-23-82 12-29-82	CA2H	66.55 67.05	220.00	
Buy	1- 3-83 1-13-83	REN	67.10 68.40	616.00	